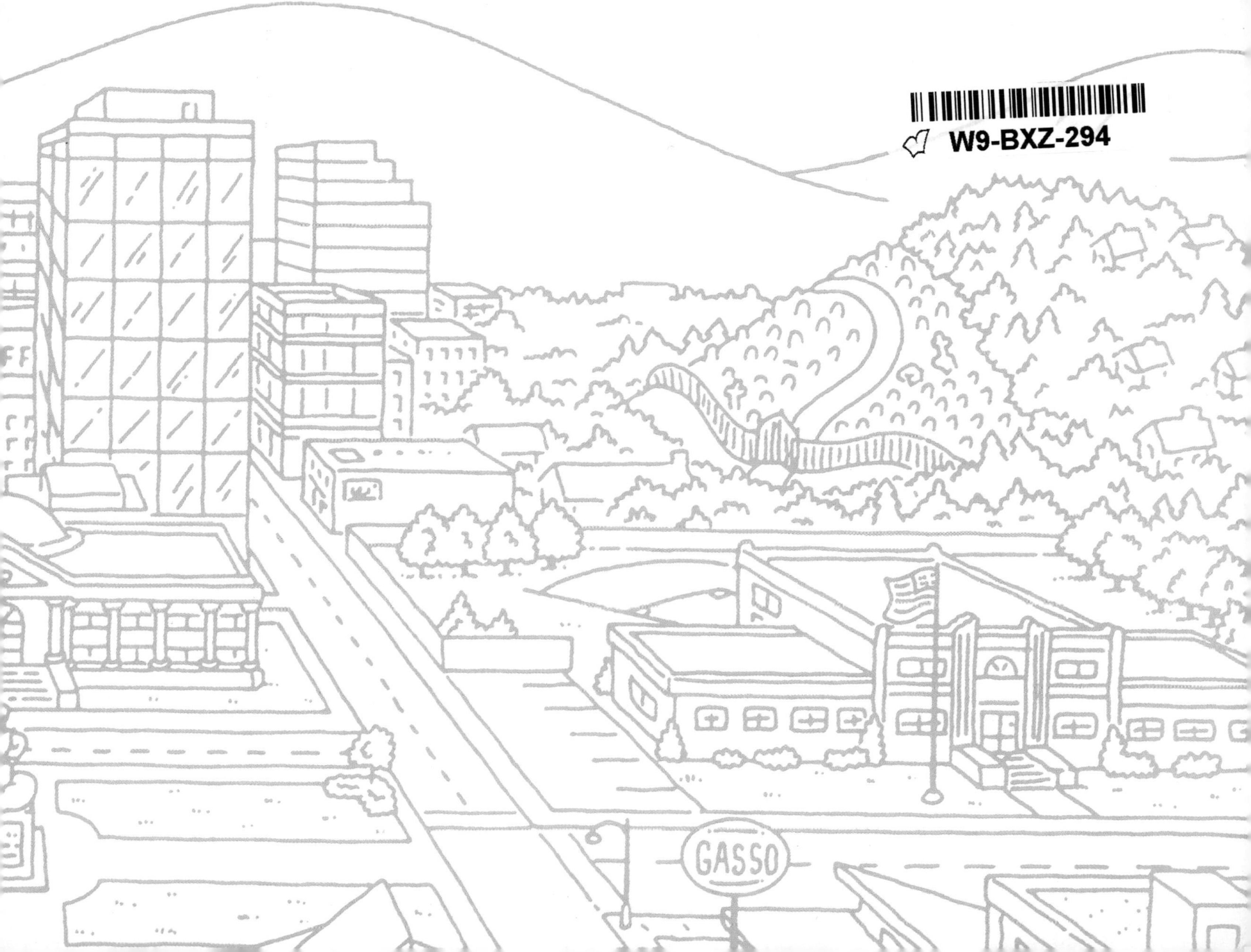
GASSO

MATT GROENING'S

THE SIMPSONS™ Guide to

SPRINGFIELD

HarperPerennial

A Division of HarperCollins*Publishers*

http://www.harpercollins.com

ARE WE THERE YET? THE SIMPSONS: GUIDE TO SPRINGFIELD
Copyright © 1998 by Bongo Entertainment, Inc. and Matt Groening Productions, Inc. All rights reserved. Printed in the United States of America. No part of this book may be used or reproduced in any manner whatsoever without written permission except in the case of brief quotations embodied in critical articles and reviews. For information address HarperCollins Publishers, Inc. 10 East 53rd Street, New York, NY 10022.

HarperCollins books may be purchased for educational, business, or sales promotional use. For information please write: Special Markets Department, HarperCollins Publishers, Inc., 10 East 53rd Street, New York, NY 10022.

First Edition

ISBN 0-06-095282-2

98 99 00 01 02 RRD 10 9 8 7 6 5 4 3 2 1

Editor/Concept/Art Direction
Bill Morrison

Writer
Scott M. Gimple

Design
Christopher Ungar

Computer Production/Design
Christopher Ungar and Karen Bates

Contributing Artists
Karen Bates, Tim Bavington, Chris Clements, Terry Delegeane, Luis Escobar, Tim Harkins, Bill Ho, Chia-Hsien Jason Ho, Abel Laxamana, Jim Massara, Bill Morrison, Kevin M. Newman, Phil Ortiz, Julius Preite, Chris Roman, Jennifer Sindon, Steve Steere, Jr., Erick Tran, and Christopher Ungar

HarperCollins Editors
Susan Weinberg and Trena Keating

Legal Guardian
Susan M. Grode

Special thanks to:
Annette Andersen, Jeannine Black, Serban Cristescu, Claudia De La Roca, N. Vyolet Diaz, Jarrett Grode, Jason B. Grode, Shelly Kale, Deanna MacLellan, Christine Shinn, and Robert Zaugh

We, the editors of *Are We There Yet?* Travel Guides would like to first thank you for purchasing this guide to one of America's most reviled and thus underappreciated cities, Springfield. We also would like to take this opportunity to state publicly that we assume no legal liability for any injuries, diseases, mental breakdowns, loss of faith in humanity, P.D.D.N.S. (Persistent, Disgust-Derived Nausea Syndrome), muggings, loss of property, loss of soul (as in funk), and any other misfortunes suffered by those who opt to visit this quaint-yet-troubled city.

Within this guide, you'll find candid essays written by Springfield natives, reviews of dozens of stores and restaurants, a guide to the many attractions of Springfield, a survival guide, and much, much more.

Special features of this guide include: "What's Right With Springfield?" sidebars that showcase Springfield natives sharing with travelers their favorite Springfield spots and the "Springfield Artifacts" bottombars, which catalog some of Springfield's most important historical treasures. Plus, handy "page numbers" help mark each page individually, so that the reader may shut the book and return to their place without endless searching.

In short, we at *Are We There Yet?* Travel Guides hope to serve you up a steaming slice of Springfield à la mode, (the à la mode being a bright, glossy cover and book binder's glue). Enjoy!

(At right) Attorney and Realtor, Lionel Hutz, chasing an ambulance shortly before being loaded into another one.

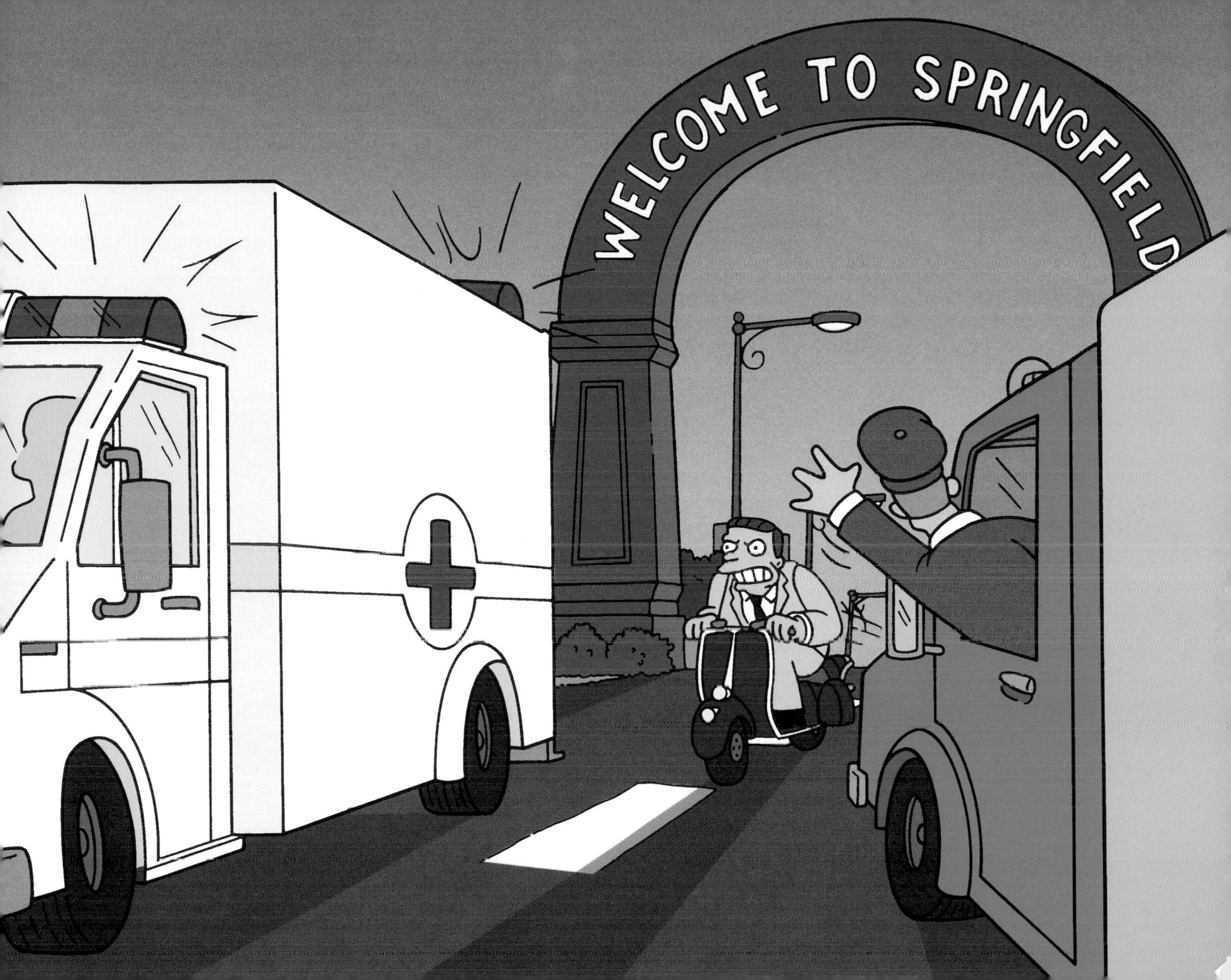
WELCOME TO SPRINGFIELD

O Springfield! My Springfield!

A Historical Perspective of the Greater Springfield Area
by Hollis Hurlbut, Curator, Springfield Historical Society; Chairman, Springfield Tourism Board

Was it really so long ago that an intrepid frontiersman led his band of opportunity-seeking pioneer brethren to this greenish-beige valley, this blessed mound of dirt, this Springfield? No. It was but one hundred and sixty years ago (or two hundred, depending on which supermarket encyclopedia you own) that coonskin-capped Jebediah Obediah Zachariah Jedediah Springfield tossed away his walking stick and proclaimed: "Here—here is where we shall build a teeming, colorful metropolis that offers free, convenient parking that serves local delicacies such as Toothless Joe's Gum-Flavored Chewing Product, whose mayor often wears a sash identifying him as "Mayor," that features more Krustyburger locations per square mile than any other place on Earth, and that, due to a near-constant economic state of recession, gives more bang for the tourist buck than Beirut and Tijuana combined!"

Of course, Jebediah didn't actually say all that, but if he came to present-day Springfield in some sort of time machine, and then returned to that founding day—I can guarantee that words such as those would have come out of his mouth. But how did this wonderful vacation destination come to be? What were the critical moments that shaped this great city, a city extremely lenient on visitors who break the law, whose officials even look the other way on most tourist misdemeanor offenses? I'm glad you asked.

Springfield would be a far different place if not for a fateful argument that occurred on the day the town was founded. According to spotty historical records, half of the pioneers—led by Jebediah

Springfield—were searching for a place where they could freely pray, justly govern, and farm hemp for rope making and blanket weaving. The other half—led by Springfield's partner, Shelbyville Manhattan—wanted to found a town that would give them the freedom to marry their cousins without fear of persecution. The party split, with Manhattan's faction forming the nearby town of Shelbyville and Springfield's followers forming the town of Springfield.

Folklorists galorists have woven tales of Jebediah Springfield killing a bear with his bare hands, taming the mighty buffalo, building the town's first hospital from mud and logs, saving the entire population during the Great Blizzard of '48, and even being, in actuality, a silver-tongued pirate [see sidebar].

But bear or no bear, silver prosthetic tongue or normal fleshy one, he founded a town that coasts along to this very day. Despite the aforementioned shakiness of the current Springfield economy—which, for tourists, means bargains, bargains, bargains!—Springfield at one time had streets paved with gold, literally.

During the postwar era, the town enjoyed unbridled prosperity from its own unusual export: the Aquacar! Part-car, part-boat, and part-crazy-person vehicular device, this four-wheeled amphibimobile took the world by storm for two insane months. Sadly, due to design flaws, every single Aquacar had to be recalled when it was discovered that they

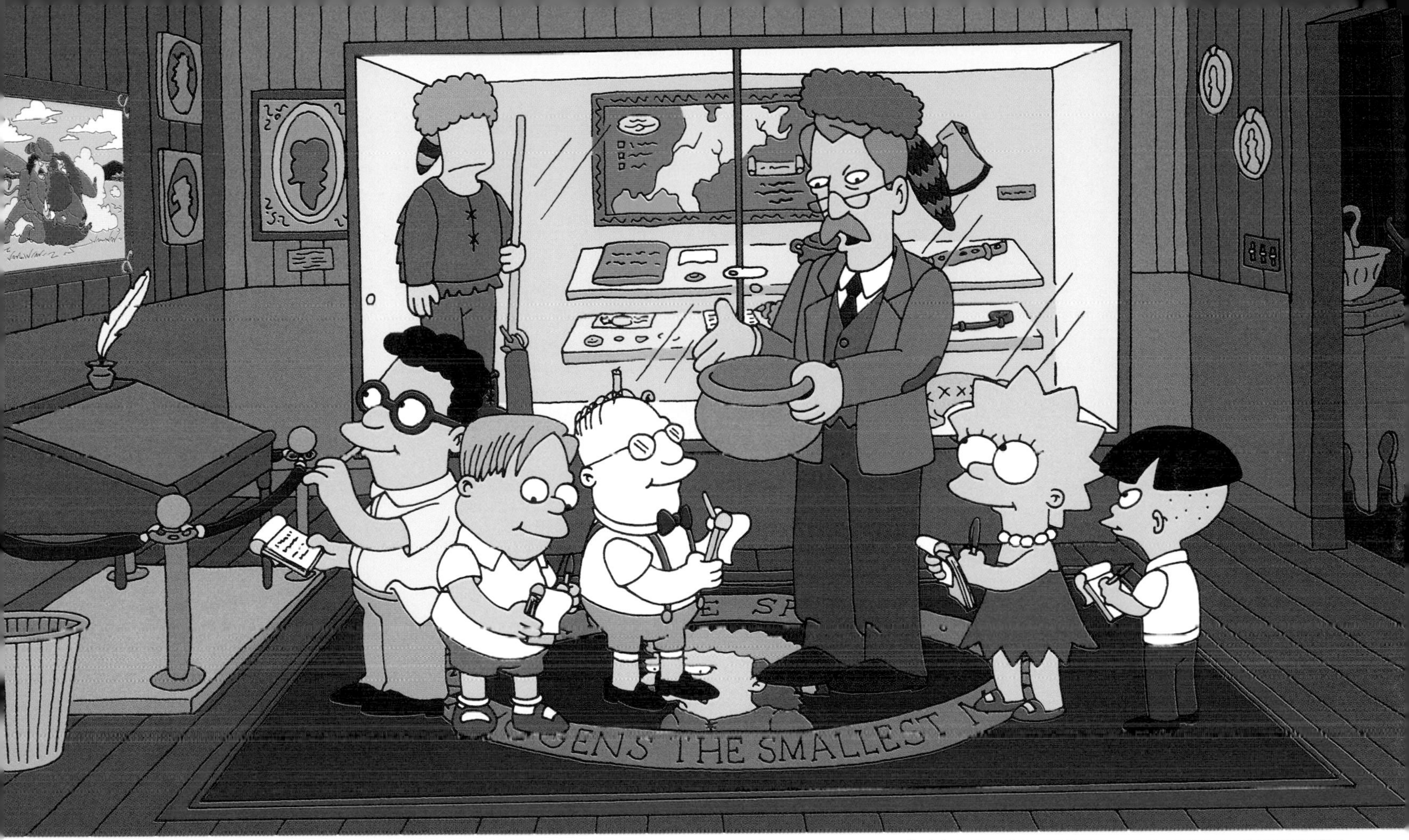
THE SMALLEST

Town historian Hollis Hurlbut shows geeky children the wonders of Jebediah Springfield's chamber pot at the Springfield Historical Society.

were subject to spontaneous explosion after 600 miles and/or knots. It was a dark time for Springfield: dozens of people were thrown out of work, the streets were repossessed and sold to the Sultan of Brunei (who subsequently melted down the gold to encase one of his many elephant herds), and the town's all-you-can-eat free-chicken Fridays were permanently discontinued.

Since that time, Springfield has persevered, however tenuously. Besides the ignition of the world's longest-burning tire-yard fire—as of this printing, it is still aflame—the last fifty years have witnessed the opening of the Springfield Nuclear Power Plant as well as chocolate, cracker, and cardboard box factories. Springfield's economy can be tied to the fortunes of two of its richest, most influential citizens:

C. Montgomery Burns and, to a lesser extent, Krusty the Clown (born Herschel Krustofski).

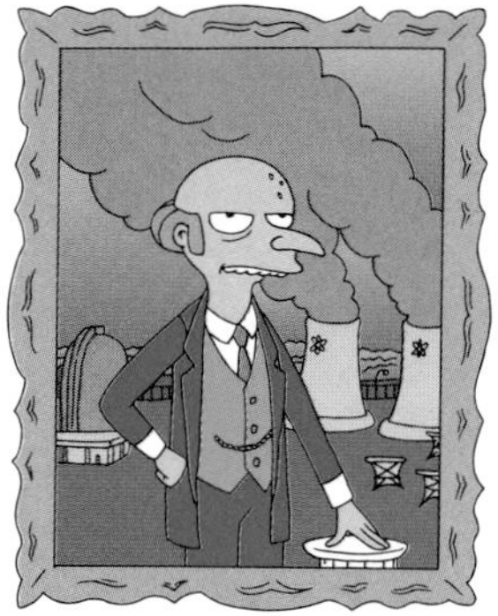

Burns, the heir to the ancient Burns nuclear-and-intimidation fortune, owns not only the power plant which employs hundreds of Springfielders, but he also has holdings in the town's electric company, railroad, and hotels. His generous kickbacks to city officials help keep them from dipping further into Springfield's depleted coffers, and his ointment expenditure alone accounts for one-fifth of the city's gross municipal product. Mayor Diamond Joe Quimby may be considered Springfield's crown prince, but C. Montgomery Burns is its king.

Springfield's King of Komedy, Krusty the Clown, has also become a major force in the city's economy. His popular television show helped launch his wildly successful—if not heavily litigated—fast-food chain, Krustyburger. The scad of Krustyburger locations throughout Springfield employs three hundred sullen teens and bitter old men and women yearly. Krusty the Clown merchandise is often produced in Springfield's sweatshops, accounting for at least 90 percent of Springfield's child labor employment and 68 percent of the town's monkey labor employment (coincidentally, Burns employs the other 22 percent of Springfield's monkey population). Besides revenue and employment from his various subsidiaries, Krusty's gambling problems have helped keep Springfield Downs solvent, his wild shopping sprees have proved a boon to the city's adult bookstores and seltzer wholesalers, and his plans to expand the Krustylu Studios Tour may very well bring in even more tourist dollars to Springfield, where visitors aren't considered guests—they're family!

Economics notwithstanding, Springfield is a dynamic, vibrant city, with museums, theaters, and cultural events such as the annual Springfield Chili Cook-Off. It is home to Springfield National Forest, Springfield Harbor, and the Springfield Speedway. Its semi-annual film festival is known for launching the short-lived career of Barney Gumble, the Springfielder who nearly got the chance to direct his own feature film until he threw up in Steven Spielberg's Porsche. It has the county-renowned Springfield Pops, a community theater that really tries, and colorful billboards aplenty. There's swanky shopping at the South Street Squidport and not-so-swanky bargain hunting at the Springfield Swap Meet—the same flea market where a woman found a copy of the Magna Carta in the lining of a shiny Cleveland Browns jacket (the document was later found to be a fraud, but we all had an exciting afternoon).

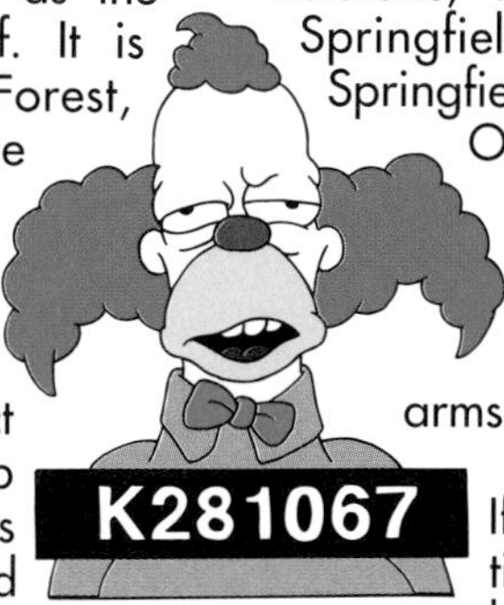
K281067

Yes, Springfield is all this, but above all, Springfield is about people: the people who live and work and play and sleep in Springfield. Their foibles are the foundation upon which this city is built (I mean that metaphorically, of course). Springfield community life often centers around meetings—meetings to decide how to spend the rare budget surplus, to hear the candidates debate, to warn the public about a strange new viral hybrid that's been introduced into the town's water supply from the nuclear power plant. But it's not all meetings and contaminated water; to Springfieldians, fun is fundamental: they pack Springfield Stadium to cheer on the Springfield Isotopes, they relive the past in Olde Springfield Towne, they take in monster truck rallies at the Springfield Coliseum. They drink and eat and tend to their lawns and welcome tourists with open arms and valuable coupon books.

If only Jebediah could have that time machine! If only he could see this alabasterish city that was but a glimmer in his good eye! And yet, it is you, the reader, who may now take Jebediah Springfield's place—it is you who may discover Springfield once more! Read on, and remember: Springfield's merchants are always happy to make change for those who need money for the parking meter! Happy Springfielding!

Hollis Hurlbut
Summer, 1998

ATTRACTIONS

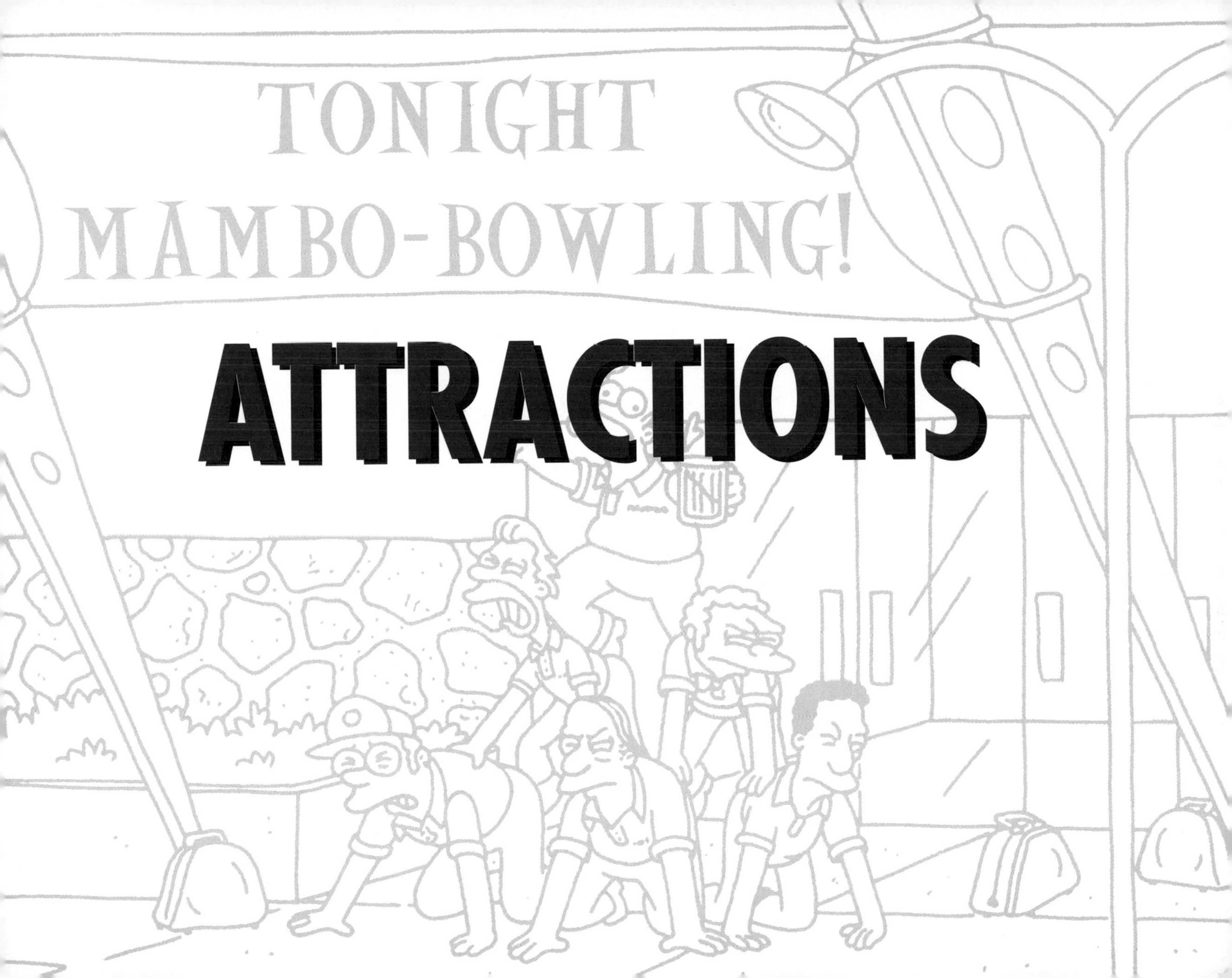
TONIGHT
MAMBO-BOWLING!

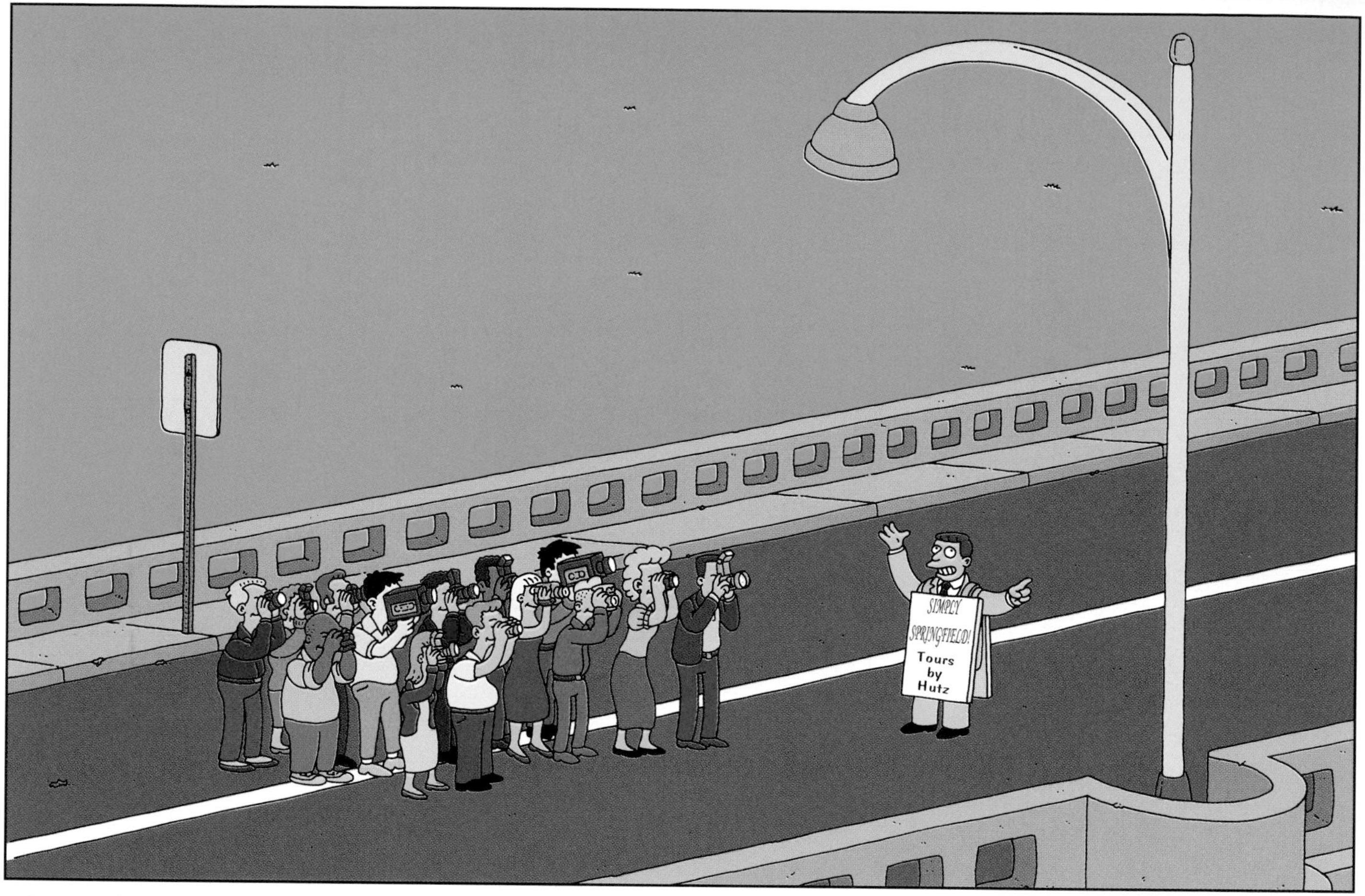
SIMPLY
SPRINGFIELD!
Tours
by
Hutz

Sometime lawyer and entrepreneur Lionel Hutz leads visitors to an ordinary lamppost, claiming it is made of metals recycled from the Spruce Goose.

If Springfield were a gigantic, warm, chewy pretzel, one could say it was virtually salted with exciting, unique attractions to quicken the pulse, lighten the wallet, and possibly leave mental (and physical) scars. That humongous pretzel, with all its salty-attraction-goodness is no metaphor—it's yours for the eating and visiting and picture taking! (Save for the fact that it's not a pretzel, but rather a town.)

What to do, what to do, what to do? Springfield is replete with places to go, things to ride, and things to see while standing behind some sort of fence. Want to see the glorious wonder of nature? Springfield's got it! Care to witness sugary candy being mass-produced for overweight children? Springfield's the place! Wanna gamble? Ride dangerous amusements? Play loud video games? Dodge crumbling concrete? You can do it all in Springfield!

Perhaps the best place to look for fun and excitement in Springfield is where the town literally begins—at the **Springfield Bridge**. Due to poor civic planning, rampant corruption, and an overly yokelized workforce, the only way in or out of Springfield is across the bridge that bears its name. The bridge was rebuilt several years ago after it was destroyed by a misguided missile that was intended to destroy a comet threatening the city. Afterward, city planners went to great lengths to restore the bridge's old-style architecture and charm, even adding re-creations of its original, innovative graffiti, such as "Class of '78 Rules!," "Marge I Love ~~Marge~~ You," and "El Barto Hired Someone That Was Here."

A NOBLE SPIRIT EMBIGGENS THE SMALLEST MAN

Within a stone's throw (Springfield Bridge's many hobos thank you for not actually throwing stones) is the **Springfield Hydroelectric Dam**, the site of the extremely wet Springfield Hydroelectric Dam Disaster. Still the subject of a great deal of conjecture, we do know this: some years ago former children's TV host and psychotic, Sideshow Bob, and his brother, Cecil, were implicated in a scheme in which the dam was blown to smithereens. To pay for the dam's reconstruction, the town sold the billboard rights to the structure. Visitors entering Springfield can now see the largest outdoor advertisement in the state, proclaiming, "Duff—Dat's Dam Good Beer!"

Moving from the outskirts to the inskirts of Springfield, what better place to begin than the center of town, at the **Springfield Town Square**. An irregular rectangle of grass and trees, the square is home to the large statue of Springfield's homely founder, **Jebediah Springfield**. Posed atop the carcass of a freshly killed bear, Jebediah stands proudly, as if to say, "I just killed this bear with my bare hands. Anyone want a piece of this, I'm right

WHAT'S RIGHT WITH SPRINGFIELD?

"I like the **Springfield Morgue.** It lets me get away from my troubles and there's always people down there to listen to me without talking back and bringing me down. There's no people saying, 'Hey, you forgot to stitch me up!' or 'You were supposed to give me artificial hips and you just put in two Lite-Brites!' I guess you could say my best friends in life are the dead people down in the morgue."

—Dr. Nick Riviera, M.D.

here, baby." Locals often refer to the statue as "the dud with the cub" and "that silly coonskinned jerk with the dead grizzly." This is the perfect place for a picnic, but do plan ahead, as the square is sprayed twice daily with malathion. Lasting the better part of an hour, these sprayings occur sometime between 10 A.M. and 2:30 P.M. and 2:37 P.M. and 5:00 P.M.

From the Town Square, follow the cacophony of digitized gunfire and death knells to Springfield's favorite hangout of perennial kids and sullen teenagers, the **Noise Land Video Arcade**. Often reaching levels of sound too loud to keep glass or human eardrums intact, the Noise Land Video Arcade is the site of many a famous event in Springfield's history. Here, for example, local bully Jimbo Jones performed his 10,000th wedgie.

Up the street, around the corner, and past the glue factory is Springfield's own **Duff Brewery**. Though smaller than its larger Capital City counterpart, fat lushes have no  problem getting drunk on its free samples. Because most visitors to the brewery leave with a greater-than-.16 blood-alcohol level, the only way to visit is via the official Duff Brewery shuttle (also called "the Big Ol' Bus for Drunks") which picks up visitors from a stop at Springfield Town Square. The shuttle features vinyl seats, a video presentation on the dangers of drinking called "Drink Duff Daily—But Don't Get Drunk" (starring recovering alcoholic Troy McClure), and motion-sickness bags aplenty.

Visitors looking to sleep off the results of their trip to the Duff Brewery will find sanctuary at

the nice, quiet, dimly lit **Mt. Swartzwelder Historic Cider Mill**. Here, surrounded by the nonthreatening beauty of nature, visitors can learn about the remarkable journey of apples from the orchards to cider bottles to our stomachs and beyond. The free samples here don't have the same consequences as those offered at the Duff Brewery, but do look out for the "Tart Months" of February and August, when the mill can produce cider sour enough to give any American a permanent French accent.

Moments from downtown Springfield, and the third stop in our free-sample triumvirate, is the **Ah, Fudge! Factory**. Here, visitors can witness the amazing machinery of the factory in action as it

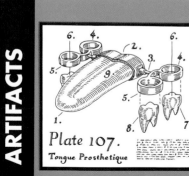

JEBEDIAH SPRINGFIELD'S SILVER TONGUE:

Plate 107.
Tongue Prosthetique

Cultural Significance:
Possibly great. There are some who say that Jebediah Springfield, town founder, was, in fact, a marauding pirate known as Hans Sprungfeld. Sprungfeld was one of the most evil, violent men of the 1780s, and he wore a black pirate hat with a skull and crossbones on it. He also wore a silver prosthetic tongue after he lost his real tongue during a groghouse fight. Thus, the metallic tongue, supposedly taken out of Jebediah Springfield's skull when he was exhumed during the Springfield

Bicentennial Celebration, may be the only evidence to support the theory that he may have led a double life.

Where to See It:
Nowhere. In fact, this highly controversial piece of history may not even exist. Rumors abound that the mayor uses it as a paperweight in his home office.

Estimated Value:
After it's been properly sanitized, in the tens of millions.

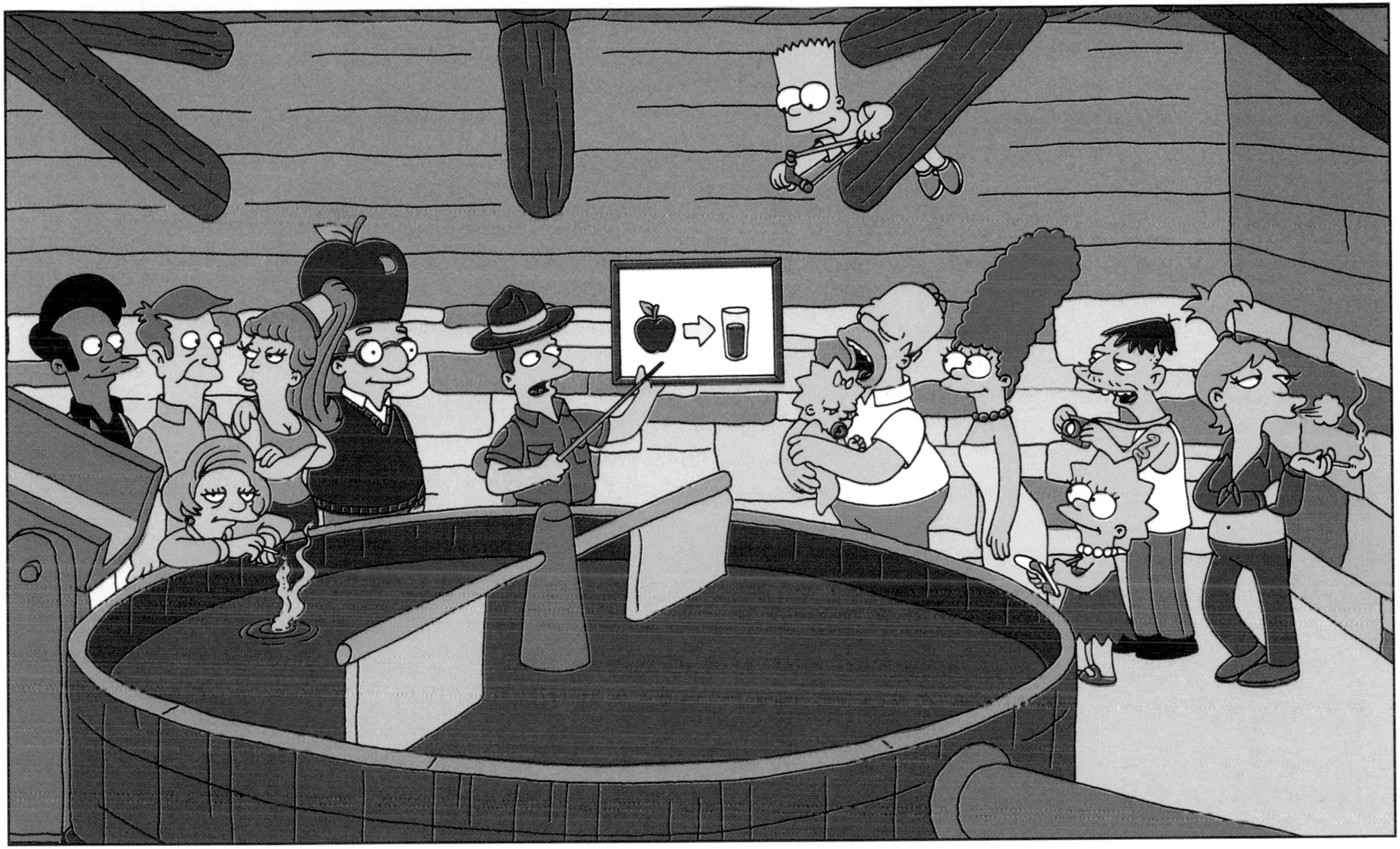

transforms dry milk, cocoa powder, and highly caustic chemicals into chocolate-flavored confections. Especially lucky children may get to catch a glimpse of "Cocoa Beanie" himself, the anthropomorphic cocoa bean who's the living embodiment of joy, cocoa, and whatever else the company currently stands for. *Note:* Children are not allowed within three feet of Cocoa Beanie until their parents sign documents promising that their offspring won't beat, kick, or spit on the aging choco-mascot; he's just had too many bad experiences.

Springfielders listen to the thrilling story of cider at the Mt. Swartzwelder Historic Cider Mill.

WHAT'S RIGHT WITH SPRINGFIELD?

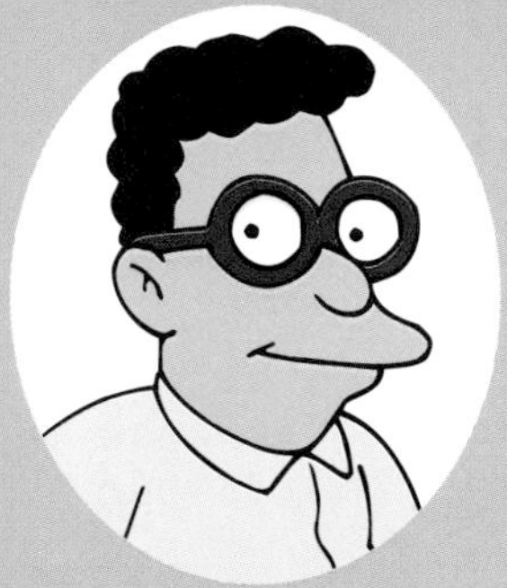

"The Springfield Observatory. Big mirrors and bigger fun!"

—Database, age 8

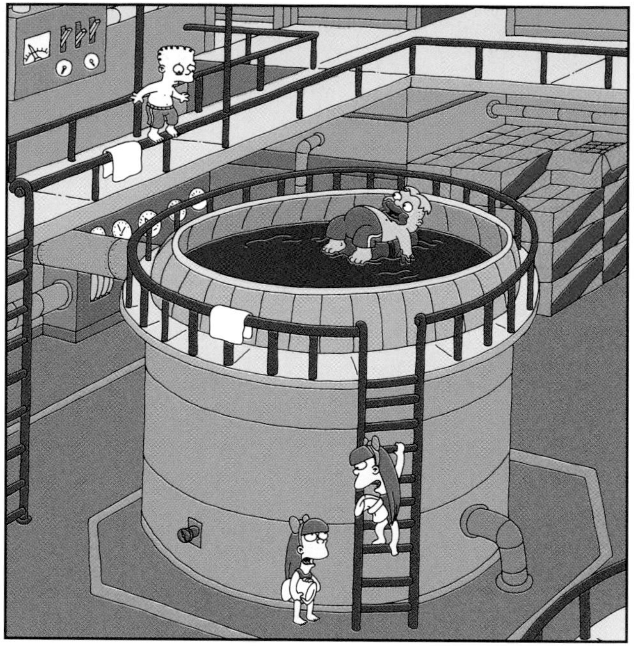

Visiting children frolic among vats of cooling chocolate at the Ah, Fudge! Factory.

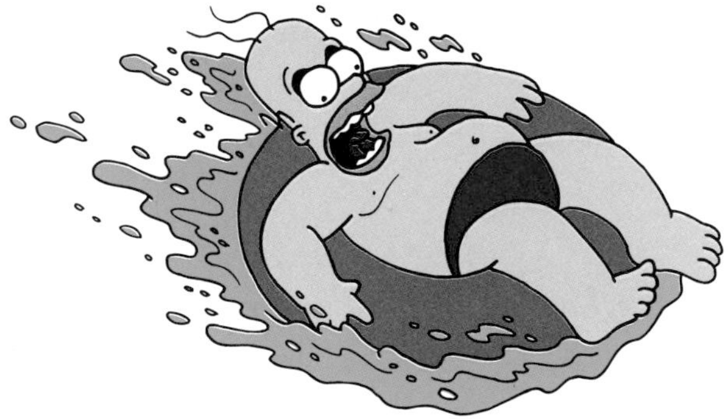

Those well-behaved kids who choose not to take a swing at Cocoa Beanie can be rewarded with a trip to Springfield's foremost waterpark and dunkery, **Mt. Splashmore**. Boasting "the most ways you can be shot hundreds of feet into the air by a geyser of highly pressurized water," Mt. Splashmore is a haven for kids too young to know fear and risk-takers looking for a way to beat the heat. But be careful. Lives are in the hands of bored sixteen-year-old lifeguards who have only casually glanced at the various rules and procedures of the park. Lax safety regulations on the part of Springfield City Hall have given license to the most thrilling, pulse-pounding, and potentially injurious slides in the industrialized world. A favorite among daring visitors is "The Devil's Gullet," which begins three hundred feet in the air and drops screaming patrons down at a ninety-degree angle before suddenly shooting them into a complex network of intensely curvy tubes and then propelling them quickly through the tank of a great white shark, over an alligator pit, and finally, into a lukewarm, extra-foamy Jacuzzi.

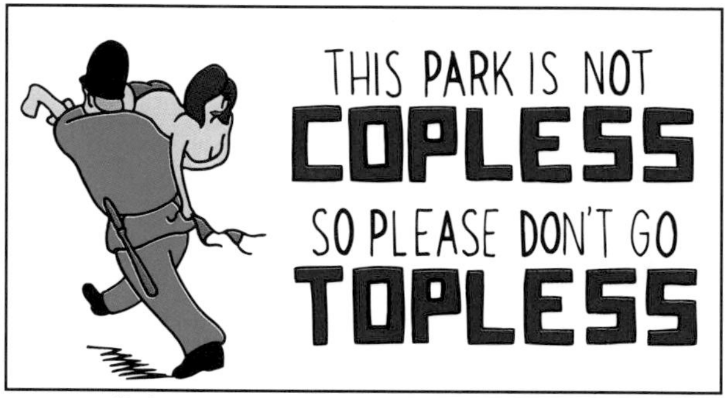
THIS PARK IS NOT
COPLESS
SO PLEASE DON'T GO
TOPLESS

If one doesn't find religion in the thrills of Mt. Splashmore, the **Springfield Mystery Spot** may

The Springfield Mystery Spot successfully nauseates over 650 paying customers per year.

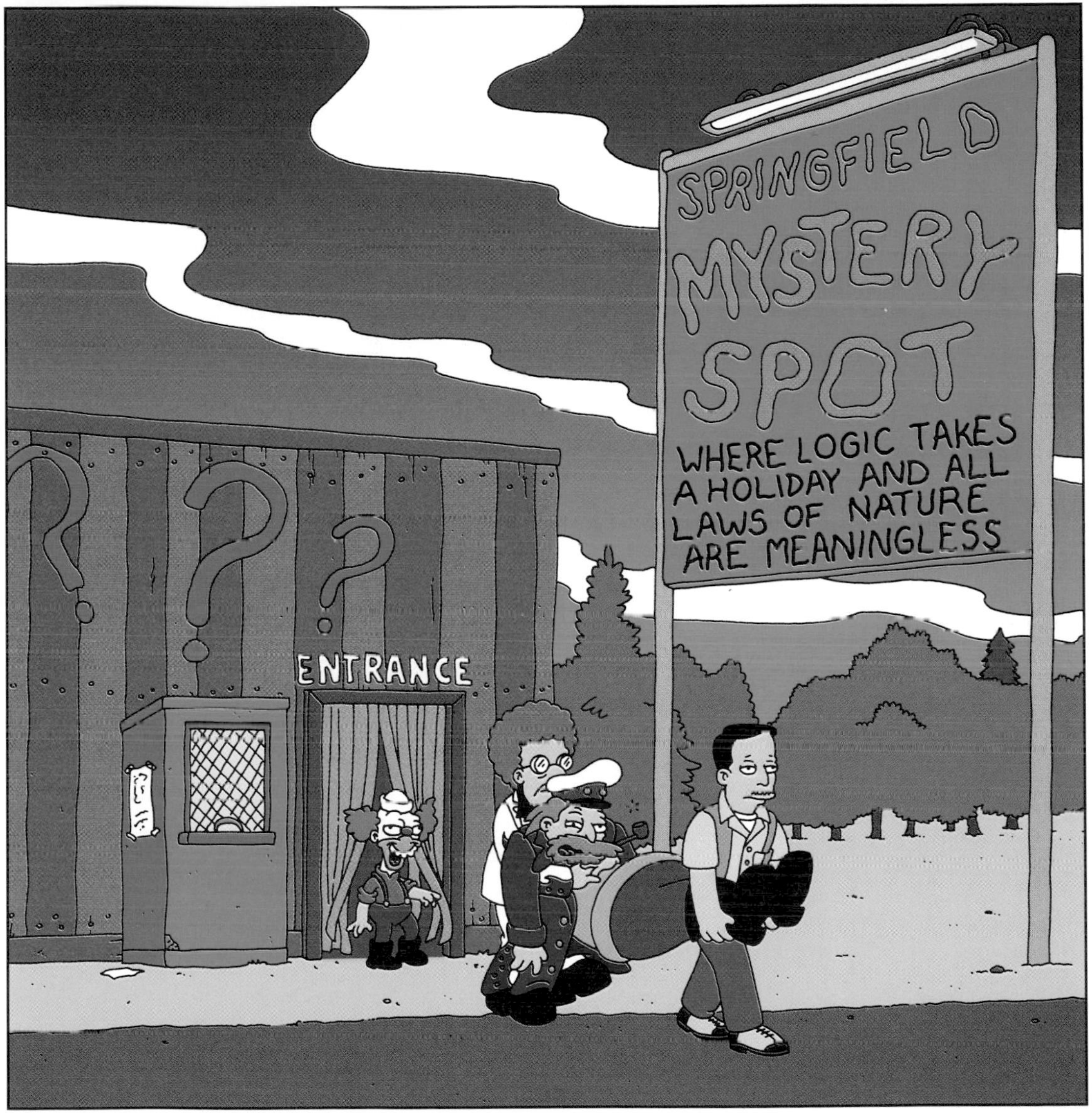
SPRINGFIELD
MYSTERY
SPOT
WHERE LOGIC TAKES A HOLIDAY AND ALL LAWS OF NATURE ARE MEANINGLESS
ENTRANCE

satisfy the hungry soul. Here, past visitors have claimed to see the face of God, to speak in colors, to shed their corporeal bodies and become floating spirits, and to take pictures that don't have that annoying red-eye effect. Basically a shack in the middle of nowhere, the site is an undefinable, unthinkable tourist stop for those who aren't afraid of the unknown or don't mind getting milked out of ten bucks. Some scientists claim that the Springfield Mystery Spot is a nexus between the time-space continuum of several dimensions intersecting in a horrible vortex of chaos. Others say that it's just the effects of the shack's wicked paint fumes.

Few things can complement horrible vortexes of chaos, but psychologists around the world agree that the calming influence of the hot pastrami and half-done pickles of Springfield's

WHAT'S RIGHT WITH SPRINGFIELD?

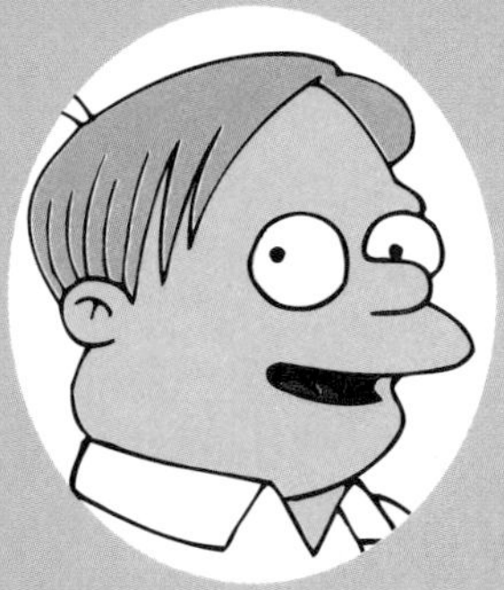

"The water lilies of the **Springfield Arboretum** sing to my soul and help ease the pain of the daily wedgies, swirlies, and liver pummelings that I receive at school."

—Martin Prince, age 10

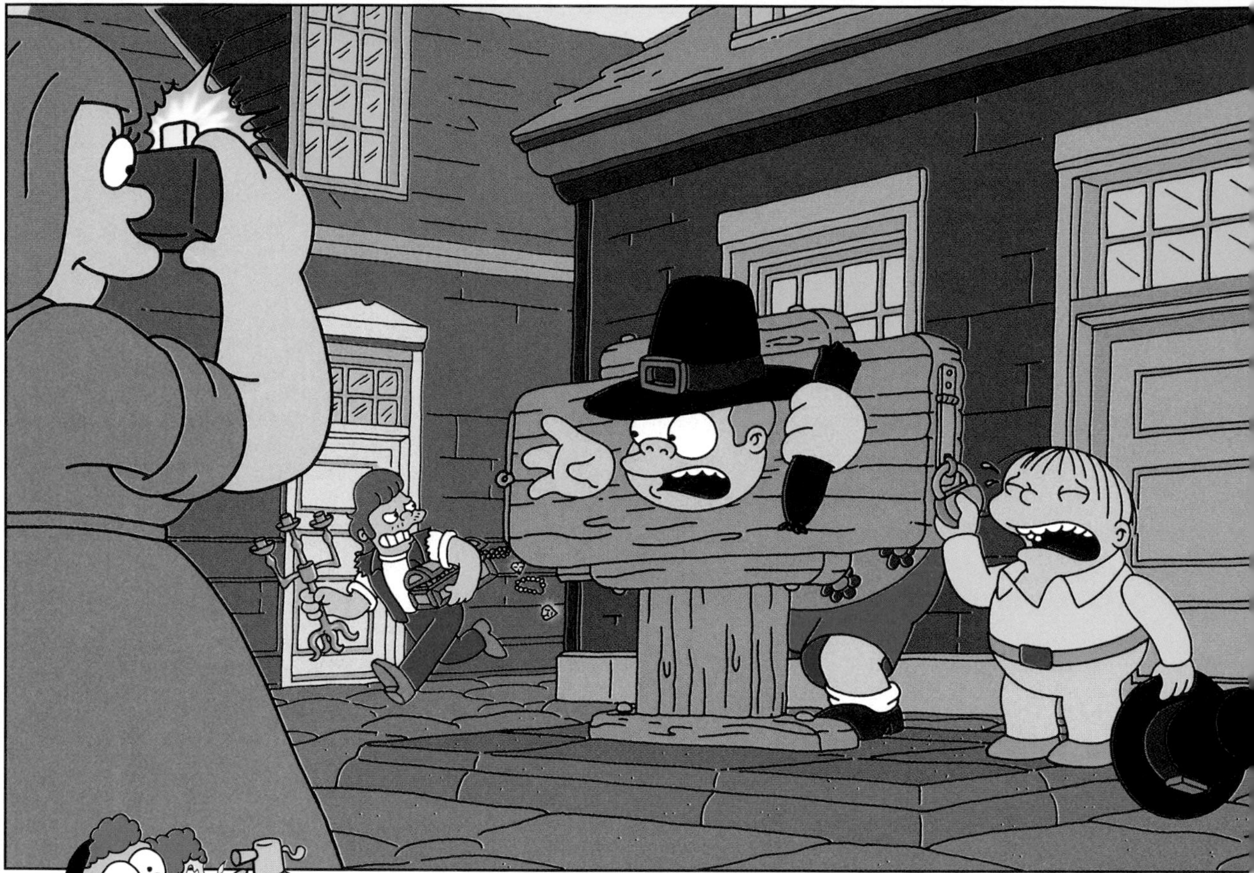

Police Chief Clancy Wiggum, dropping the ball on a family outing/stakeout at Olde Springfield Towne.

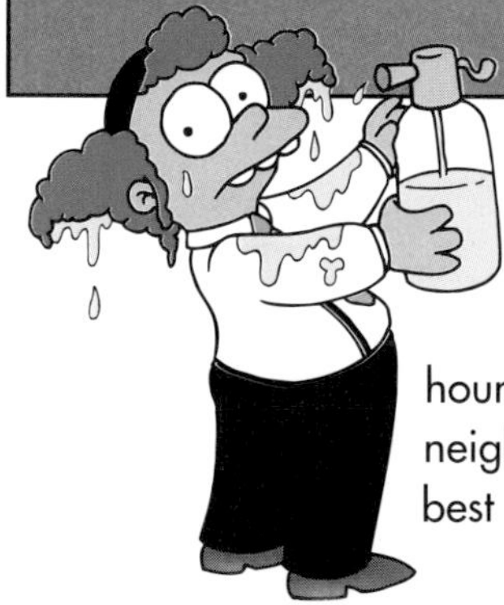

Lower East Side can whisk away the effects of post-traumatic stress disorder inside a lunch hour. Tannen's Fatty Meats, a neighborhood favorite, is the best spot in all of Springfield for such a feast. Just down the street from Tannen's is the Krusty the Clown Birthplace Tour and Gift Shoppe. Called "the Graceland of Jewish Clown Fans," the tour takes you from the carpet Krusty did his first pratfall on to the bathroom he

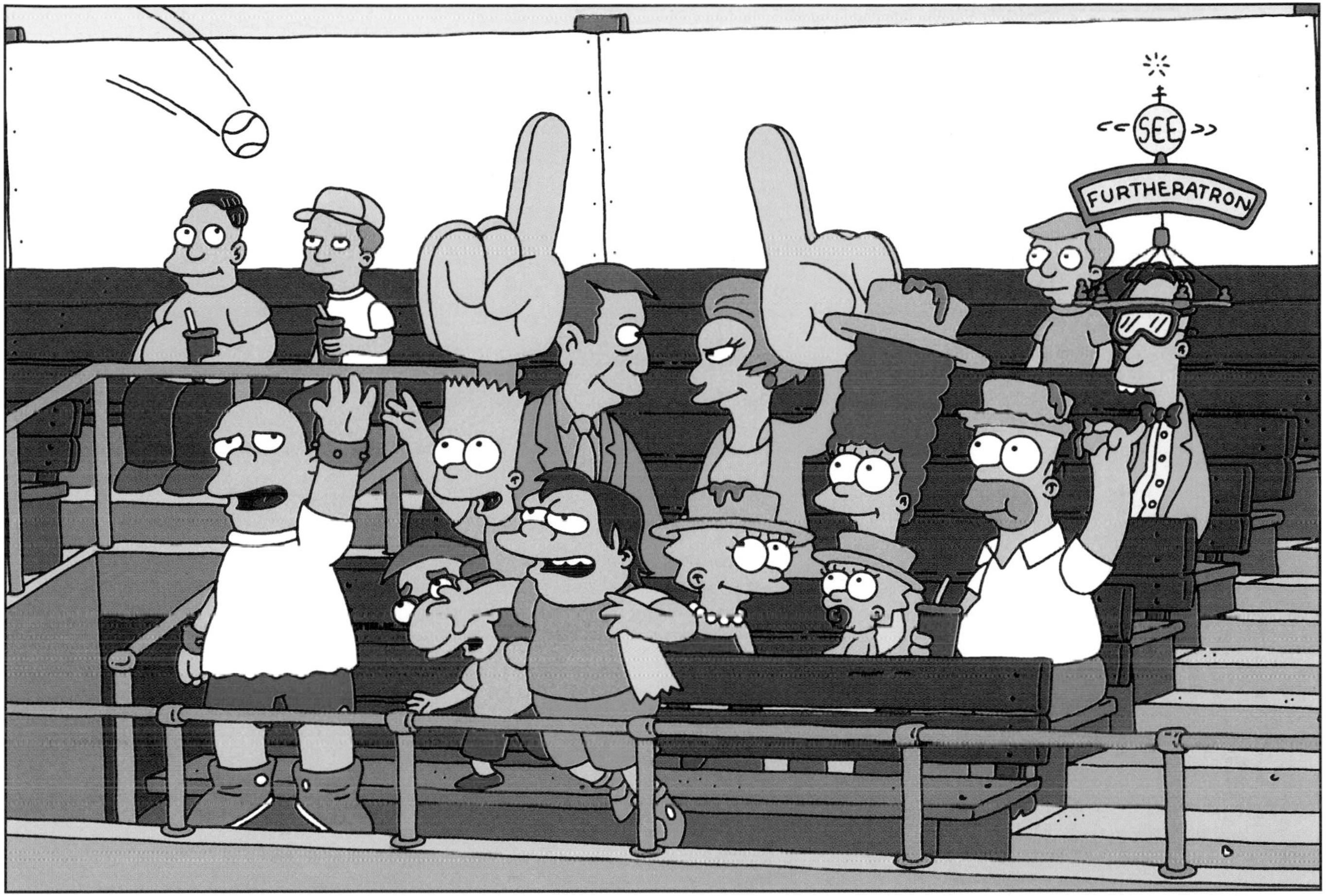
SEE
FURTHERATRON

practiced seltzer tricks in to the back alley where he learned how to swear.

Approximately five miles in some direction from the Lower East Side lies **Olde Springfield Towne**, a for-profit historical park replete with glass blowers, candlemakers, and wig powderers. In response to recent complaints by educators that the park is "just too boring," the Towne's proprietors have given it a minor facelift and restructuring. However, scholars are quick to point

Springfielders vie for a baseball, enjoy Nacho hats (and a Li'l Nachee), and watch minor-league play at the Springfield War Memorial Stadium.

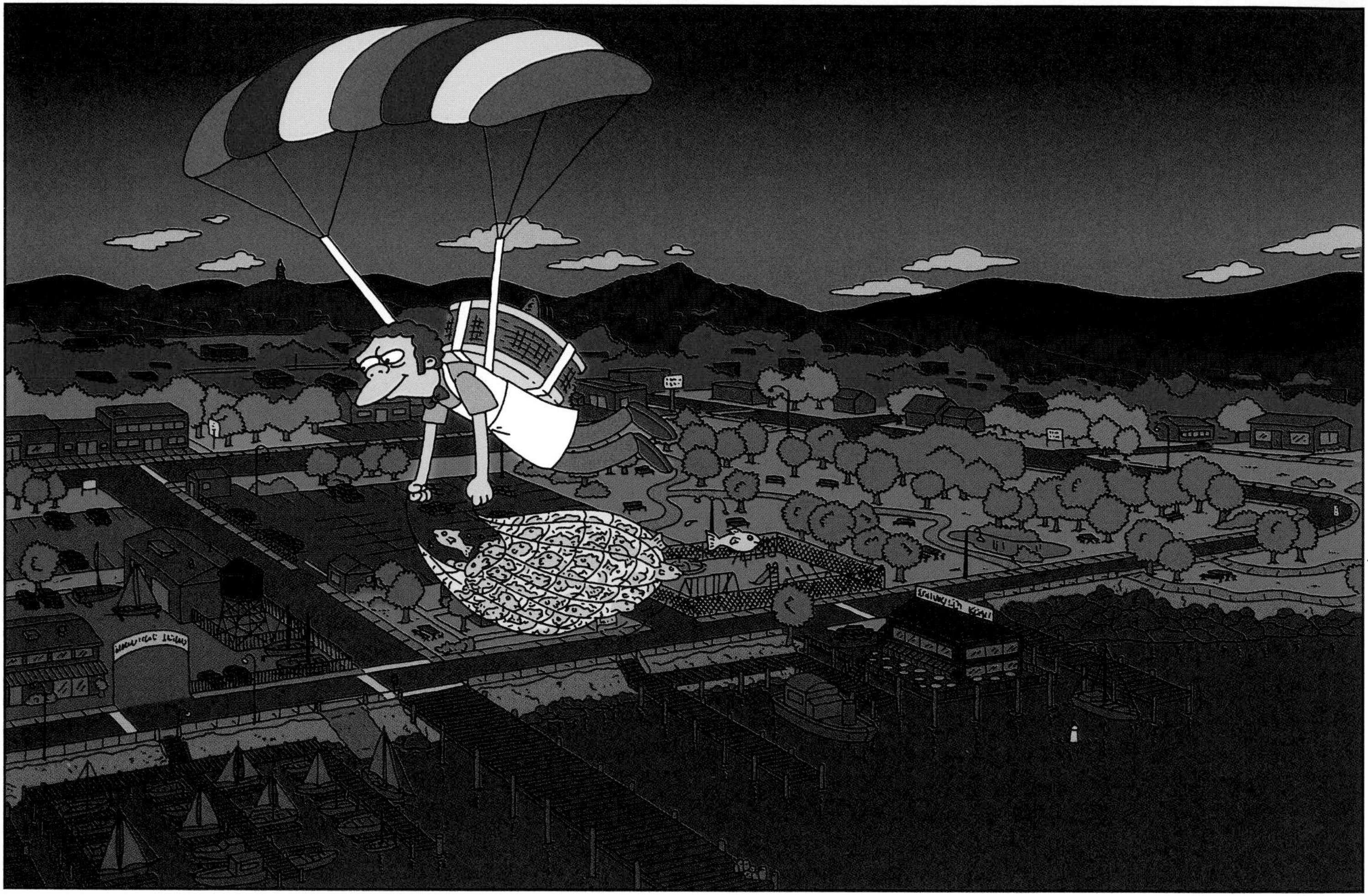

out recently added anachronisms: Colonial Springfield did not use muskets with laser sights, three-cornered hats were never used as "ninja star"-type weapons, and tavern waitresses did not wear hot pants. Regardless of what did and didn't go on in bygone Springfield, a day in Olde Springfield Towne is about as exciting as history can get. Admission includes four eggs to huck at unruly children who

Moe Szyslak hauls his latest illegal pollack catch back home.

Truckasaurus, the monster truck monster, noshes on the Springfield Elementary School bus.

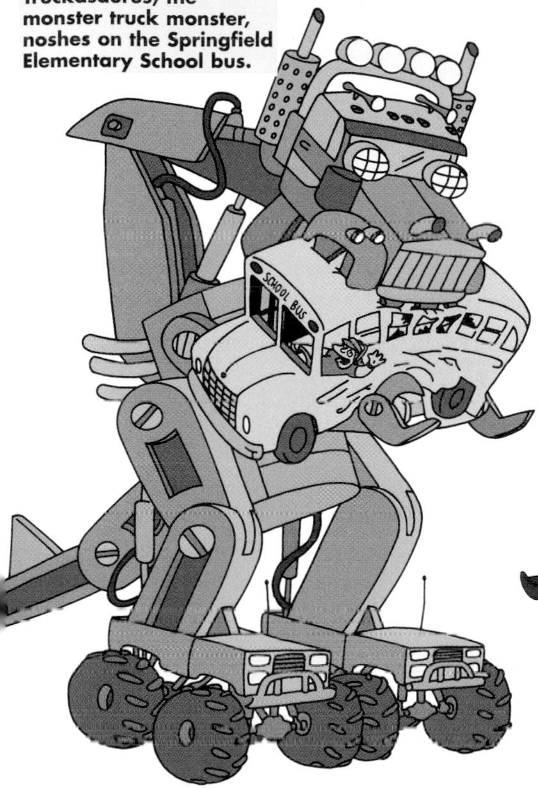
SCHOOL BUS

are put in the stocks throughout the Main Street area.

After a day of faux-history, who can resist the simple, continental charms of nitro-burning cars hurtling dangerously around curves at speeds exceeding 150 MPH? Fortunately, two places in Springfield provide this awesome spectacle: the big freeway interchange just outside town and the **Springfield Speedway**. Though equally harrowing, the corn dogs at the Speedway are better. Visitors there can witness any number of reckless events, including drag racing, daredevil life-risking, or a visit from Truckasaurus, the fire-breathing metallic monstrosity that eats other cars to provide captivating family entertainment.

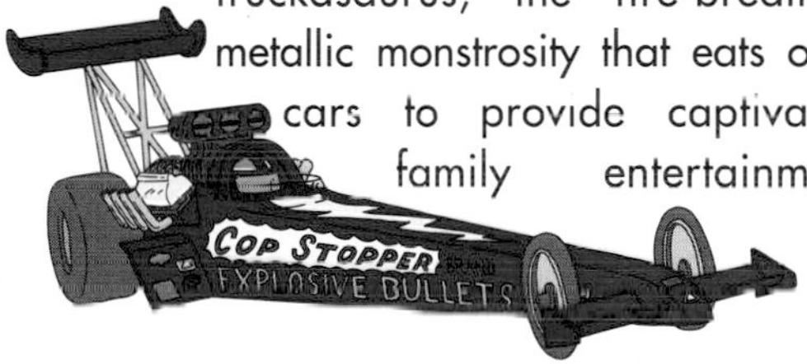
COP STOPPER
EXPLOSIVE BULLETS

(Those who have been attacked by fire-breathing, metallic monstrosities in the past might want to stay behind, as the show is sure to revive bad memories.)

Another terrific sit-down activity is a baseball game at the **Springfield War Memorial Stadium**, the current home of the Springfield Isotopes. Though the Isotopes have never enjoyed a winning record, scientists do calculate that it is possible and could happen sometime during the next thirty years. Of course, some predict that a non-losing season would be the sign of an upcoming apocalypse, but really, who's to know? Among the unique concessions available at the stadium are buffalo wings

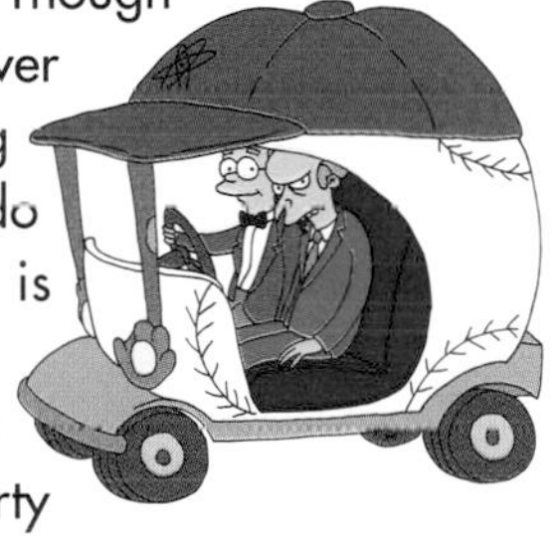

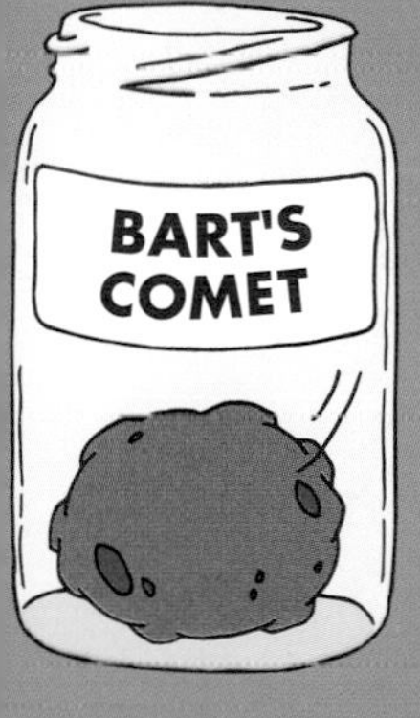
BART'S COMET

THE SPRINGFIELD COMET:

The Story Behind the Space Stuff:
When a comet threatened to destroy Springfield, the city's extra-thick inversion layer of smog and nuclear vapor helped burn it up and reduce it to the size of a Chihuahua's head. The tiny cometette landed in Springfield without destroying anything but a vandalized (and thus obscene) weather balloon and an empty, poorly constructed bomb shelter.

Why It's Worth Seeing:
This wee comet that fell to Springfield is a testament to the city's dumb luck and near-criminal environmental policies.

Where to See It:
At the Simpson family home on Evergreen Terrace. Ten year-old Bart Simpson will show it to anyone who asks, provided they can pay him five dollars and do a dead-on impression of Huckleberry Hound.

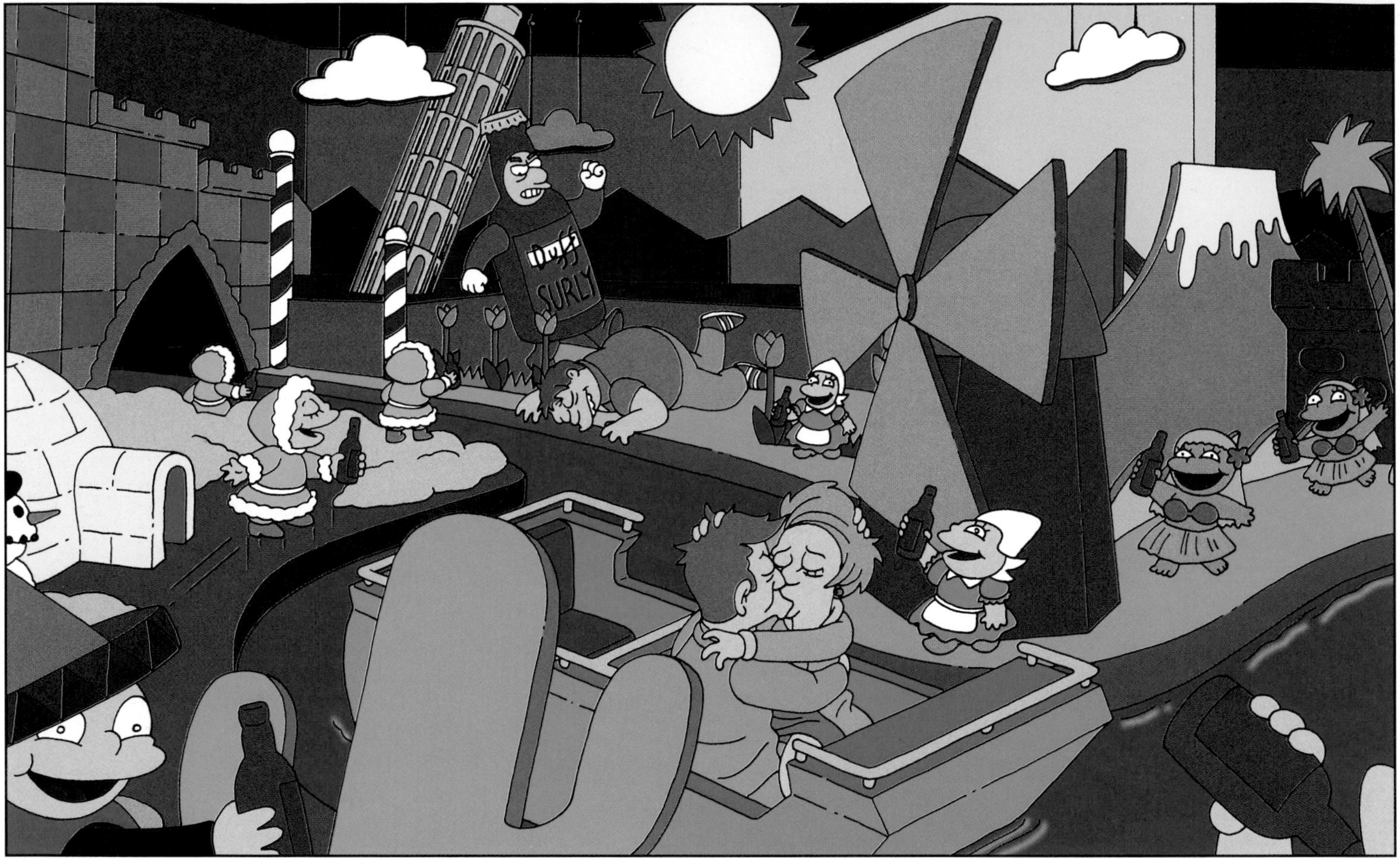
Duff
SURLY

The "Little Land of Duff" ride at Duff Gardens, enjoyed by lovers and alcoholics alike.

(not chicken but the actual wings of a buffalo/bird hybrid that recently mutated into existence at a Springfield farm downstream from the Springfield Nuclear Power Plant) and marzipan putty for children.

Virtually around the corner from the Springfield War Memorial Stadium is **Springfield Harbor**, famous for its squid gutteries and brine clarification plants. At this salty, fishy, and generally abandoned harbor, where the barnacles are free for the taking, visitors will find a fine, firsthand look at the effects of NAFTA and declining scungilli consumption in the United States. An upscale shopping promenade known as the **South Street Squidport** has taken over most of this ruined harbor. Filled with trendy, demographically correct stores like Turban Outfitters, Just Rainsticks, It's a Wonderful Knife, and Malaria Zone, the Squidport is a terrific place to put a dent in the vacation budget while picking up absolutely unnecessary items.

After a day or two of the hustle and bustle of Springfield's sophisticated streets, it's a good idea to make a brief escape to the bucolic (and deceptively alcoholic) wilds of **Duff Gardens**, located a few dozen miles outside of the city. Featuring rides and attractions that either promote alcohol consumption or simulate inebriation or both, Duff Gardens can dizzy and disorient even the most jaded amusement seeker and/or experienced drinker. The Barrel Roll recently underwent a complete redesign, making it one of the most jarring, internal-organ-shifting rollercoasters on the face of the Earth. Each car comes with motion-sickness bags, smelling salts, and a Unitarian Bible. The Barrel Roll is so fast, steep, and curvy, pregnant women are advised to not even look at it.

Duff
SLEAZY

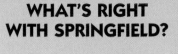

If the amusement bug continues to bite, put some calamine lotion on said bite and consider taking a day trip to **Itchy & Scratchy Land**. While the kids frolic at Torture Land, Explosion Land, Searing Gas Pain Land, Unnecessary Surgery Land, and the upcoming BloodClot Center (projected opening: 2002), parents can unwind at the aptly named Parents' Island. Here, parents can pursue their interests in consuming alcoholic beverages, learning new recipes, hammock-loafing, watching hours of

TORTURE LAND
EXPLOSION LAND
UNNECESSARY SURGERY LAND
SEARING GAS PAIN LAND
CHILI

WHAT'S RIGHT WITH SPRINGFIELD?

"The floor of Moe's has kept my back straight for aught-BRAAAP!"

—Barney Gumble, entrepreneur

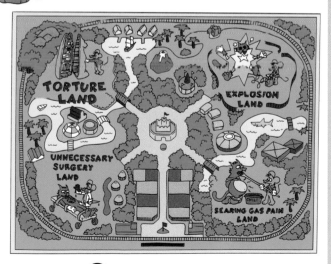

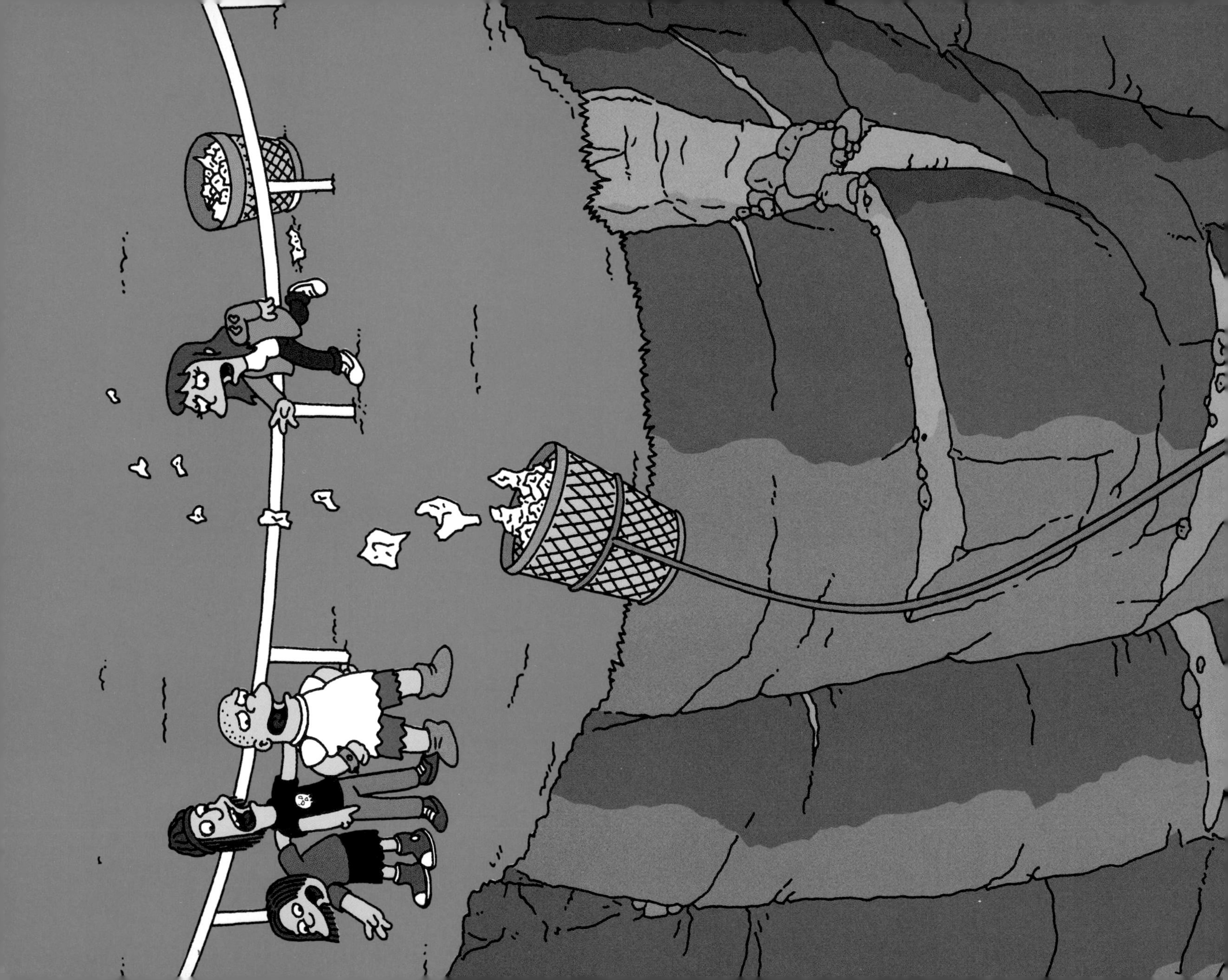

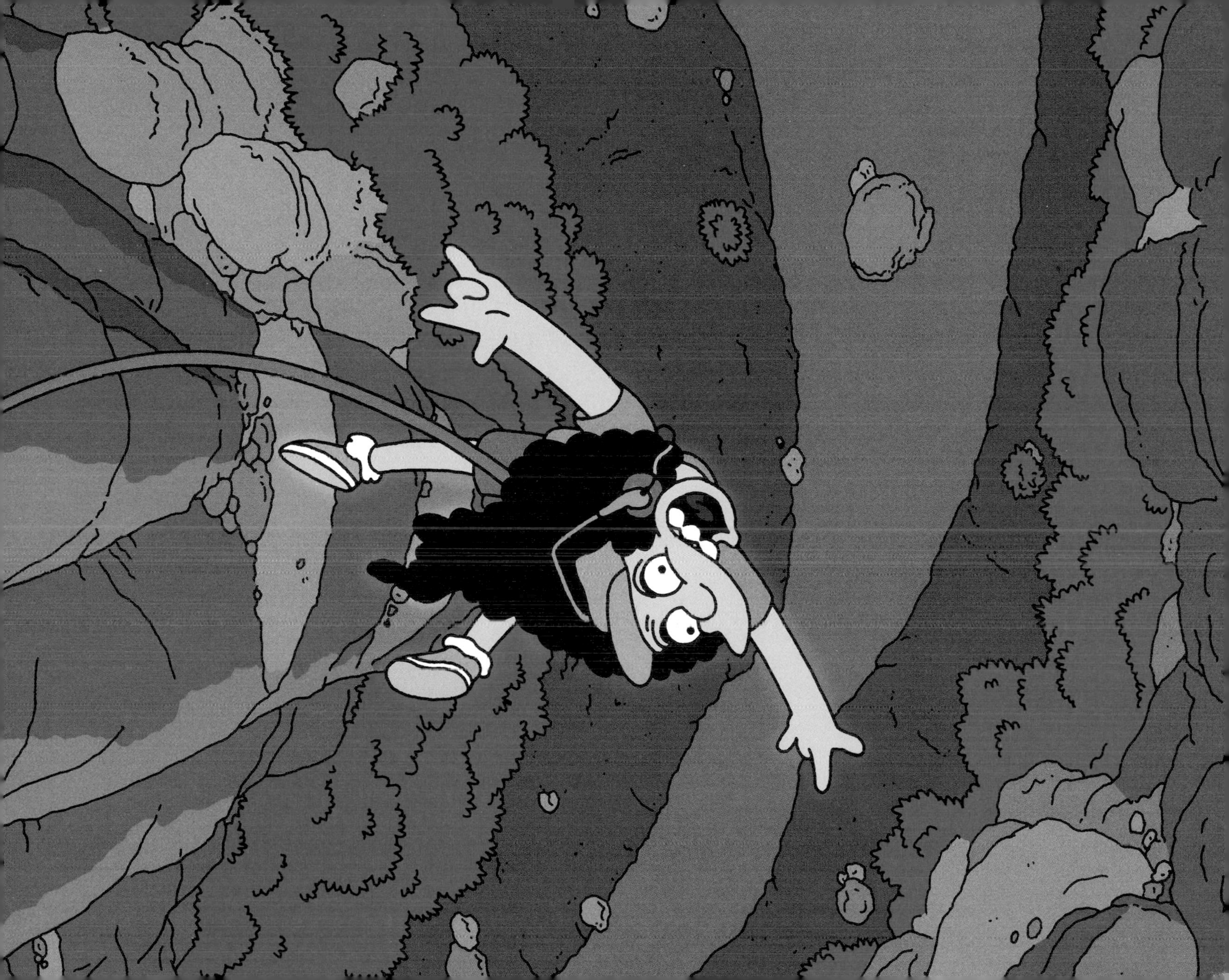

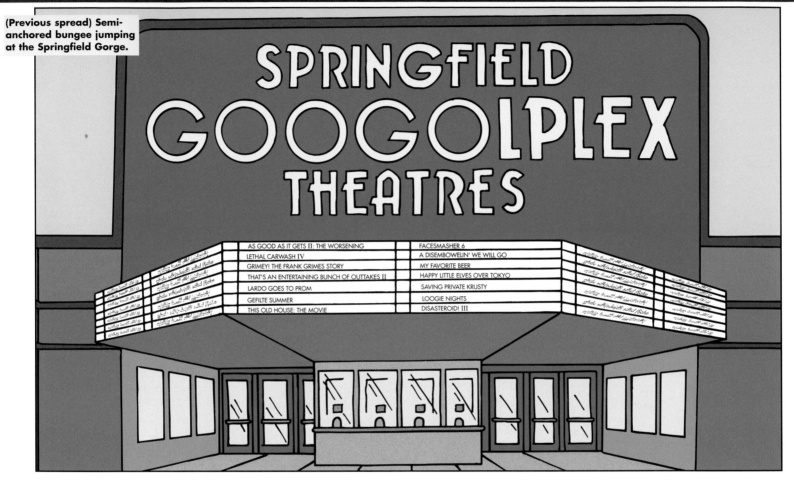

(Previous spread) Semi-anchored bungee jumping at the Springfield Gorge.

SPRINGFIELD GOOGOLPLEX THEATRES

AS GOOD AS IT GETS II: THE WORSENING	FACESMASHER 6
LETHAL CARWASH IV	A DISEMBOWELIN' WE WILL GO
GRIMEY! THE FRANK GRIMES STORY	MY FAVORITE BEER
THAT'S AN ENTERTAINING BUNCH OF OUTTAKES II	HAPPY LITTLE ELVES OVER TOKYO
LARDO GOES TO PROM	SAVING PRIVATE KRUSTY
GEFILTE SUMMER	LOOGIE NIGHTS
THIS OLD HOUSE: THE MOVIE	DISASTEROID! III

television, or deluding themselves that they are still living in the 1970s. Also featuring the finest amusement-park-run ER and triage center in the state, Itchy & Scratchy Land boasts a 95 percent survival rate for its emergency organ transplants and tracheotomies. Of course, no one wants to have an amusement-park-related accident, but if you must have one, consider having it at the "Violentest Place on Earth."

(At right) Children loiter around the Aztec Theater, preparing to go inside, while movie star Troy McClure makes an impromptu personal appearance.

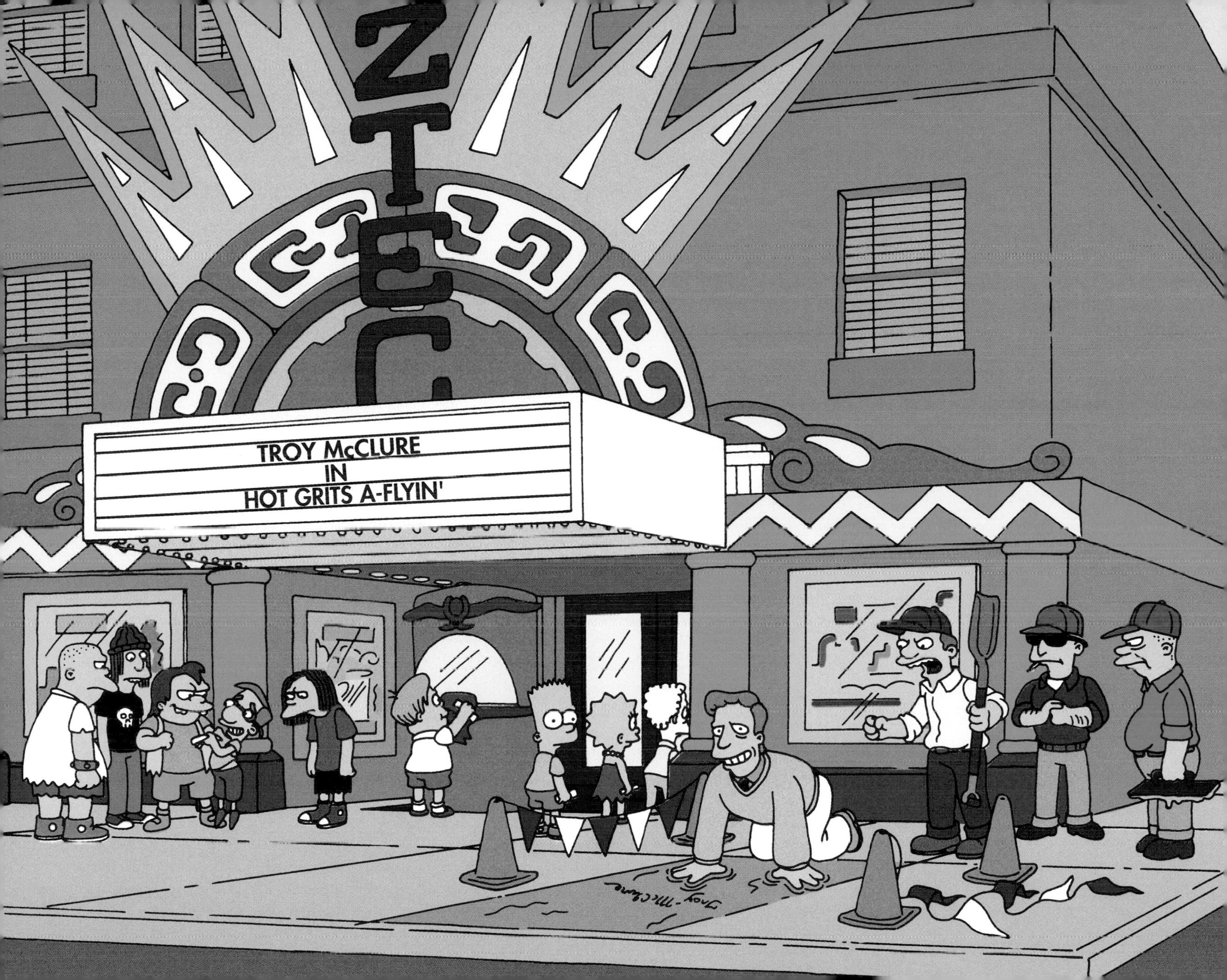
AZTEC
TROY McCLURE
IN
HOT GRITS A-FLYIN'
Troy McClure

WHAT'S RIGHT WITH SPRINGFIELD?

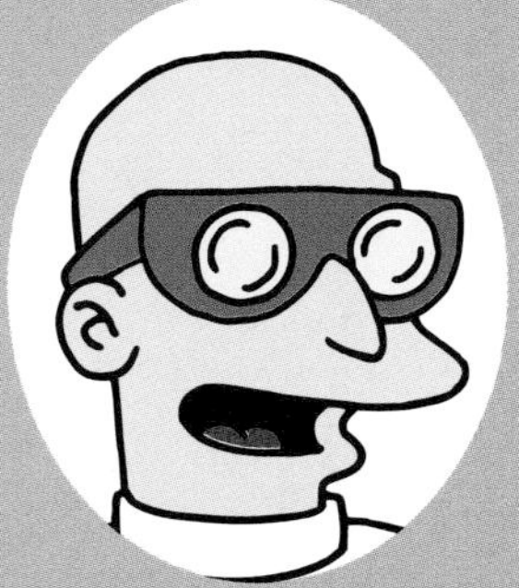

"Though I am capable of creating laser weapons that could vaporize entire armies, I often find myself browsing the aisles of Herman's Military Antiques, immersing myself in the weapons of a simpler time, when men killed each other with simple, elegant tools like bayonets and military-issue oyster forks."

—Dr. Colossus, professional supervillain

The one (legal) thing visitors won't find at Itchy & Scratchy Land is America's favorite pastime: gambling. For that, visitors must actually cross the state line to find Springfield's nearest risk-a-teria, **Plato's Republic Gaming Casino and Pleasure Domiarium.** Crapsheads rejoice: The casino at Plato's houses the world's longest craps table, measuring two hundred feet long. (Sorry, seniors: To throw the dice you must qualify by taking a rigorous battery of physical tests, including lifting the filled coin receptacle out of the Philosopher King-Sized Slot Machine.) Also, patrons can stuff themselves silly at the Golden Trough, Plato's fabled buffet, now salmonella-free for its third straight year. (The management is feverishly working on its botulism record, so avoid the oysters and the cocktail wieners in brine.) Plato's Pleasure Domiarium also attracts some of the finest entertainers who are either considered "has-beens" by most of the American public or were in a drunken stupor when they accepted a gig at Plato's Republic. Currently, Paul Revere & the Raiders and Dean Martin, respectively, hold the records for the largest number of performances at Plato's.

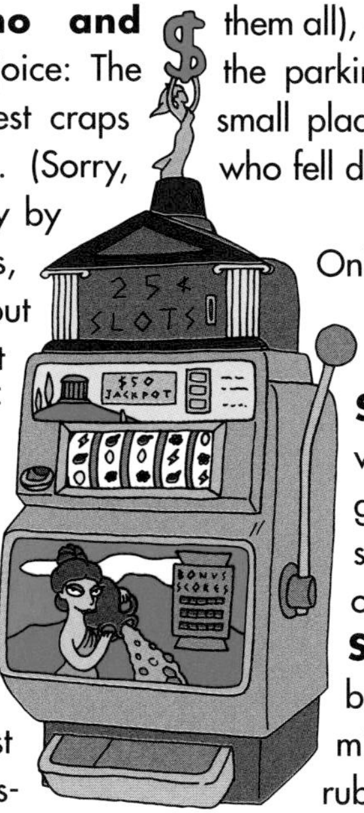
2 5 4
SLOTS
$50
JACKPOT
BONUS
SCORES

After a visit to Plato's, perhaps a less expensive itinerary may be desired. There isn't an attraction cheaper in Springfield than the **Springfield Gorge**. Here, visitors can pass countless minutes standing and staring at the mild semi-majesty of what has been called "Springfield's Really Big Creekhole." Though fairly uninteresting as far as gorges go (because, really, if you've seen one gorge you've seen them all), admission is free. An interesting area near the parking lot called "Homer's Leap" features a small plaque that details the story of a local man who fell down the gorge twice in one afternoon.

Only a lottery win can catapult ordinary visitors from the Springfield Gorge to where wealthy Springfielders gorge: the **Springfield Millionaire's Club**. For visiting millionaires, no trip to the atomic gables of Springfield is complete without stopping at one of this city's most exclusive organizations. Here, high atop the **Springfield Trade Center** (the tallest building in town), millionaires, multi-millionaires, and the occasional billionaire rub elbows, using state-of-the-art loofas to exfoliate themselves before mealtime. And what mealtimes they are! Fifteen-course dinners are served nightly, featuring the most expensive foods available: caviar, bluefin tuna, and premium Lorax steaks. From the club's gleaming faucets run Bordeaux wines: a

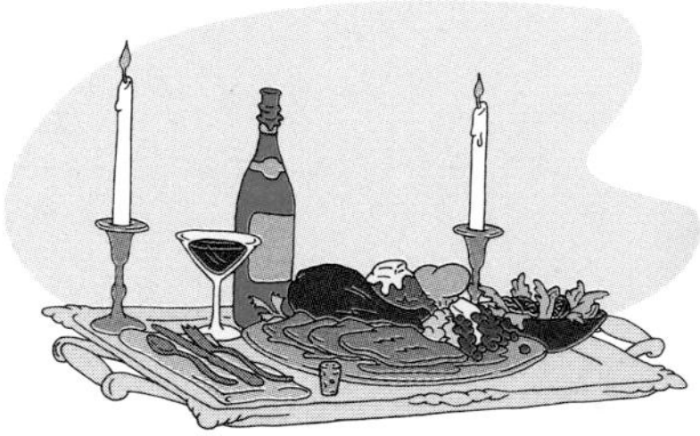

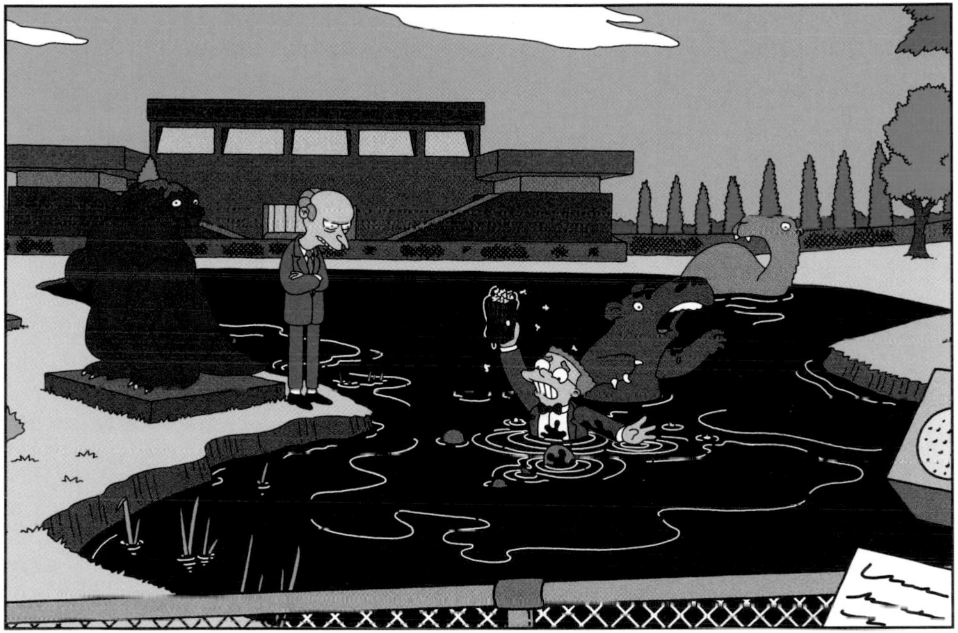

Rescuing a 98¢ box of popcorn at the Springfield Tar Pits.

'62 Chateau Lateur and a '54 Raison Segler replace hot and cold water, respectively. In the club's rumpus rooms, CEOs and CFOs play cutthroat games of Ping-Pong and Hungry Hungry Hippos, wagering their companies and their hundred-thousand-dollar hair-weaves to increase the stakes. Sadly, most visitors to Springfield will never see this modern-day Mount Olympus, although reports of snooty washroom attendants who expect a tip just for handing guests a paper towel seem to indicate it may not be that big a loss.

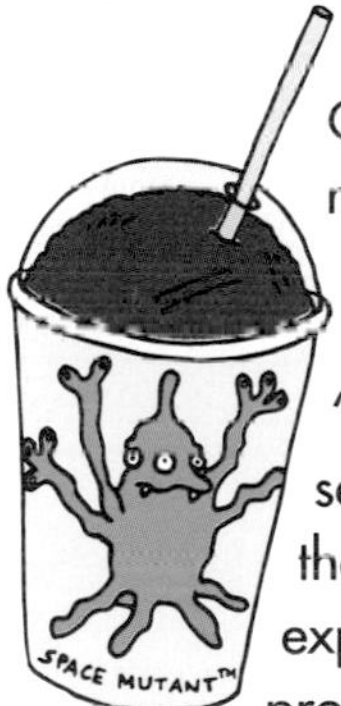
SPACE MUTANT™

Climate-controlled luxury for millionaires and nonmillionaires alike can be found at the **Springfield Googolplex**, the local version of the Taj Mahal. "Down at the Goog," patrons enjoy stadium seating in over thirty theaters (as of this writing, there are plans to increase the Googolplex's annual expansion from three to six theaters a year—it is projected to have over seven hundred screens by the year 3000), state-of-the-art projection, and, for an additional charge, shiatsu massage during the trailers and/or closing credits. The Googoplex's upscale concessions are truly wow-inspiring, offering hot foods from corn dogs to osso buco, while a chef carves freshly roasted turkey, prime rib, and Red Vine loaf. Each seat is equipped with a pause button that allows individual audience members to freeze the film while they get up to stretch their legs or go to the bathroom. *Note:* This feature may be discontinued soon, as it has led to several riots and three popcorn-tub smotherings.

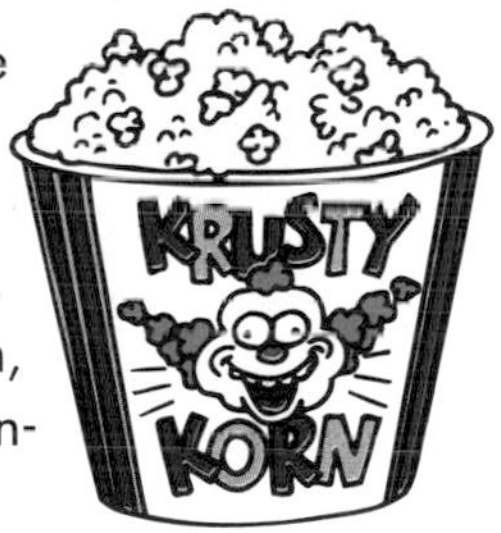
KRUSTY
KORN

Closer to the center of town, the **Aztec Theater** delivers an old-fashioned moviegoing experience, with a single large theater and Milk Duds that were purchased in bulk back in 1968. The Aztec's seats are worn, the floor is beyond sticky (those with loose-fitting shoes should be advised to either tighten

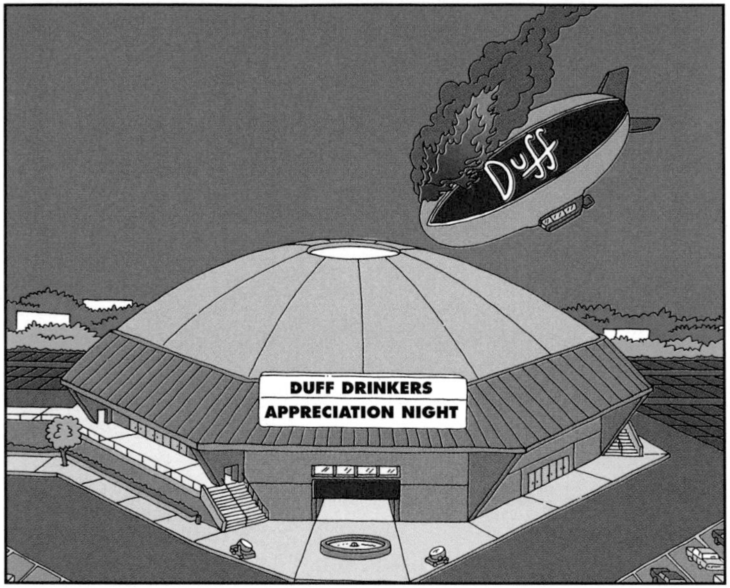
Duff
DUFF DRINKERS
APPRECIATION NIGHT

Bitter irony at the Springfield Coliseum.

their laces or prepare to part with their soles), and the screen occasionally falls over during the film. But theatergoers enjoy many benefits: There are no competing sounds from another film in an adjacent theater, the Aztec rarely sells out, and the marquee boasts a kick-ass display of neon wonderment.

Aficionados of the old-fashioned may want to walk several blocks from the Aztec to the **Springfield Historical Society**, where the dusty smell of history fills the air. Here, cases and cases of Colonial items are on display for curious eyes: Cutlery and plates sit side-by-side with centuries-old bottles and shoelaces. If that isn't excitement enough, the society's curator, Hollis Hurlbut, occasionally shares his johnnycakes with lucky visitors.

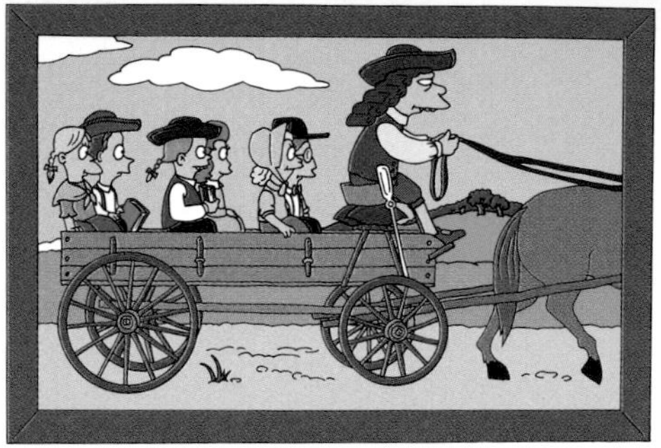

Heading north on the "Educational, Nonprofit Foot-trail"—a blue line painted on Springfield's downtown sidewalks that leads visitors to especially boring, underfunded attractions—leads to

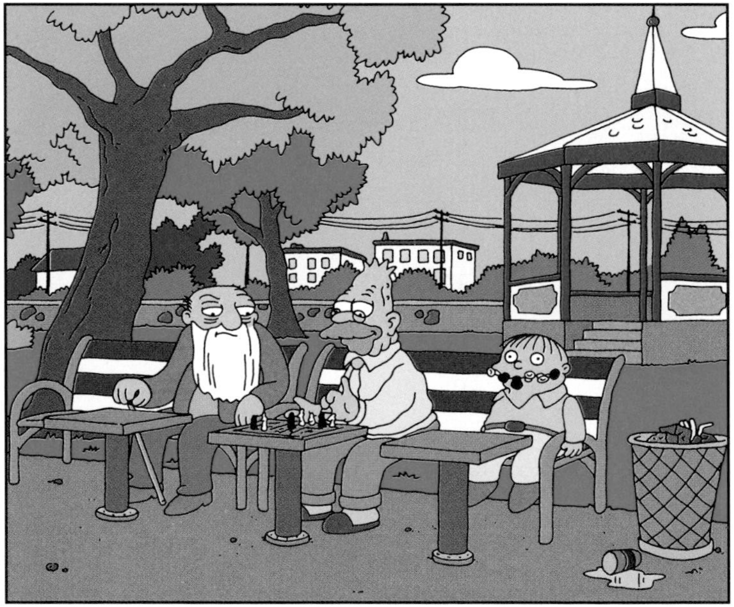

Seniors enjoy a rare day outside as an unidentified boy sucks on several pawns and a rook.

(At right) Krusty laments over a busted trifecta at Springfield Downs.

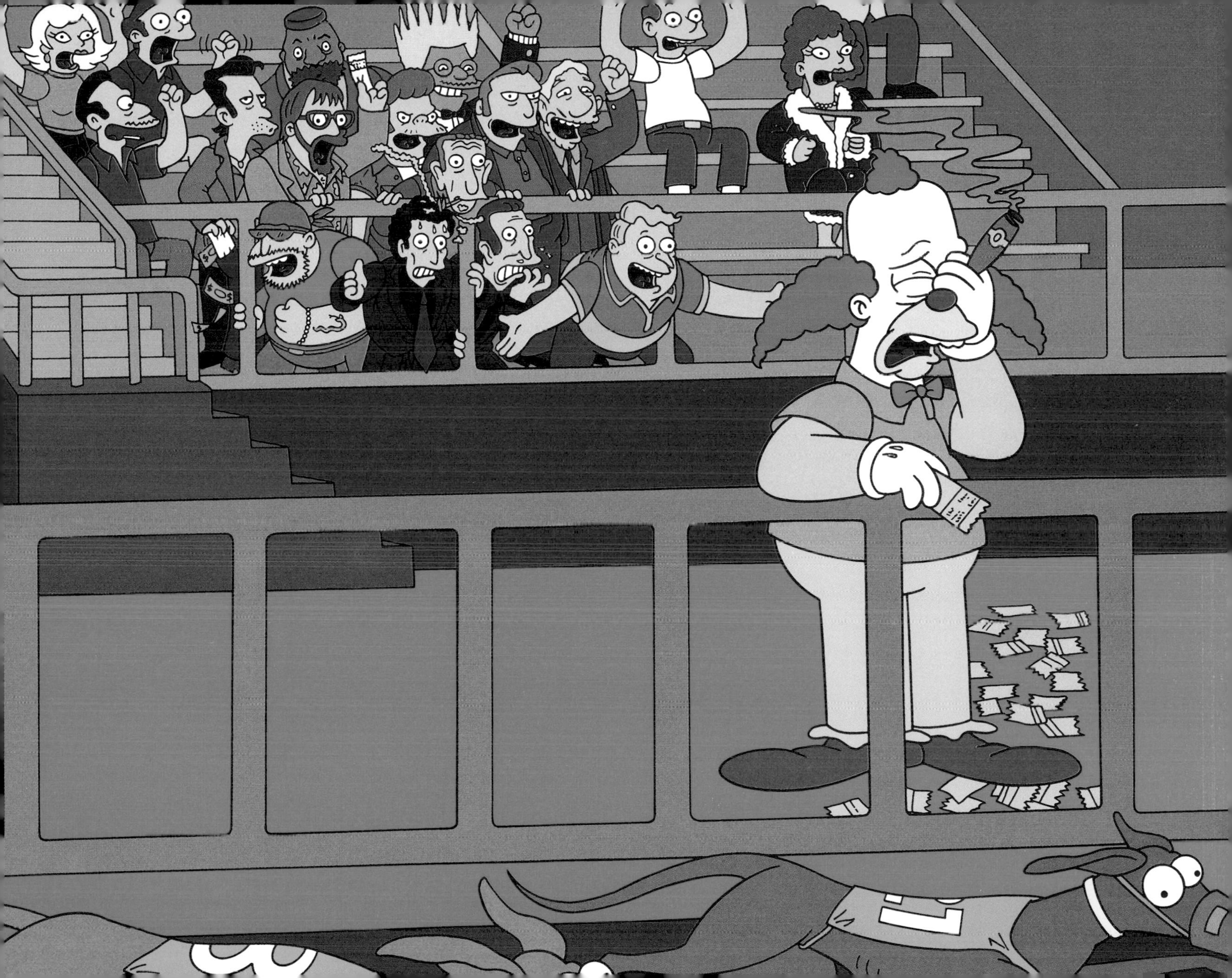

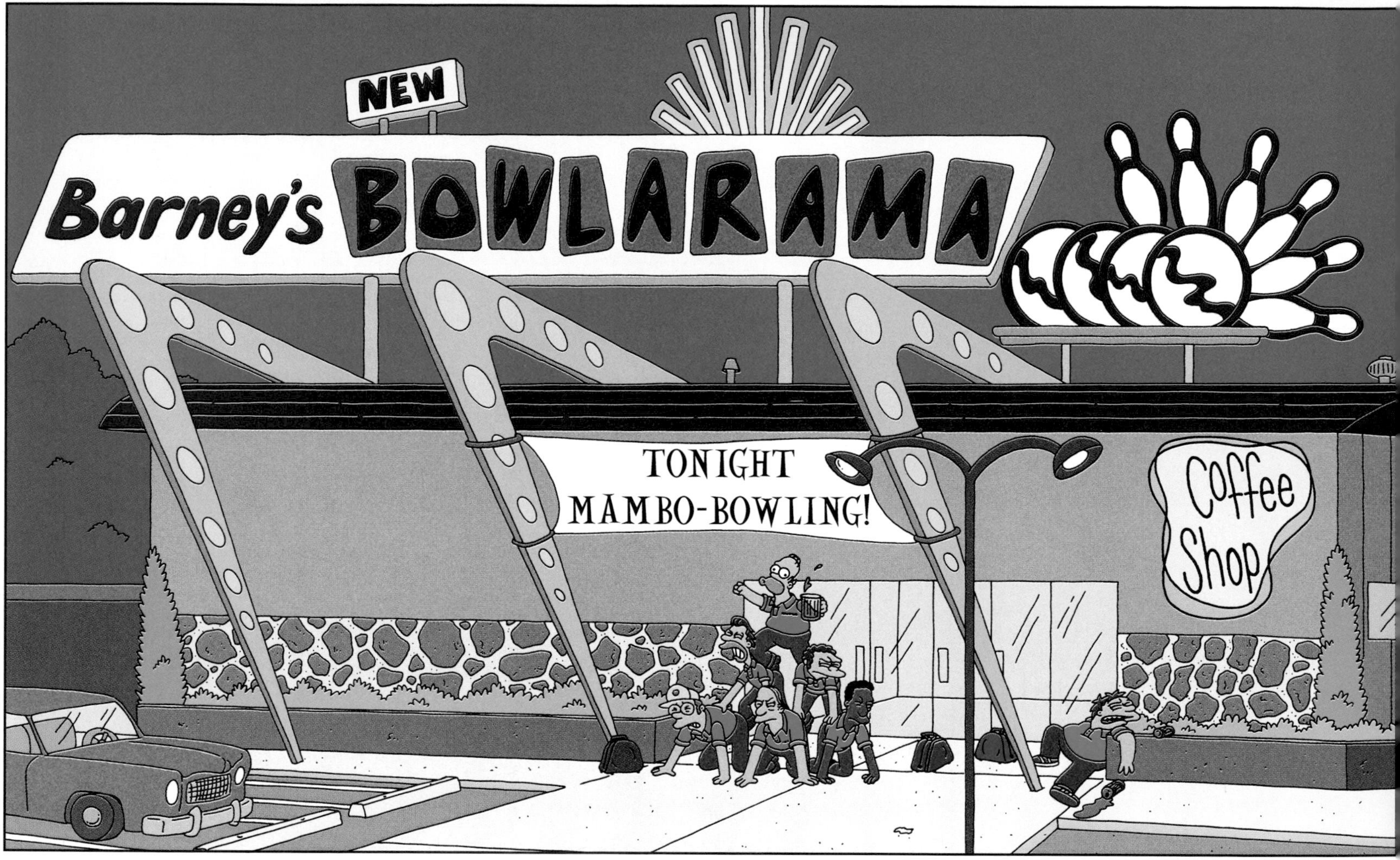
NEW
Barney's BOWLARAMA
TONIGHT
MAMBO-BOWLING!
Coffee
Shop

Beer-fueled revelry at Barney's Bowlarama.

the **Springfield Natural History Museum**. Visitors will marvel at simulated dinosaur bones and mounted fish and observe a real live caveman community portrayed by natives of the hills of nearby Spittle County. The museum also features the preserved bodies of local Springfield fauna displayed in faux-authentic

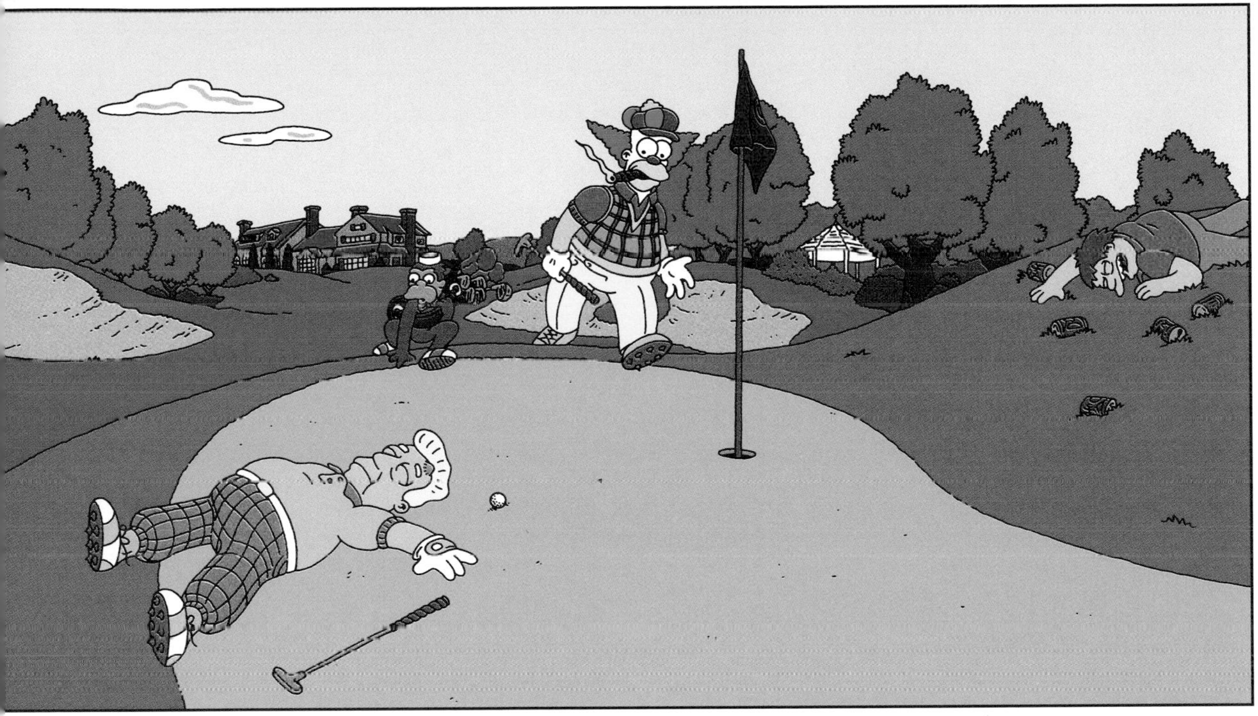

Krusty the Clown and his chimp-caddy, Mr. Teeny, play through at the Springfield Glen Country Club.

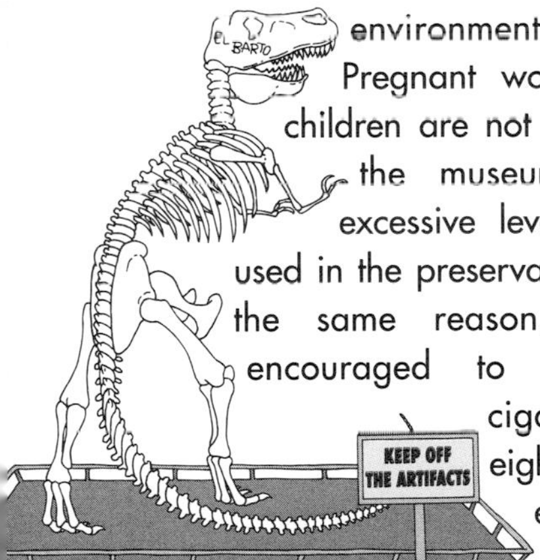
EL BARTO
KEEP OFF THE ARTIFACTS

environments. *Warning:* Pregnant women and small children are not advised to enter the museum due to the excessive levels of chemicals used in the preservation process. For the same reason, smokers are encouraged to avoid lighting cigarettes within eight feet of museum exhibits.

To find naturally preserved (yet still toxic) animals, one needs only to venture a few blocks from the Springfield Natural History Museum to the **Springfield Tar Pits**. Here, the distant past is submerged under several cubic tons of black, foul-smelling, gas-emitting black stuff. Visitors to the tar pits—chosen as one of the top "Ant-Free Picnic Sites" by *Springfield Magazine*—are given the opportunity to bring the excitement home: Included in the price of

WHAT'S RIGHT WITH SPRINGFIELD?

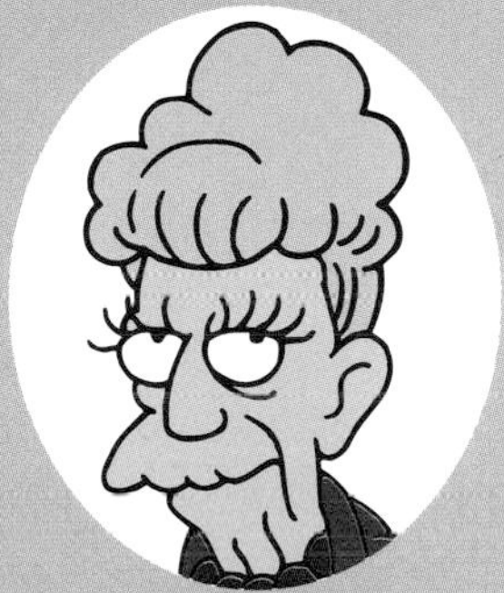

"I like going to the **Springfield Swap Meet** for antique ashtrays. They're fun to look at and you can fill them with mints you take from restaurants."

—Agnes Skinner, widow

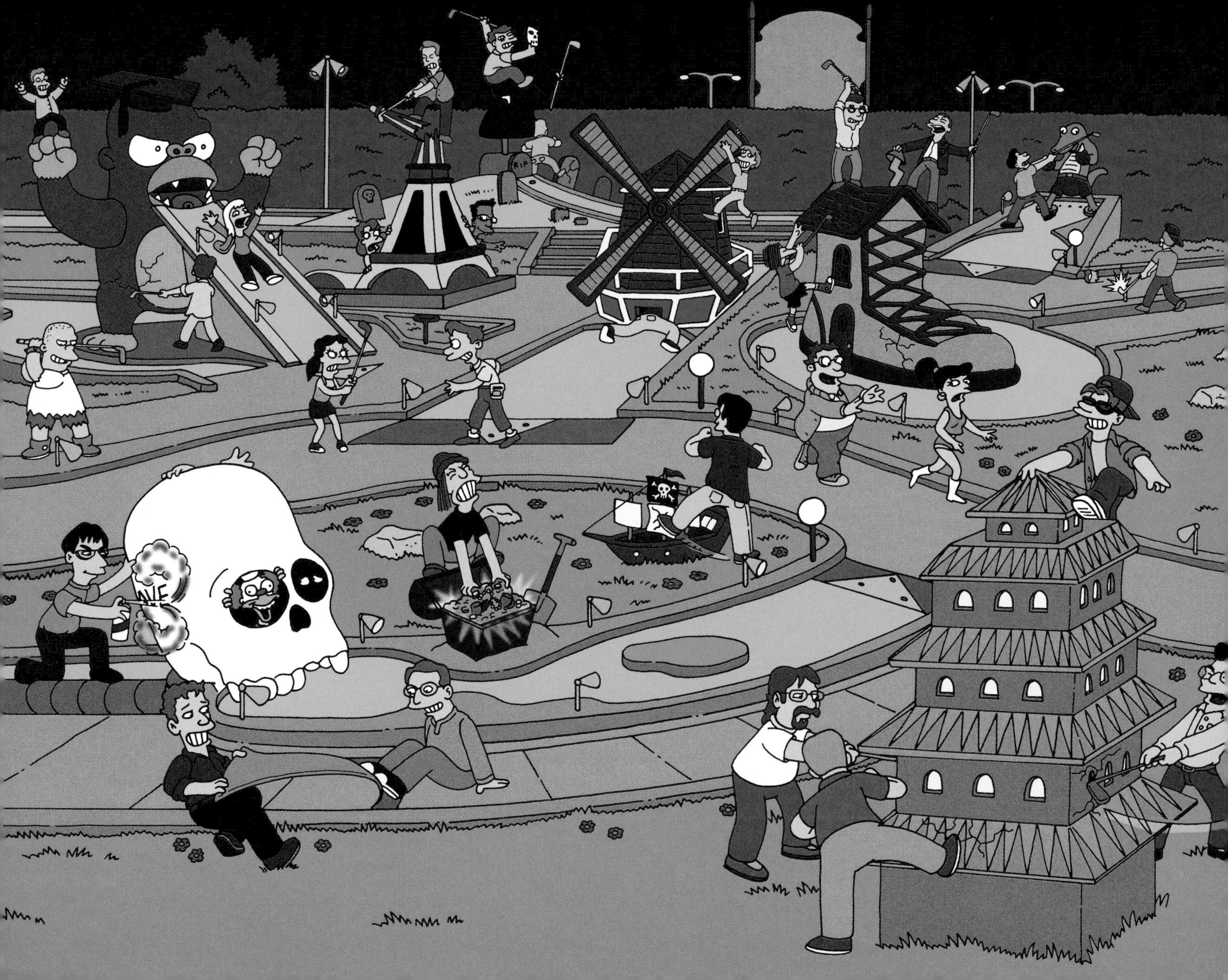

(At left) Teens and not-so-teens unwind during Youth Night at Sir Putt-a-Lott's Merrie Olde Fun Center.

admission is a free bucket of tar. *Note:* There is a limit of one tar bucket per person; professional roofers and candy machine saboteurs are excluded from this offer.

Of course, one can see live animals in Springfield as well. The top animal-looky-lookery in town is the **Discount Lion Safari**. Stocked with retired circus lions and several former mascots of the Metro-Goldwyn-Mayer studios, the Discount Lion Safari specializes in getting visitors in, getting a lion in front of them, and getting visitors out. After the crackdown brought about by the Cowardly Lion Scandal of 1993, actual live lions, not out-of-work actors in cheap costumes from *The Wizard of Oz*, are guaranteed.

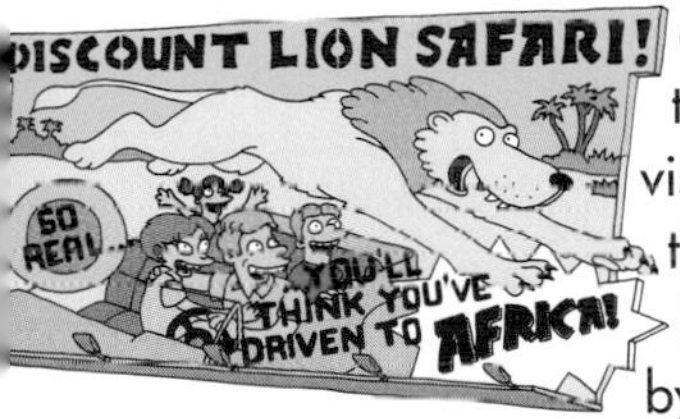
DISCOUNT LION SAFARI!
SO REAL!
YOU'LL THINK YOU'VE DRIVEN TO AFRICA!

Elephants are the main attraction at the **Springfield Animal Refuge**, where seventeen pachyderms—left over from radio contests, laid off from bankrupt circuses, and on the lam from Krustyburger meat-packing plants—frolic, romp, and gore to their hearts' content. *One thing to consider:* Due to the refuge's tight budget and shortsighted management, the only thing keeping the elephants from charging at helpless visitors is a weak chain-link fence that was originally designed for chinchilla farming.

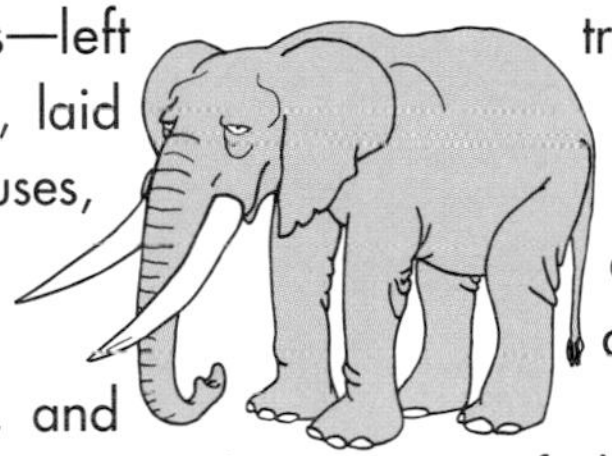

Visitors who prefer to see animals hurtling forward with reckless abandon, desperately trying to outpace one another in a savage, hopeless struggle to catch a mechanical bunny, can grab their binoculars and make their way to **Springfield Downs**. Post time at this dog track is at 1:00 P.M. daily. Losing dogs are given away immediately after the last race, and due to racetrack regulations, all men over forty have to wear ugly shirts and smoke at least one cigar while there.

If dog racing is one of Springfield's most popular pastimes, the semi-high culture of the **Springfield Opera House** is probably the least. The SOH recently adopted a controversial policy to attract more patrons: Only grotesquely obese singers will be featured in the house's productions. Although ticket sales have improved, the stage has collapsed twice and the songs

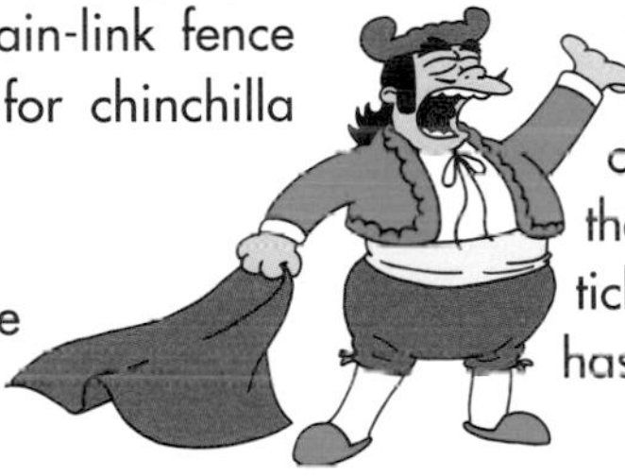

THE BURNS BULLET:

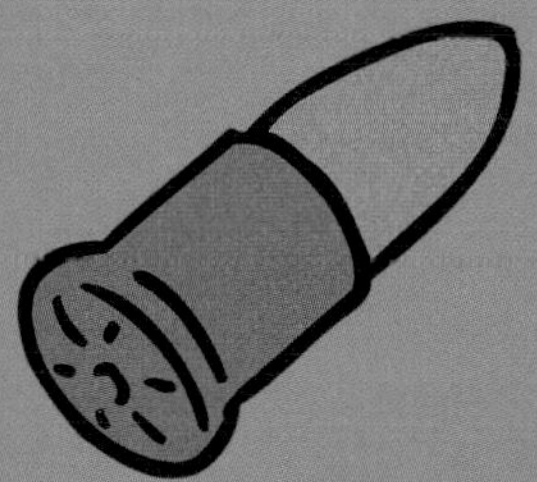

What it is:
The bullet used in the most famous gun-related accident in Springfield. It was removed from the city's richest (and some say, most evil) man after it was mistakenly fired by infant Maggie Simpson.

Its Significance:
After Burns was shot, Springfield was consumed by mystery-hysteria (the *Springfield Shopper* referred to the town during this period as a "myster-hysteriteria"), over the identity of the culprit. The bullet was not only a key piece of the puzzle, but it is the first piece of recovered ammunition that was not taken from Apu Nahasapeemapetilon.

Where it can be seen:
Amongst all the fired rounds in Chief Wiggum's "Box o' Used Bullets." It's not labeled, but it's in there somewhere.

WHAT'S RIGHT WITH SPRINGFIELD?

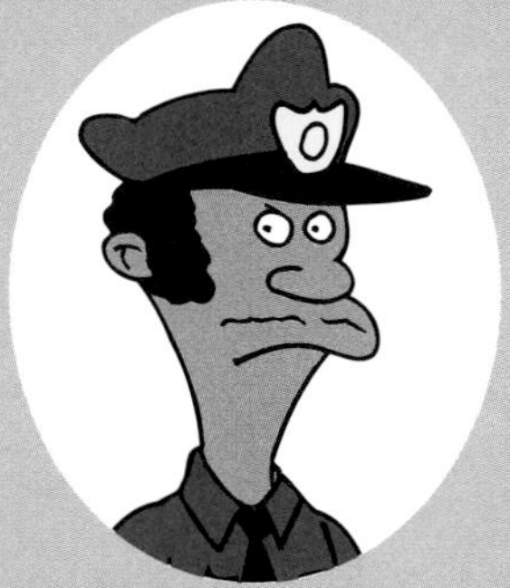

"Springfield A&M. I've been pursuing my ballistics degree on the police department's dime. I don't really go to classes, but the fact that I'm a student helps get us kick-ass seats to the football games."

—Lou, police officer

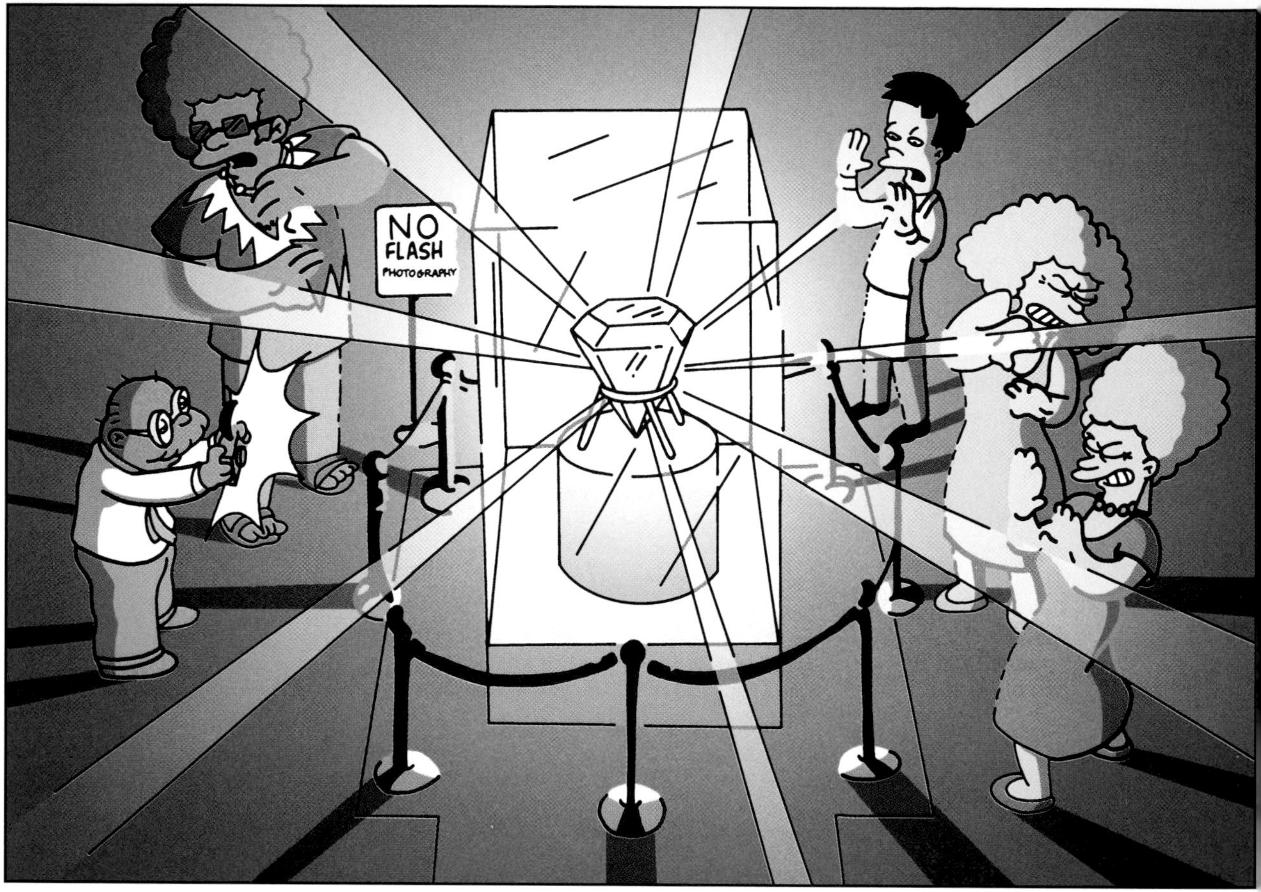
NO
FLASH
PHOTOGRAPHY

A feeble Springfield resident temporarily blinds his fellow townspeople at the Springfield Museum.

themselves have been occasionally upstaged by the loud sound of rippling fat. Still, the combination of quality opera and gruesome freak show does provide visitors some benefit: While the adults enjoy the subtler pleasures of *Der Ring des Nibelungen*, little kids can stare in wonder at the sight of a 400-pound woman dressed like a Valkyrie.

Visitors whose kids aren't interested in opera or obesity can be dropped off at Springfield's own **Diz-Nee-Land**. Though not affiliated with Disneyland,

(At right) Uninhibited fun at Jebediah Springfield Park.

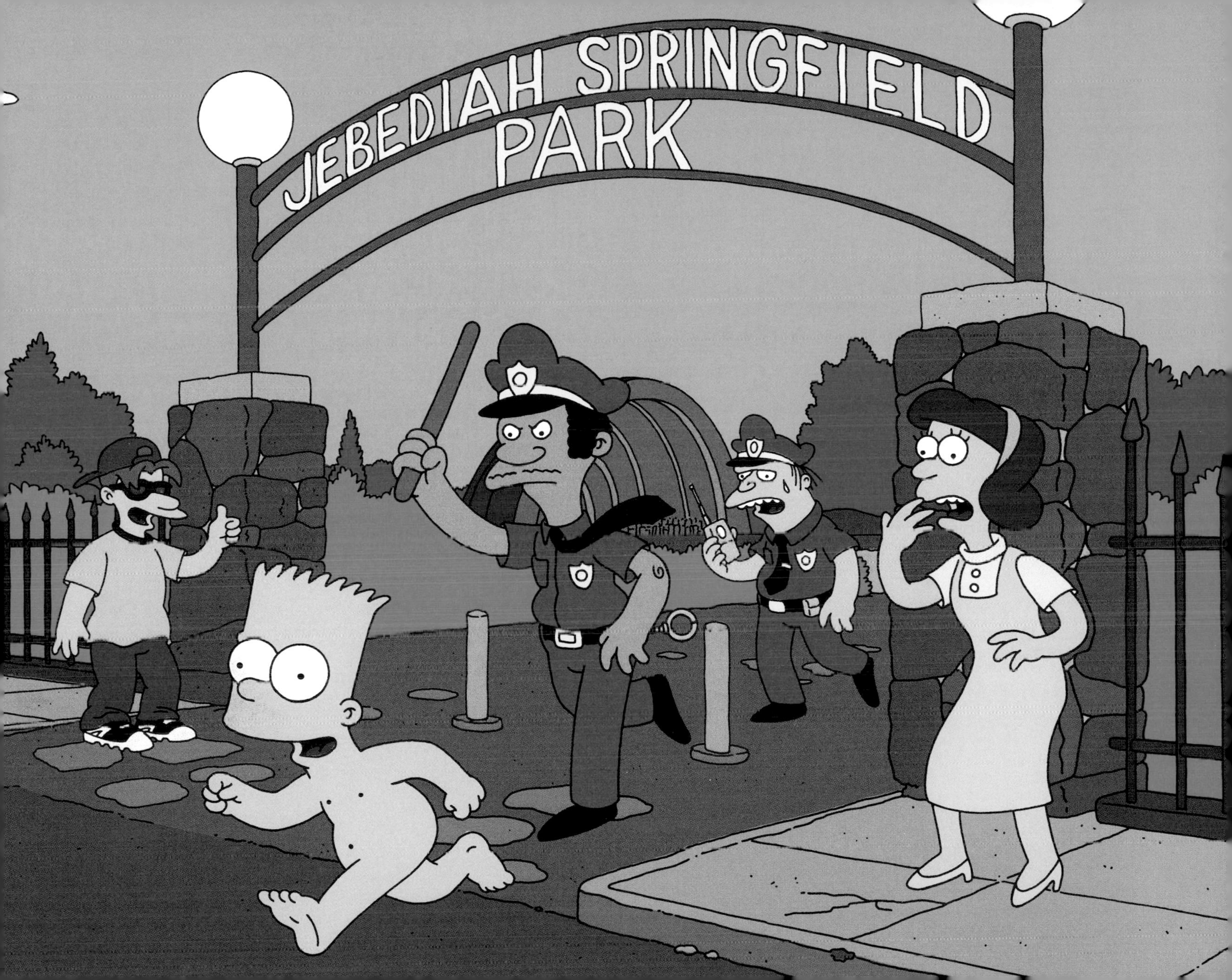
JEBEDIAH SPRINGFIELD
PARK

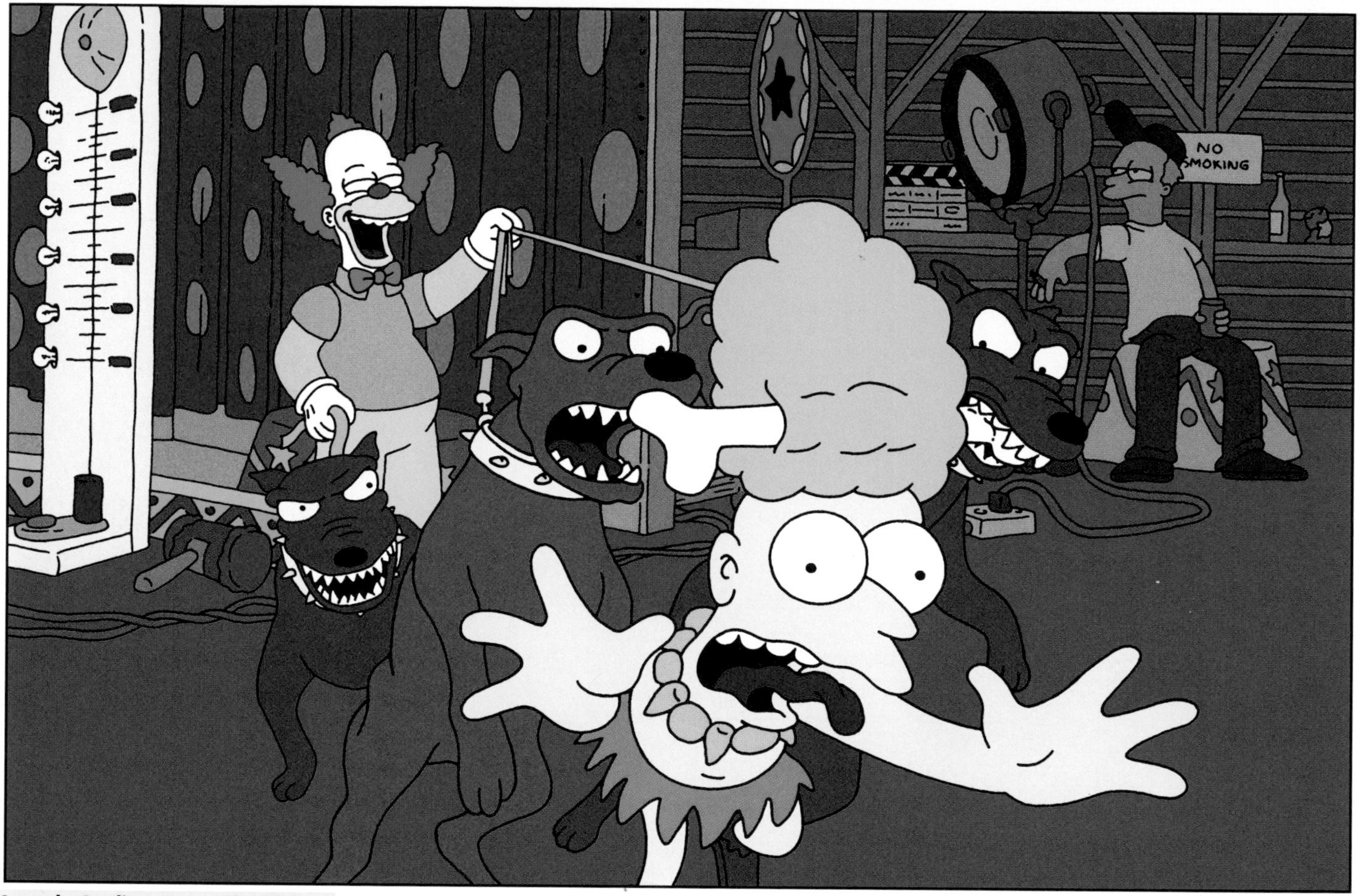
NO
SMOKING

At Krustylu Studios, Krusty the Clown unwinds and has some fun with his erstwhile partner, Sideshow Mel.

Disney World, or any other enterprise of the Walt Disney Company, Diz-Nee does have the brand-new Screamin' Hurlinator—a rollercoaster designed with one purpose in mind: to get people to buy lunch twice. But beware, as the park is filled with disturbingly derivative costumed characters (i.e., Mitchy Mouse, Danny Duck, and Goophee the Mandog), and lawyers taking depositions are a common sight. This applies to nearby

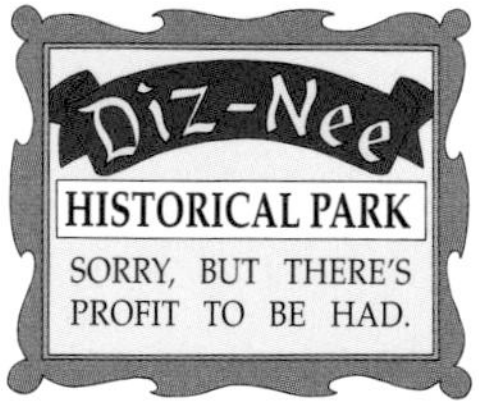
Diz-Nee
HISTORICAL PARK
SORRY, BUT THERE'S
PROFIT TO BE HAD.

Diz-Nee Historical Park as well, but it's unlikely that the kids will go anywhere near this edutainment mecca.

Care for a simple evening of amusements? What could be simpler than hucking a heavy ball to knock down a bunch of pins? And there's no finer place to heavy-ball knockdown-pin-huck than at Springfield's legendary crashateria, **Barney's Bowlarama**. What makes the Bowl-arama great is not its thrice-fried onion rings, the surprisingly good-smelling shoe rentals, or the free pencils with every scorecard. It's the glistening, ultraflat lanes—fabled alleys of polished wood on which even a small, anemic child can, with just a small push, make a ball roll fast enough to jump fifteen cars.

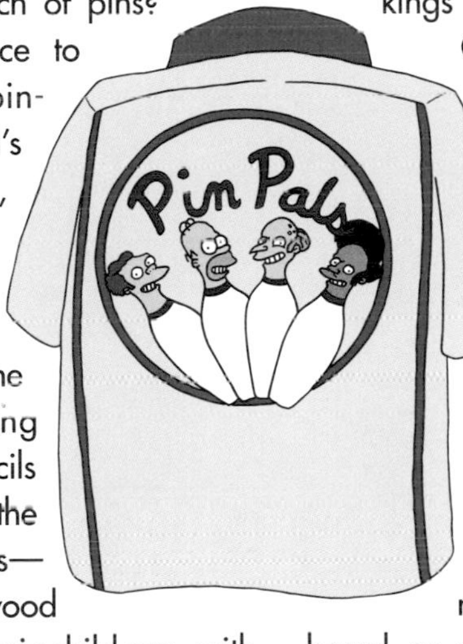
Pin Pals

Afraid of heavy bowling balls? Prefer something a little lighter and somewhat more dignified? Try the totally unique sport of mini-kings at **Sir Putt-a-Lott's Merrie Olde Fun Center**, just blocks away from the Bowlarama. Featuring a remarkable "miniature" version of golf (don't worry about clubs, this game requires only putting) complete with hilarious, fanciful obstacles, Sir Putt-a-Lott's is a place unlike any other on Earth. Picture yourself trying to putt a ball under a boxing alligator, or into the opening-and-closing mouth of a monkey in a mortar-board, or even between the legs of the Great Emancipator, Honest Abe Lincoln! Town officials agree: A trip to Springfield would be stupid and horribly irresponsible without at least one try at this astoundingly original game.

A calmer, simpler, less innovative environment than the pulse-pounding, teeth-gnashing, spleen-irritating excitement of Sir Putt-a-Lott's Merrie Olde Fun Center is the **Springfield National Forest,** where the trees are big, the squirrels are well-fed, and illegal campfire-starters are shot on sight. Scholars argue whether Robert Frost penned his poem, "That's One Freakin' Big Tree" while in the forest and even question whether it was actually Frost or Robert Klein who wrote it. Nevertheless, the Springfield National Forest has some of the most beautiful views in all of Springfield, and

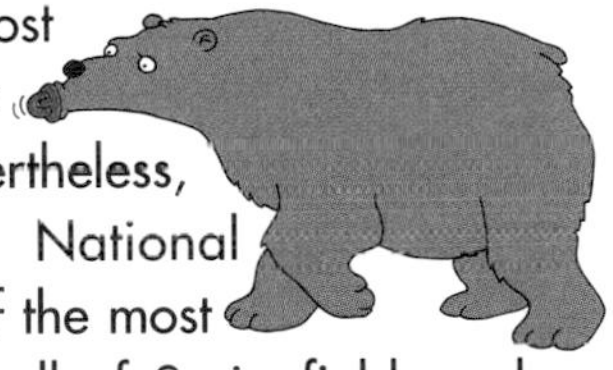

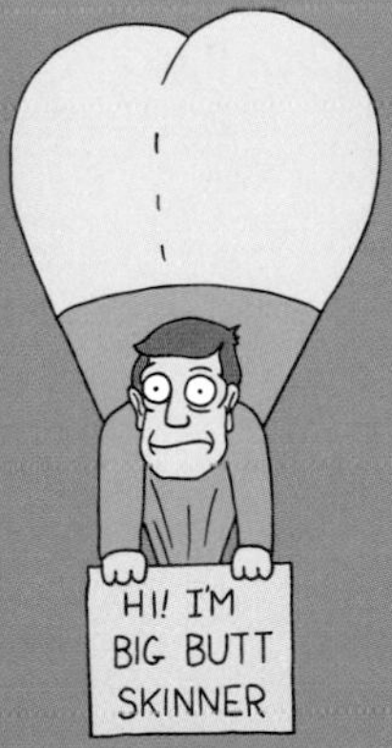
HI! I'M
BIG BUTT
SKINNER

BUTTZILLA:

What It Is:
The aforementioned vandalized (and thus obscene) weather balloon. Originally launched as part of a Springfield Elementary Science Week, the balloon was altered to resemble the school's own Principal Skinner, bending over and exposing his butt. The vandal, a little boy named Bart Simpson, also included a caption, "Hi! I'm Big Butt Skinner." As a punishment, Simpson was sentenced to helping Skinner with an astronomy project. That in turn led to the discovery of the Springfield Comet.

Its Worth:
About six bucks. (If you can find someone in need of a bunch of industrial strength mylar plastic sheeting.)

Where to See it:
Hanging in the vandalized weather balloon wing of the Springfield Natural History Museum.

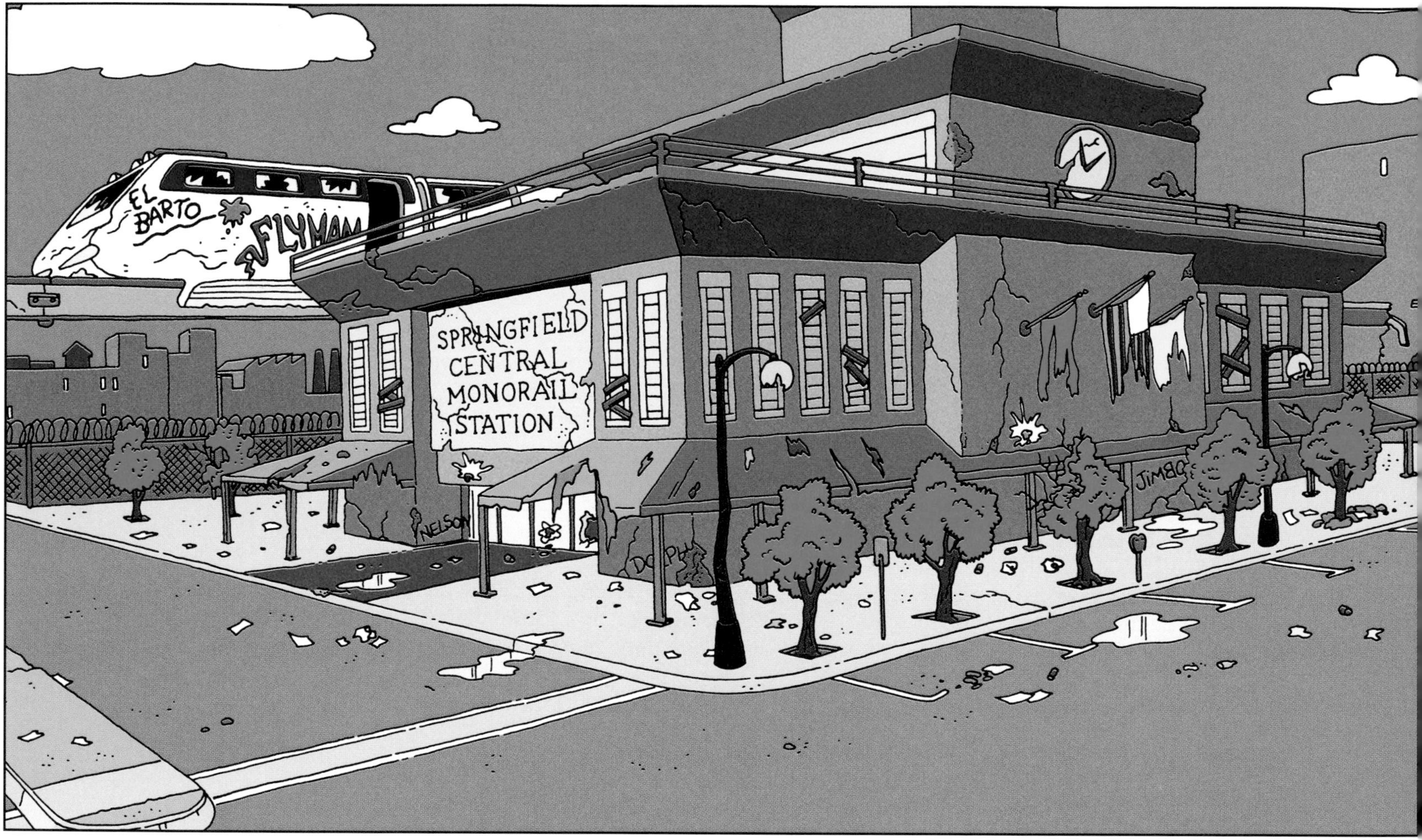
EL BARTO
FLYMAN
SPRINGFIELD
CENTRAL
MONORAIL
STATION
NELSON
DOLPH
JIMBO

The still-decaying Springfield Monorail Ruins.

it's the only place in town where the rank, acrid fumes of the tire-yard fire aren't quite so noticeable.

The quiet, semi-interesting halls of the **Springfield Museum** provide a nice, gradual transition from the peaceful world of nature back to Springfield's civilized chaotic charge. The museum houses the largest cubic zirconia in the world, easily twice the size of "Hacksaw" Jim Duggan's head. The museum also displays lithographs and high-quality place mats of some of the greatest works of art in the world. Its gift shop, though unremarkable in almost every other respect, sells artist action figures, including Deranged, Kicking van Gogh and Break-dancing Keith Haring.

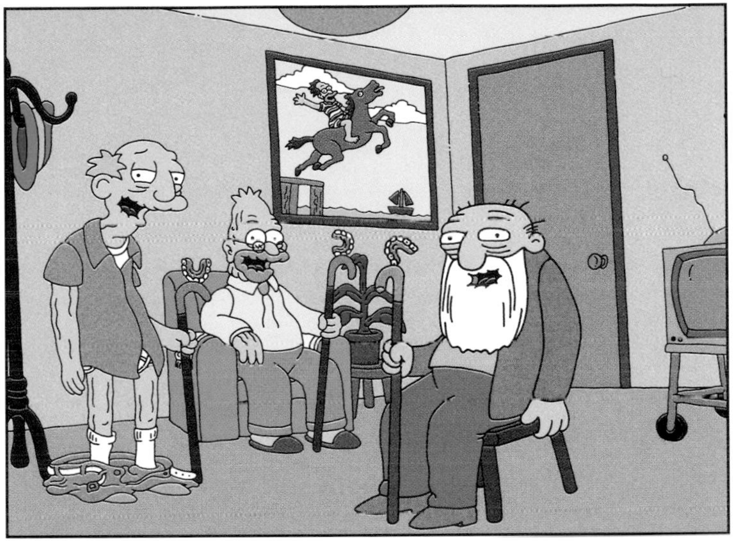

Denture-tricks with residents of the Springfield Retirement Castle.

Just around the corner from the Springfield Museum is an educational experience that kids might actually enjoy: the **Springfield Knowledgeum**. Full of loud exhibits that shake, shoot fire, and/or demonstrate the human reproductive process, the Knowledgeum excites children about various "-ologies" by disorienting them and making science their only path back to sanity. Current exhibits include "From Seed to Sausage: The Curious Journey of Mustard" and "The Vacuum of Space Surprisingly Sucks."

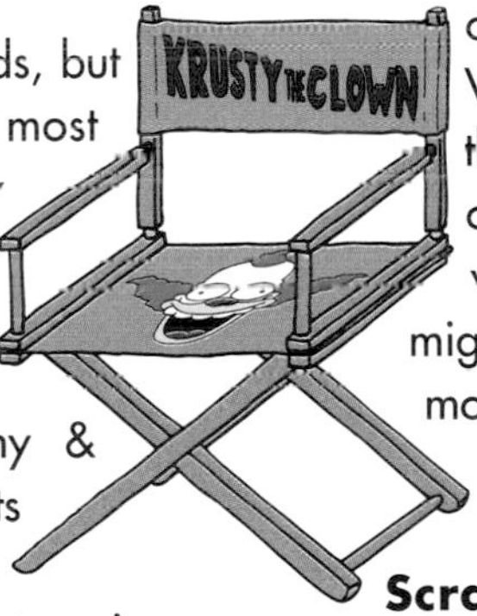
KRUSTY THE CLOWN

The Knowledgeum may be a gateway of fun for kids, but **Krustylu Studios** is by far Springfield's most meaningful juvenile attraction. Tickets to *The Krusty the Clown Show* are regularly available, provided that Krusty is well and not at a rehabilitation facility. Those unfamiliar with the program are in for a treat: *The Krusty the Clown Show* features Itchy & Scratchy cartoons, toy commercials, and comedy skits in the "cream pie/seltzer/chemically imbalanced chimpanzee in a fez on rollerskates" tradition. But seeing a Krusty show is only one of Krustylu's many attractions. There's an hourly tour, a commissary, a fifteen-minute oil-change station, and a gift shop that carries nearly every Krusty product ever licensed, including those long-since-recalled products that cause chemical burns, radiation poisoning, and leprosy. Visitors who are lucky enough to bump into Krusty on the lot are encouraged to snap a picture. It will be their only proof that it was merely a bump and not the whiplash-inducing pummeling that Krusty might claim in the hopes of receiving a modest cash settlement.

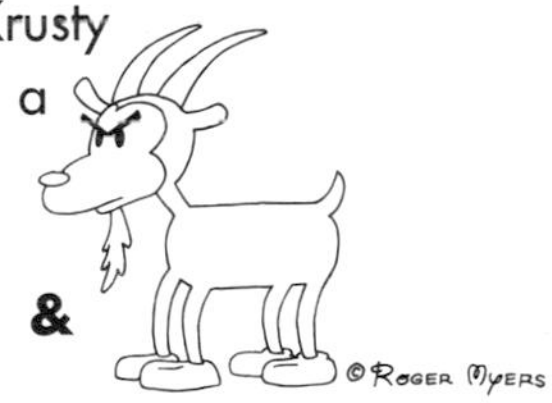
© Roger Myers

DISGRUNTLED GOAT

Mere miles from Krustylu is **Itchy & Scratchy Studios**, the supposed birthplace of the most violent cat-and-mouse team in cartoon history. Although the public is not allowed in the building, viewing the decorative

fencework alone is worth the trip. However, the janitor's entryway can be easily jimmied with a credit card, a screwdriver, and a bit of beef tallow. Visitors who make it inside are advised to act like they belong there, look people in the eye and smile. Should anyone ask, simply claim to be Hy Levine's cousin. Inside are a bunch of light-deprived, low-life animators, numerous awards lining the walls, and an incredible amount of second-hand smoke. Visitors who pose as couriers may just walk out with some highly valuable production artwork.

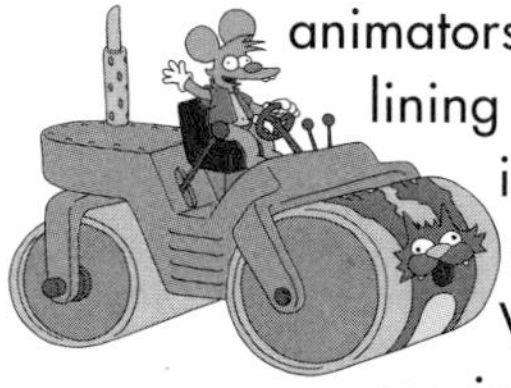

Scattered throughout Springfield are potent reminders of what town historians consider a particularly stupid period in Springfield's civic history—when the burg embarked on a half-witted attempt at mass transportation. The **Springfield Monorail Ruins** dot the city with various decaying pieces of elevated rail, dangling chunks of concrete, and rusting passenger cars that hang precariously over heavily trafficked sidewalks. Although the ruins make for excellent pictures, step lively, as four to six monorail cars crash to the ground every month in twisted, horrible explosions of metal and glass.

A site that makes a particularly good ending to a trip to Springfield is the **Springfield Lemon Tree**. Originally planted by town founder Jebediah Springfield, the tree has been a source of civic pride, shade, and lemonade for more than a hundred years. It is the very embodiment of Springfield itself. Like Springfield, it continues to grow despite neglect and poor city management. Like Springfield, it produces radioactive by-products that cause mutations in the environment. Like Springfield, it nurtures a tough, yellow-skinned population that is incredibly sour, but who—with the right amount of sugar and water—can create something truly memorable, refreshing, useful, and sweet. Just don't pick the lemons! International law forbids any fruit from leaving Springfield, as it hosts dangerous parasites, attracts highly evolved fruit flies, and often gives off a barely-audible hum.

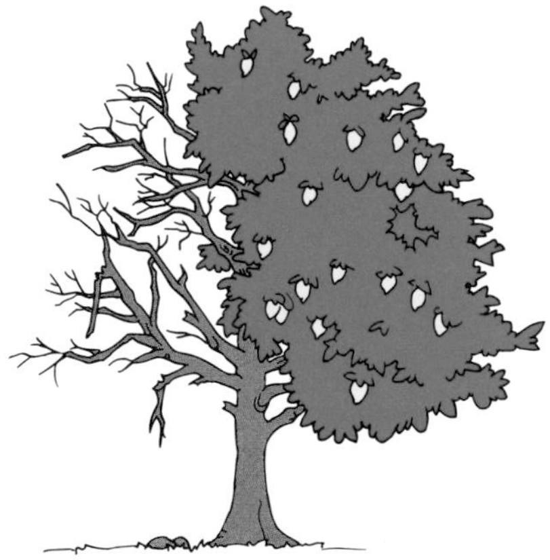

ARTIFACTS

THE SPRINGFIELD MUNICIPAL CATAPULT:

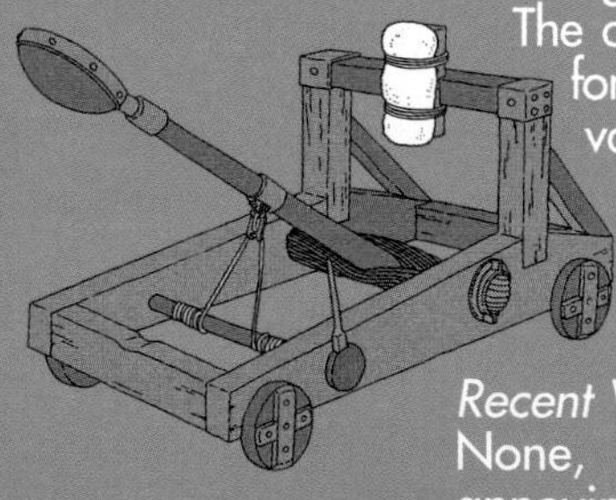

Its Origin:
The catapult was used over two centuries ago as a form of legal penalty by Springfield's founders for various vices, including the consumption of alcohol. After the town's 200-year-old prohibition law was briefly revived, the catapult was brought back as well.

Recent Victims:
None, save for an unlucky testing cat and an annoying Federal official.

Why It's Worth Seeing:
It's a well made piece of catapultery. Plus, you never know, maybe some soused-up frat boy who's showing off for his friends will catapult himself all the way to Shelbyville. Wouldn't that be a sight!?

Where to See It:
In the backyard of the Springfield Historical Society, under the blue tarp.

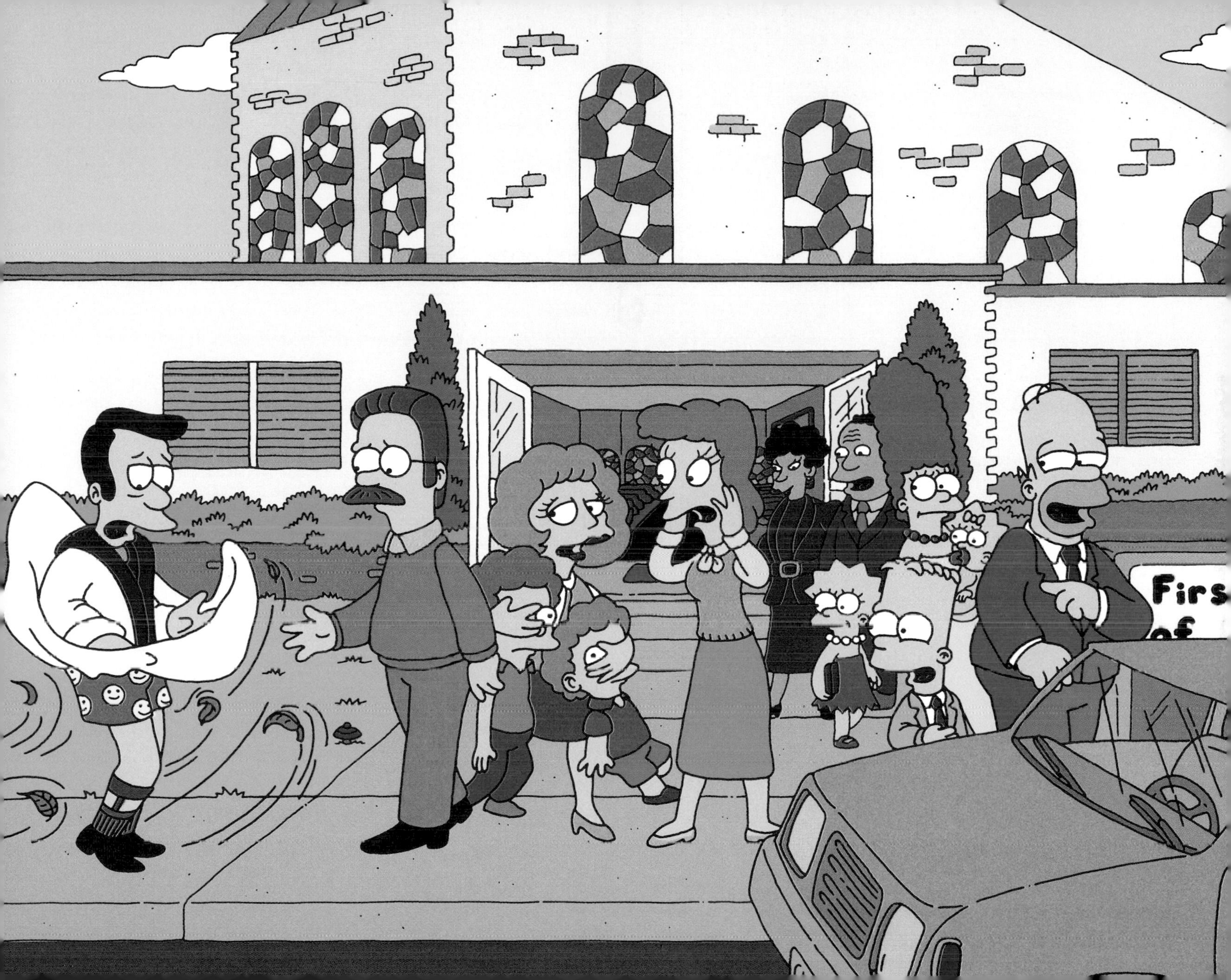
Firs

Come for the Fun, Stay for the Guilt:
A Vacationer's Guide to Worshiping in Springfield

by Rev. Timothy Lovejoy

Congratulations on your decision to visit Springfield, a city well known for its recreation and debauchment opportunities. You may be surprised to learn that it has a holy side as well. In the 23rd Psalm, David writes "Yea, though I walk through the valley of the shadow of death, I shall fear no evil, for thou art with me. Thy rod and thy staff, they comfort me" and so forth.

As Pastor of the First Church of Springfield and a longtime resident, I cannot think of a scripture passage which more perfectly describes our town. With mountains nearby, it could be viewed as a valley (from certain vantage points), and people do die here on a semi-daily basis, many of them in the shade. Yet, even more importantly, this psalm also serves as a biblical "heads up" for those planning a trip to our fair, yet insidiously evil city. But you should have no reason to fear during your visit, as long as you remember to let the Lord's rod and staff comfort you while you're here. And what better place to do that than in one of the many churches, mosques, or synagogues that dot this not-quite-godforsaken landscape?

(Previous page) Reverend Timothy Lovejoy, catching the backdraft outside the First Church of Springfield.

While you pack for your trip, meditate on whether you want to bask in the brotherly (and sisterly) love of the Springfield Community Church, or fill a pew at one of those other places. In the meantime, let's take a look at the city's venerable history, shall we? Despite its sullied reputation, Springfield has a past steeped in faith and faith-related fund raising activities. In fact, the city was founded on faith. It wouldn't even exist if not for Jebediah Springfield and his band of fearless religious zealots who left their homes in Maryland in search of a place called New Sodom. It was faith that saw them through the mild discomfort and inconvenience of the wilderness. It was faith that steered them toward the land we now

know as Springfield. And yes, it was faith that allowed them to fight the urge to go with the cousin-marrying Shelbyville Manhattan and instead remain with Jebediah who by this time smelled an awful lot like a drunken grizzly eating another drunken bear that had been dead for some time. This godly spirit is still alive today, embiggening the souls of all who worship here (even the transplanted Detroiters).

Somewhere in the Bible it says "Blessed is a man who perseveres under trial," or something to that effect. It may be in First Thessaleezians. Feel free to look it up. Anyway, the vast importance of these words is something that Springfielders know only

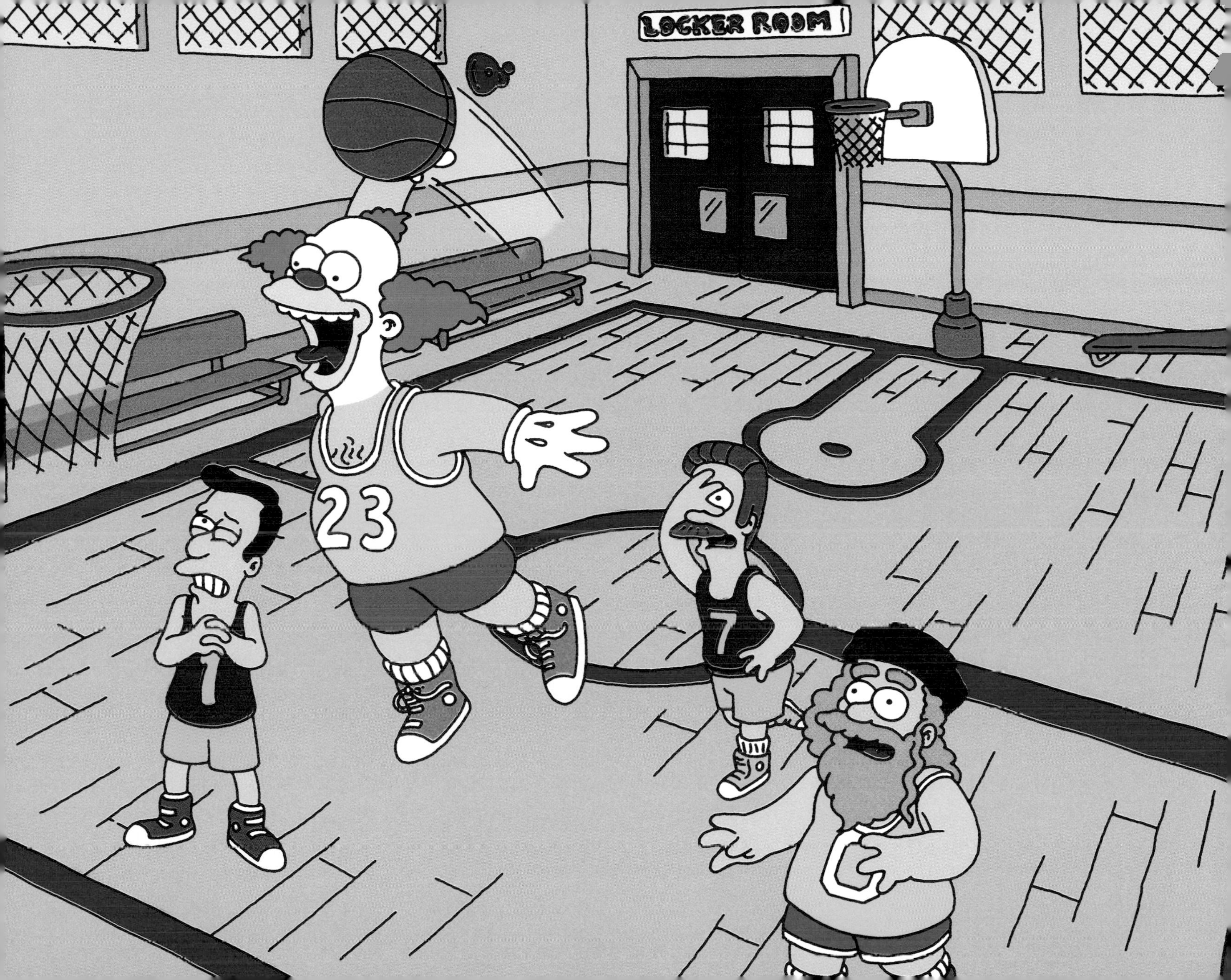
LOCKER ROOM
23
7

too well. A partial list of recent tribulations which our townspeople have endured includes: Hurricane Barbara; the decapitation of the statue of our beloved town founder; a Do-What-You-Feel Festival; the near destruction of the city by a comet; legalized gambling; the cancellation of Whacking Day; a nuclear meltdown scare; a runaway monorail crisis; citywide participation in a false religion; a sexual harassment scandal; wild animal rampages; a "kid stuck in a well" emergency; an evil plot to block out the sun; a losing ball team; the hedonistic, rock and roll festival known as Hullabalooza; and consistently bad community theater. These trials, though irksome, have refined and strengthened our faith. We have persevered and are blessed, indeed. In fact, as my esteemed colleague Rabbi Hyman Krustofski might say, "Enough with the blessing, already! More with the noshing!"

And speaking of noshing, there's no better way to stretch your vacation food budget than by dropping in on one of Springfield's

(Previous page) Reverend Timothy Lovejoy and Ned Flanders play Krusty the Clown and Rabbi Hyman Krustofsky in the annual, Springfield Two-Man Interfaith Jammy-Jam.

many inexpensive church-sponsored dining events. For a syrup-soaked breakfast that's guaranteed to stick to your ribs, try the weekly waffle gorge at my own Springfield Community Church. If you're in the mood for something kosher, the good Rabbi Krustofski offers Gefilte Fridays down at the temple, where the Manashevitz flows as freely as an even cheaper brand of table wine. For those of you who just want to feast until you're too full to breathe, you can't beat Our Lady of Perpetual Sorrows' Fun-and-Food Fest. There's also the Kwik-E Mart, where you can worship the Hindu god Ganesha while waiting for your microwave soy dog to cook. These are but a few of the many faith and feed opportunities our town offers. Beware, however, the seductively savory smells that emanate from Springfield's various cult churches and secret organizations. Groups to look out for include The Movementarians, the Ancient Mystic Society of No Homers (formerly The Stonecutters), and a small group of people who split off from the Presbyterians to worship an Inanimate Carbon Rod. Although these unholy alliances are adept at hosting sumptuous banquets, I warn you: STAY AWAY! Their

food is not properly blessed and may cause thy bowels to writhe in fiery Hell-pain, forcing you to cry out from the depths of your eternal soul, "Thy Will be done! Oh, dear God, please, Thy Will be done!"

Other places to avoid during your stay include Moe's Tavern, Shotkickers, Duff Gardens, Stu's Disco, The Hate Box, The Jazz Hole, the Duff Brewery, Plato's Republic Gaming Casino and Pleasure Domiarium, Springfield Downs, Itchy & Scratchy Land, and a fleshy den of iniquitous entertainment known as the Maison Derriere. Also try to steer clear of vegetarianism in all its abominable incarnations.

A trip to Springfield can be informative, filling and even fun as long as you plan in advance to pacify our vengeful God (and the various other gods, who I assume are equally as wrathful) by attending church at least once while you're here. And when the offering plate comes by, remember that most local churches honor traveler's checks, and several have installed pay-as-you-pray instant credit card kiosks for your convenience.

LODGING

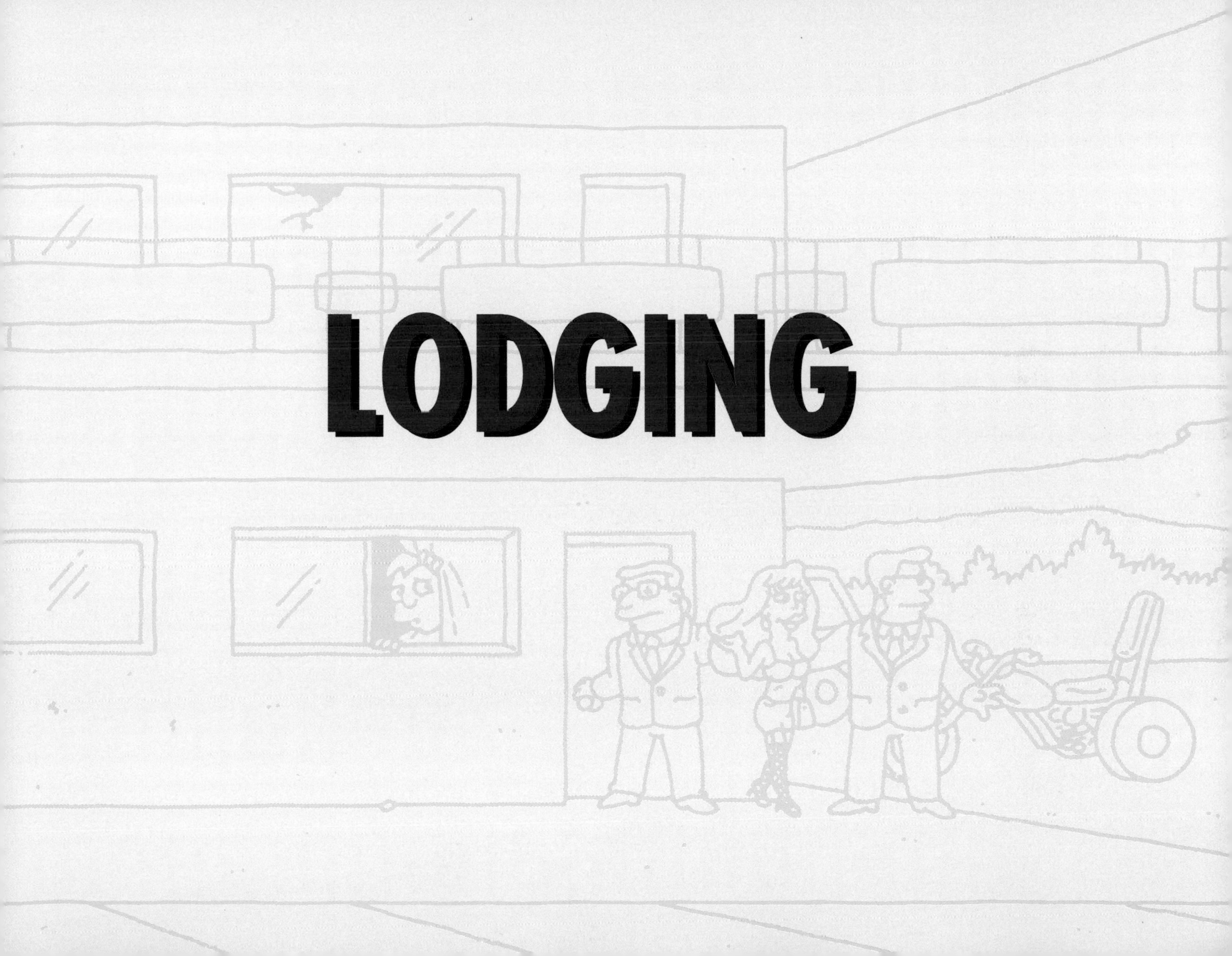

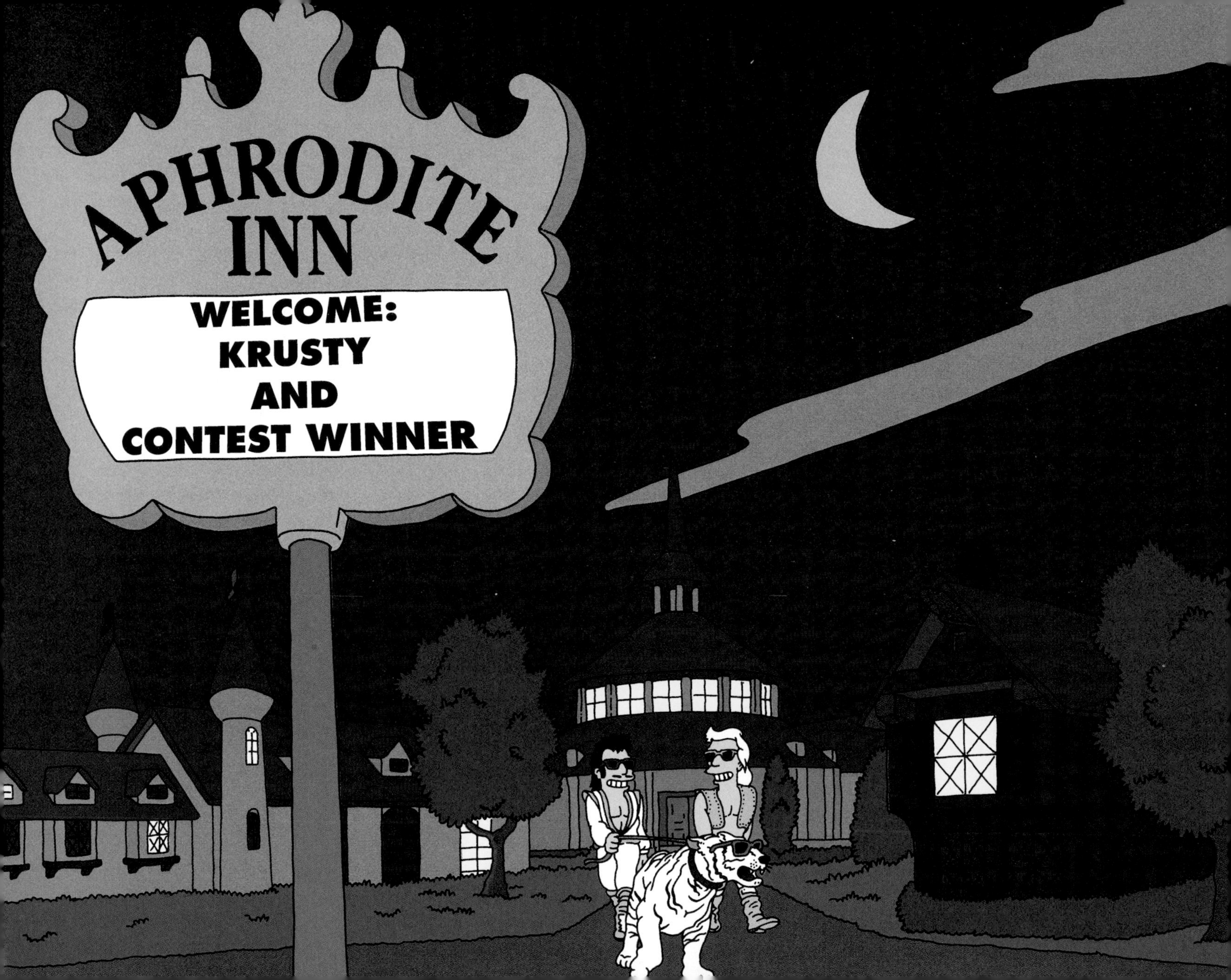
APHRODITE INN
WELCOME:
KRUSTY
AND
CONTEST WINNER

According to local legend, Beat-era writer Jack Kerouac, while passing through town, was once heard to say, "Ah, to sleep in Springfield, perchance to dream of someplace else." Obviously, he never slept in one of Springfield's delightful lodgings—if he had, he probably would have taken a shine to this pleasant little burg. More likely than not, he passed out on top of the statue of Jebediah Springfield in the town square, slept wrong, got a sore back, and thus made that hurtful, hurtful comment. Think ahead and sleep on a bed.

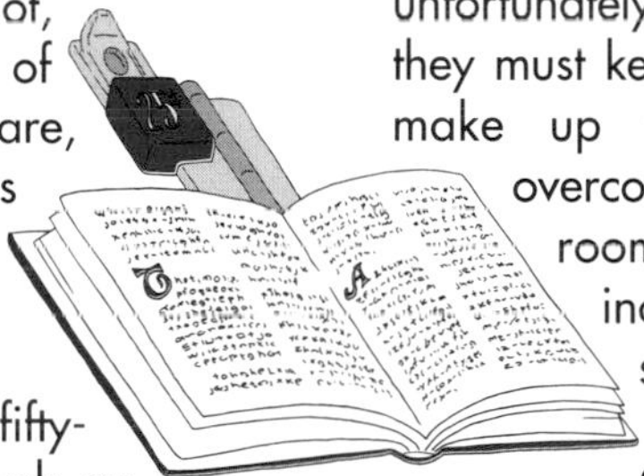

Aphrodite Inn: This hotel boasts fifty-seven individually themed rooms, such as the "Smokey and the Bandit Suite" (guests sleep in a black Trans-Am surrounded by cases of Coors) and the "Oval Office" (a near-exact replica, in which the president's desk folds out into a vibrating bed). Make reservations early, lest you get stuck with the "This Room Contains Chemicals That Are Known to Be Hazardous to Your Health Room" or the "Leaky, Dusty, Stained-Carpet Suite."

Who's to Know Motel: Made famous during Mayor Quimby's "Tartargate" (in which Diamond Joe seduced half a dozen dental hygienists, offering them municipal judgeships in exchange for their silence), the Who's to Know offers cheap, clean rooms that are swept twice daily for surveillance devices and disgruntled spouses. The hotel also serves a discreet continental breakfast in a poorly lit room for those secretive souls who don't want to miss the most important meal of the day.

(At left) Frequent lodgers Gunter and Ernst, out for a midnight stroll at the Aphrodite Inn.

The Happy Earwig Hotel: The new management of this hotel recently purchased the property with the intention of changing its name; unfortunately, the fine print on the deed specified that they must keep the moniker until the year 2157. To make up for this, the hotel's owners have overcompensated, sanitizing everything in the rooms for the customers' protection, including phones, TV remotes, Bibles, and shoehorns.

Sleep-Eazy Motel: Smelly beds and clown pictures on the wall, accompanied by the sounds of sirens, gunshots, and hopelessly lost ice cream trucks.

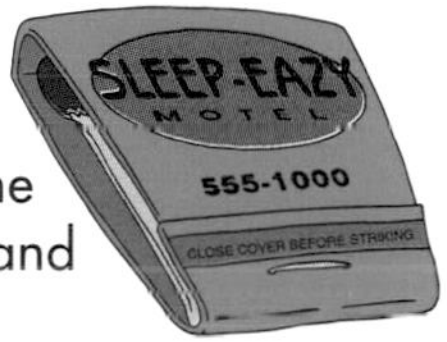
SLEEP-EAZY
MOTEL
555-1000
CLOSE COVER BEFORE STRIKING

The Springfield Palace Hotel: 1970s-style elegance in the heart of downtown Springfield, complete with pillow mints, expensive room service, and uncut movies that, outside of Springfield, aren't available due to FCC broadcast restrictions. *Sequestered Juror Magazine* recently voted the Springfield Palace one of the top hotels to be holed up in for an undetermined length of time.

The Happy Gypsy: Full of old men in tank-style undershirts, the persistent smell of beef consommé, and the sound of people playing bad klezmer music, the Happy Gypsy offers pre-war apartment-style

WHAT'S RIGHT WITH SPRINGFIELD?

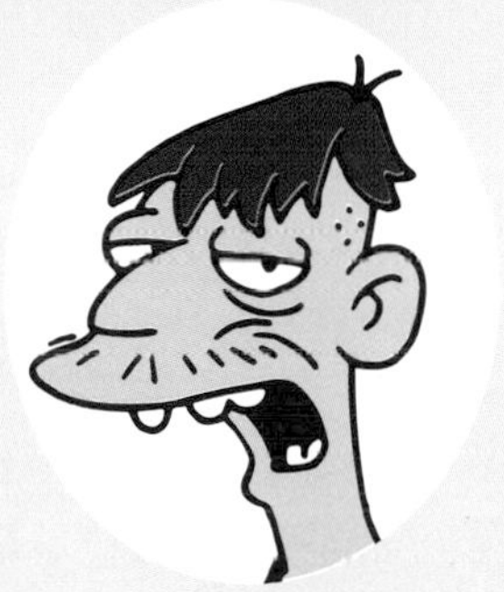

"Yous kin find mightee good bargains at that Springfield Dump."

—Cletus Delroy, slack-jawed yokel

living where "you pay by the day." Amenities include a free can of black shoe polish, a water pitcher with ceramic basin, and free clothesline access. The management advises patrons to bring plenty of cedar balls, as the building's attic has been the location of an impromptu moth sanctuary for the past thirty-six years.

Rancho Relaxo: Springfield's only two-star hotel-spa wasn't even located in Springfield until just three years ago, when the town petitioned the federal government to annex the ten acres of land in the Springfield Mountains, where the resort resides. Springfield's justification: they had no two-star hotel-spa. Since the annexation, the town can now boast its own luxury hotel, where one can bathe in mud, hot sand, and room-temperature rice pudding all in the same day.

Springfield Rescue Mission: Those looking for budget accommodations look no further—the Springfield Rescue Mission offers a cot, a pillow, three meals a day, and a complimentary delousing upon arrival, all for free. The only drawback is the extraordinarily high rate of luggage theft and being forced to pose as a homeless person throughout your stay.

Ye Olde Off-Ramp Inn: The typical economy route, complete with Magic Fingers beds, Bibles in the nightstands, and that really odd feeling one gets that something very, very wrong happened in the room one is sleeping in. B.Y.O.D. (Bring Your Own Disinfectant).

Ned Flanders's Christian Youth Hostel: If you are truly without any other alternative, you might want to try this impromptu hostel set up in this Springfield resident's basement. The Flanders are an extremely sweet, if not saccharine, family, eager to help and house Christians and non-Christians alike, as they feel it is their religious and civic obligation to do so. But this place goes far beyond mere spiritual obligation—the Flanders's basement is actually quite nice, as the family recently purchased a mattress that converts their pool table into a king-sized bed, and their bar has a multi-keg beer tap with such selections as Duff Quadruple Bock

ARTIFACTS

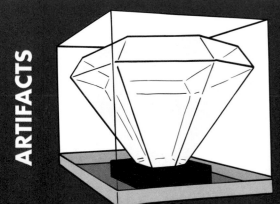

THE WORLD'S LARGEST CUBIC ZIRCONIA:

Where It's Housed:
The Springfield Museum.

Its Possible Practical Applications:
For use as a drill bit to mine immense pastries for custard; to show the newly engaged what a mistake it would be not to go with a real diamond; a conversation piece/paperweight.

Its Primary Purpose:
To serve as an exhibit in a woefully uninteresting museum.

Its Worth:
Twenty-seven bucks of cheap glass.

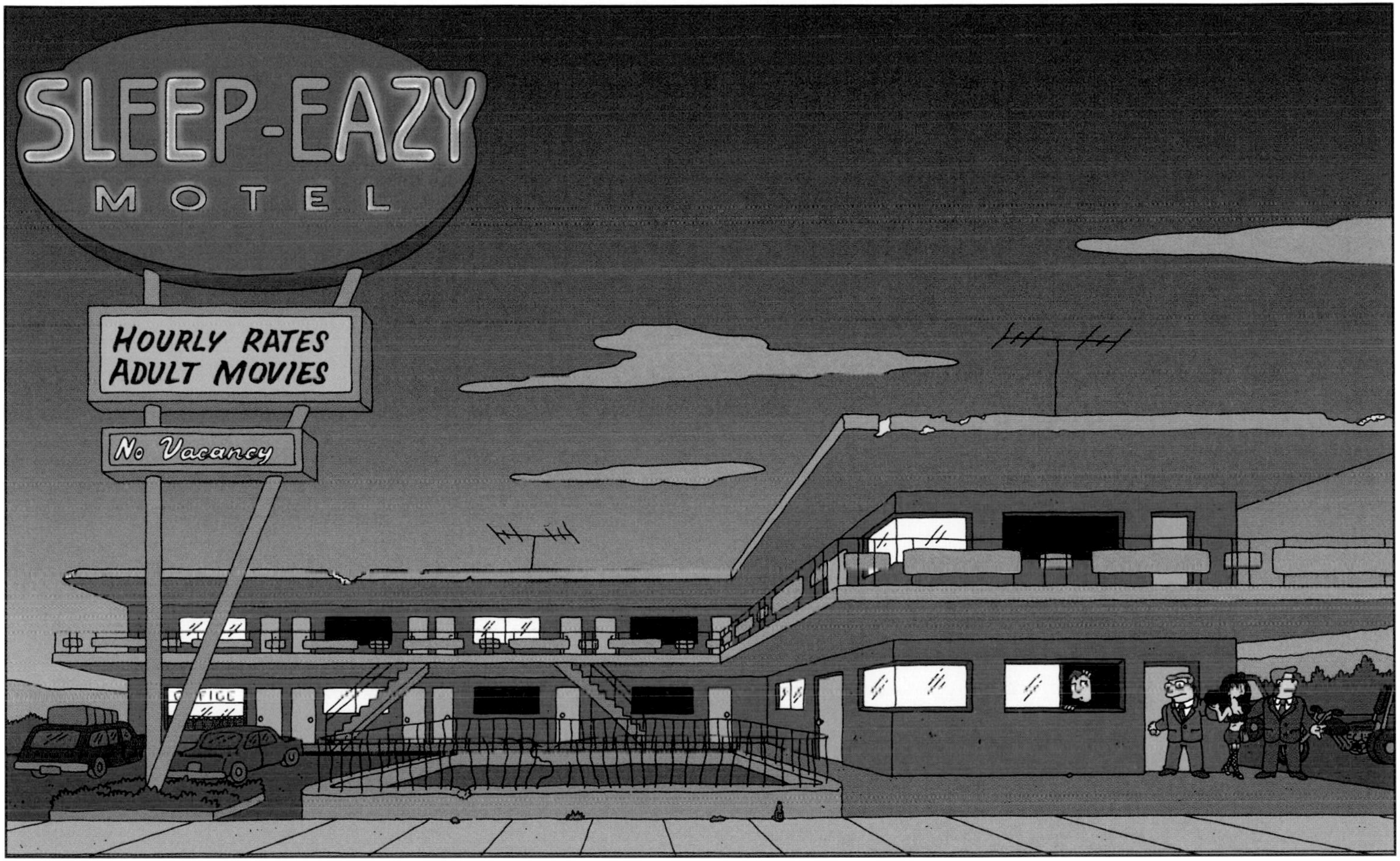
SLEEP-EAZY
MOTEL
HOURLY RATES
ADULT MOVIES
No Vacancy

Mayor "Diamond Joe" Quimby stays abreast of public affairs by polling one of his constituents at his private suite at the Sleep-Eazy Motel.

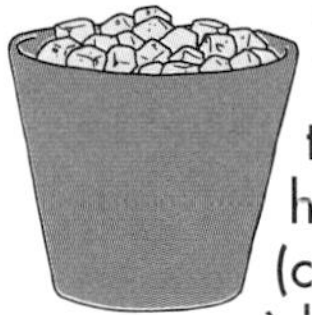

and Duff Stout. Plus, the room service is impeccable: Maude Flanders's kitchen is open twenty-four hours a day, serving up such household favorites as Flanders-style Nachos (cucumbers with cottage cheese) and Chicken Curry à la Ned (turkey bologna with ketchup and salt). The Flanders's sons, Rod and Todd, serve as concierge and bellboy, both ready to haul luggage and press pants whenever needed. Ned himself will stay home from work just to make sure you don't miss any messages. Put it all together

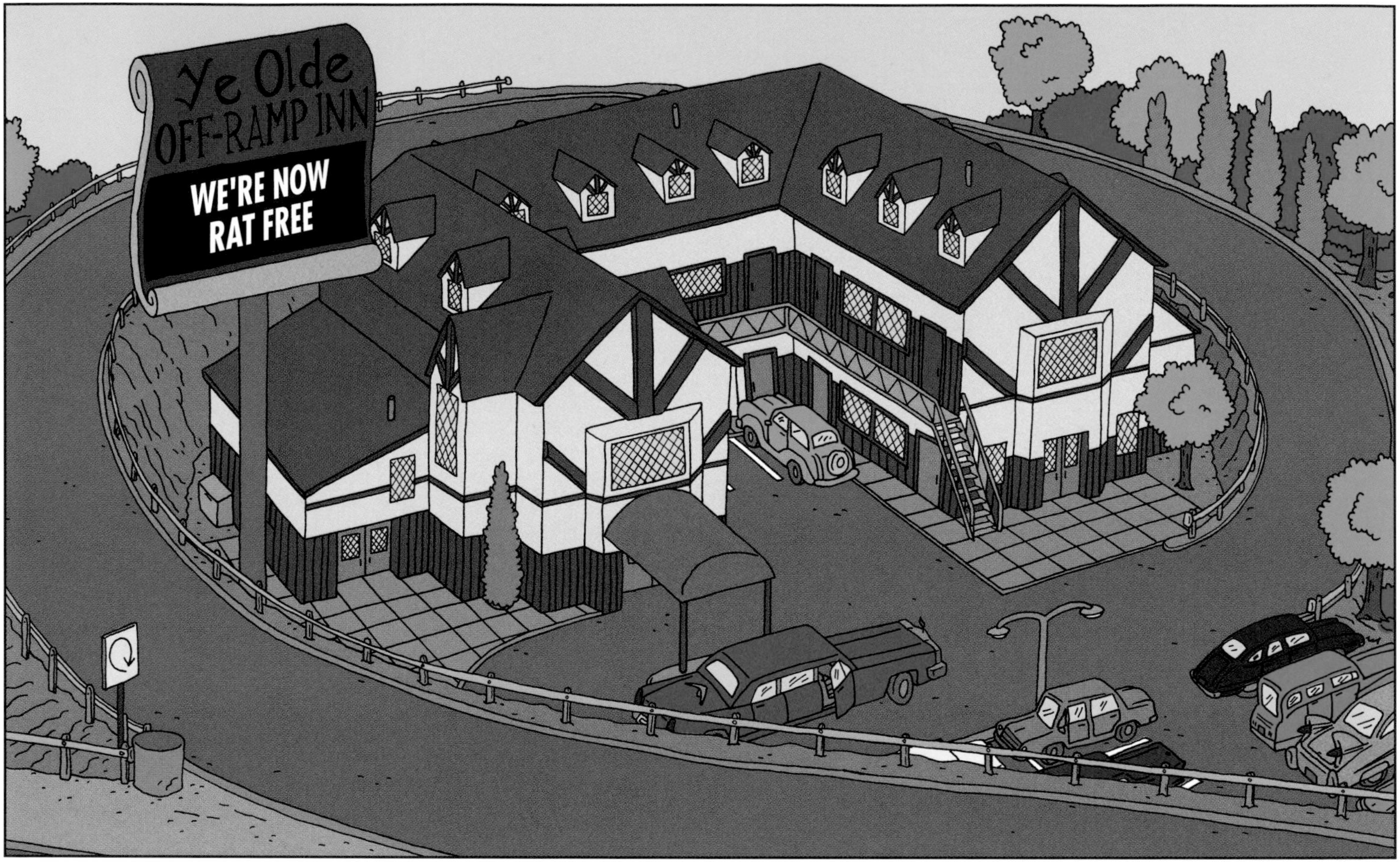
Ye Olde
OFF-RAMP INN
WE'RE NOW
RAT FREE

The parking lot at the Ye Olde Off-Ramp Inn is always full, due to the fact that so many customers can't figure out how to get back on the freeway once they arrive.

and you actually have the makings of a four-star hotel in an area zoned strictly for domestic dwellings. And you get it all for the low, low price of merely having to take a copy of *The Good News Bible* home with you when you check out.

Worst Western: A motel on the comeback trail. Last year, authorities condemned three of Worst Western's guest rooms. This year, they had to board up only one. Building on this recent success, the motel has instituted a continental breakfast composed of flour, warm water, and sugar packets from the Mexican restaurant next door.

DINING

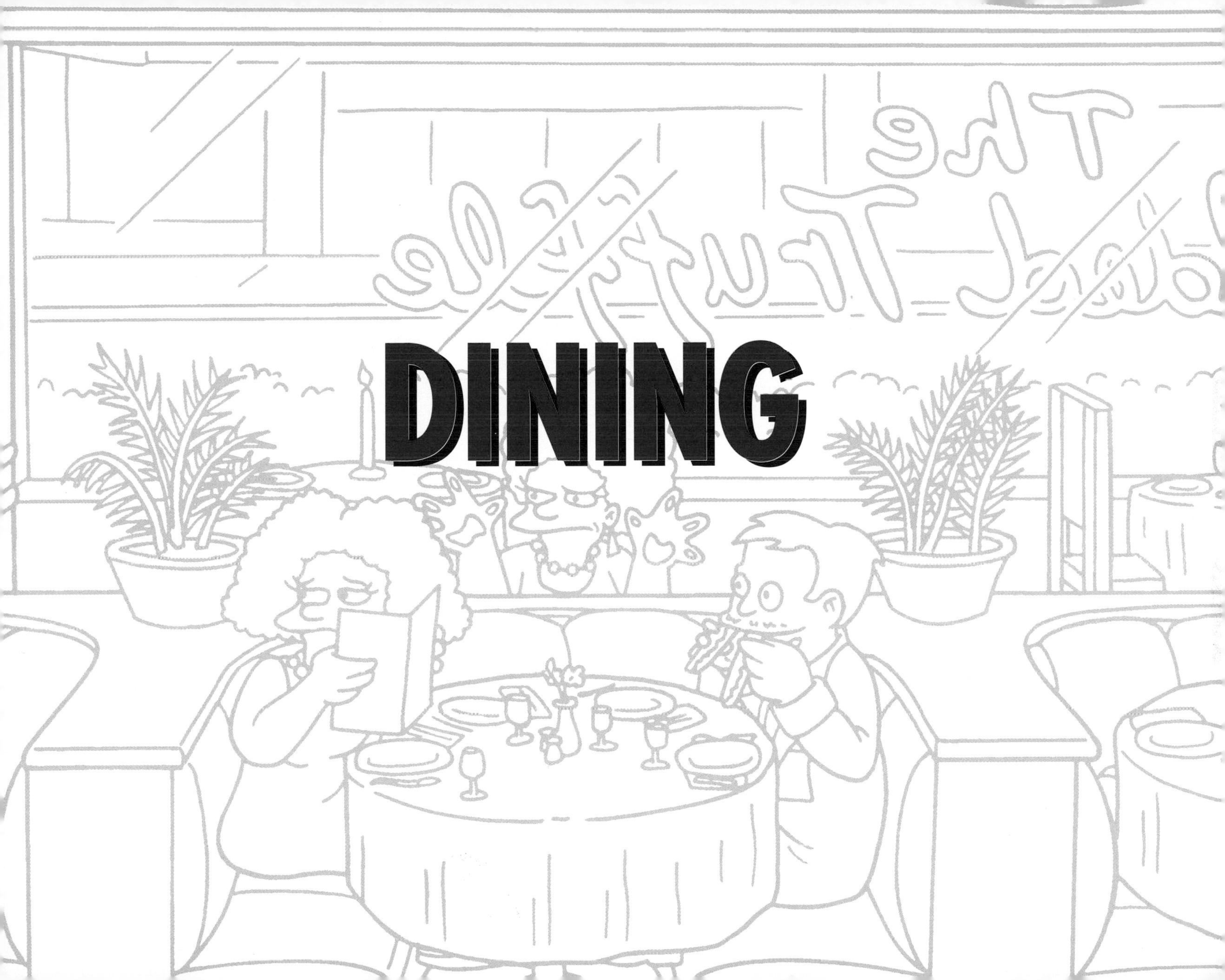

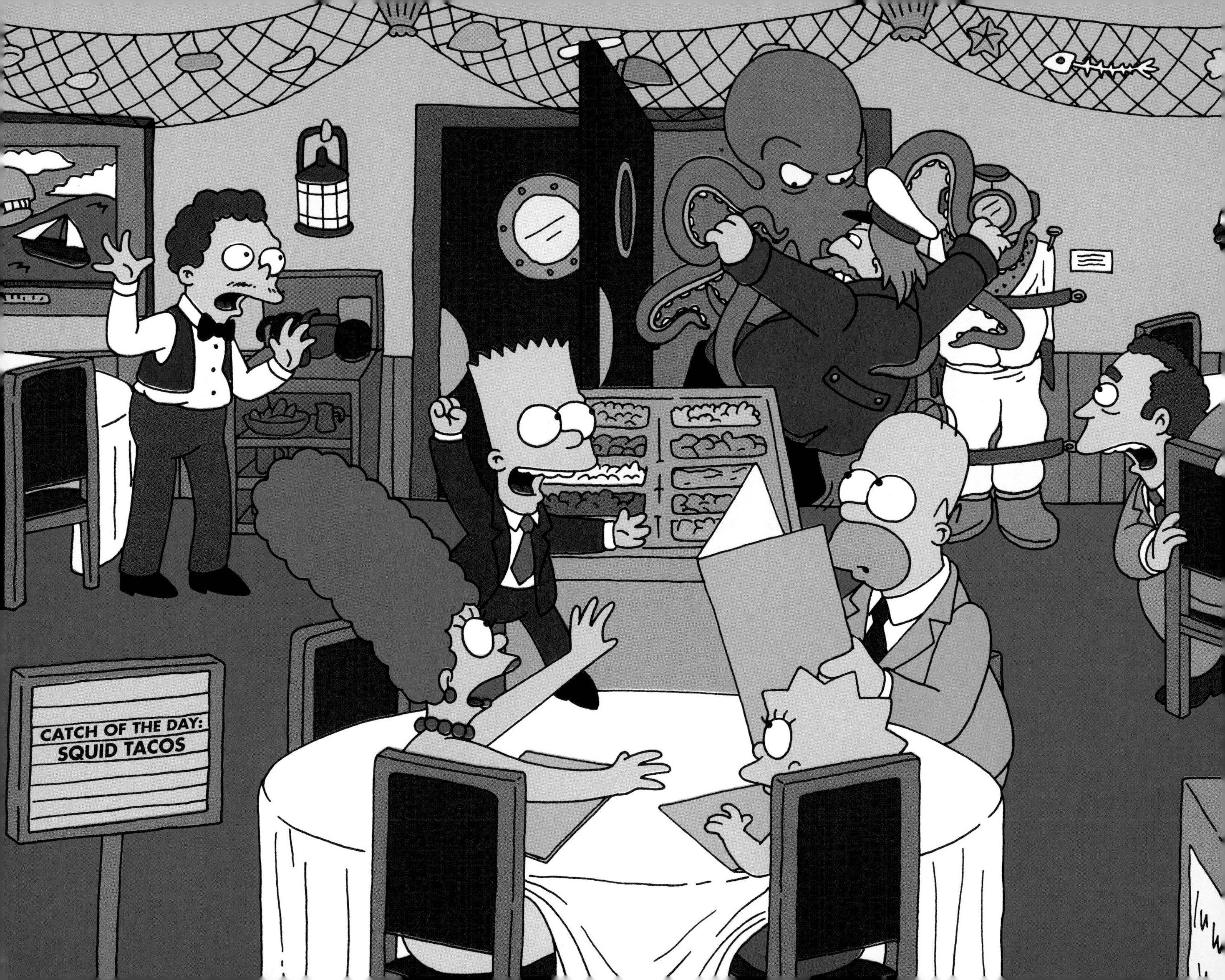
CATCH OF THE DAY:
SQUID TACOS

With the proper shots, enzyme conditioning, and psychological preparation, dining in Springfield can be a satisfying, if not challenging, experience. Some say Springfield is a blight on the culinary landscape of the United States. Sure, Springfield is a city of deep fryers and MSG drums. And yes, it's a city that has legally designated squirrel meat as poultry. And it is true that the city's health department can be easily bought off with Belgian chocolates and fortified wine. But to call this city a culinary "blight"? Please. Everyone knows that Springfield has its food-service problems, but it's also a city of bold culinary vision that gave us such victual innovations as Nacho Hats and the eye-opening, artery-closing Good Morning Burger! It's a city that takes the phrase "all you can eat" seriously! It's a city that doesn't cower from its dining obligations; nay, it offers up plates of steaming-hot foodstuffs and says, "Eat it! It's good and probably not harmful to you!" But where to eat it in Springfield? We're glad you asked.

Izzy's Deli: Recently voted the city's saltiest restaurant, Izzy's is also Springfield's premier

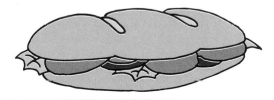

(At left) Patrons enjoy really fresh seafood at The Frying Dutchman.

delicatessen. Try the "Rainier Wolfcastle" (an edible machine gun fashioned from sauerbraten, kraut, and chopped liver), but avoid the "Troy McClure" (pickled herring and beets on day-old bread).

The Frying Dutchman: This quaint nautical eatery specializes in deeply fried seafoods. The pros: The seafood is fresh and the restaurant is owned by a genuine salty old sea captain. The cons: The seafood is from the semi-toxic Springfield Harbor and the salty old sea captain is often drunk and odd-smelling. The restaurant's boldest challenge is the creamed seafood steam table, offering such delicacies as chipped scallops on toast and macaroni and mussels and cheese. *Note:* The "all-you-can-eat" policy was discontinued after a local gentleman with an eating disorder nearly ran the place out of business.

Two Guys from Kabul: Serving the best labna this side of Vandihar, TGFK is one of Springfield's finest "constantly-smells-like-curry" restaurants. The free floorshow every night centers around the "two guys" screaming at one another, each blaming the other for opening a Pakistani restaurant in a town that considers Swiss cheese too exotic.

WHAT'S RIGHT WITH SPRINGFIELD?

"I would have to say my beloved place of employment: the **Kwik-E-Mart**. Partially because it has given me a purpose in life, a semi-livable wage, and discounted past-freshness date merchandise, and partially because I have seen little else of Springfield due to the cruelly inhumane shift lengths."
—Apu Nahasapeemapetilon, local merchant

The Happy Sumo: Excellent sushi served in all the colors of the wind, including the potentially fatal fugu (blowfish) and the famous Springfield Sushiii Roll, (it's got three eyes, get it?), consisting of salmon and yellowtail wrapped 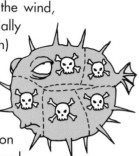 around sea urchin and served under a blacklight on a glow-in-the-dark tray. Come for the sushi, stay for the karaoke, and watch drunken Japanese businessmen slur their way through "Suspicious Minds" before they throw up, pass out, wake up, and order more Duffahama.

Phineas Q. Butterfat's 5600 Flavors Ice Cream Parlor: The gaudy, neo-chitty-chitty decor of this ice creamery is almost as sugary-sweet as its frozen confections. How can they possibly have 5600 flavors, you ask? Anything goes at Q. Butterfat's: choices include Cheddar Cheese Dream, Parsley Sorbet, and Liver N' Bacon Rhumba. Our suggestion: Stick with the Rocky Road.

Ugli: Snotty, trendy, Los Angeles-style, Euro-fusion dining. Everything can be ordered fat free or with extra contempt. Act indifferent, keep your nose at a 45-degree angle, leave your socks at home, and everything will be fine. For those with brave constitutions (and the proper shots), order the seared gefilte fish with wheatgrass polenta.

Shakespeare's Fried Chicken: Serving thousands of grease-laden, crispy fried-chicken parts daily, Shakespeare's is the granddaddy of fast-food poultry outlets in Springfield.

The eventual victor of the Springfield Chicken Wars of the late 1980s (Colonel Krusty's made a run for deep-fried dominance but failed), Shakespeare's is the most widely available bucketfood in the area.

Jittery Joe's Coffee Shop: A twenty-four-hour greasy spoon specializing in reheating frozen foods purchased from industrial restaurant suppliers. Drink your coffee, exchange some mean looks with the truckers, and get out.

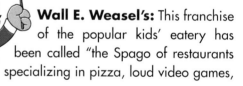

Wall E. Weasel's: This franchise of the popular kids' eatery has been called "the Spago of restaurants specializing in pizza, loud video games,

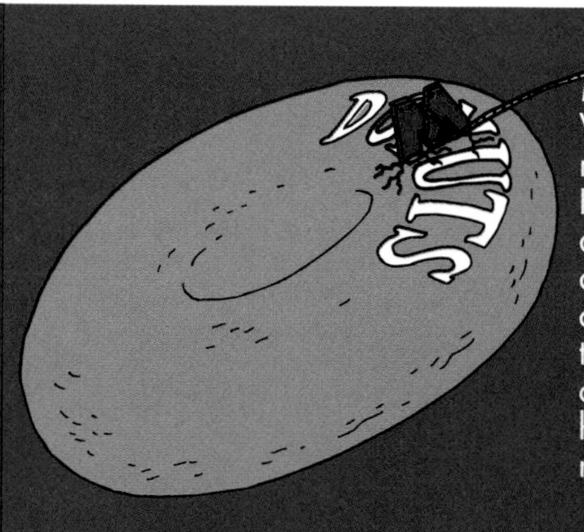

ARTIFACTS

THE DONUT-ANCHOR:

Its History:
When the city lost control of its much-heralded monorail on its maiden voyage, train operator Homer J. Simpson showed uncharacteristically quick thinking by rigging an impromptu anchor out of a large "M" from the logo outside the train's cockpit. As the space-age transportation system continued on its erratic course, the "M" finally caught onto this humorously large donut replica, bringing the runaway monorail to a stop.

Historical Significance:
Great. That cement and chickenwire faux pastry saved dozens of lives and ended Springfield's monorail madness.

Where to See it:
Anywhere from up close to miles and miles away. That's one big freakin' donut.

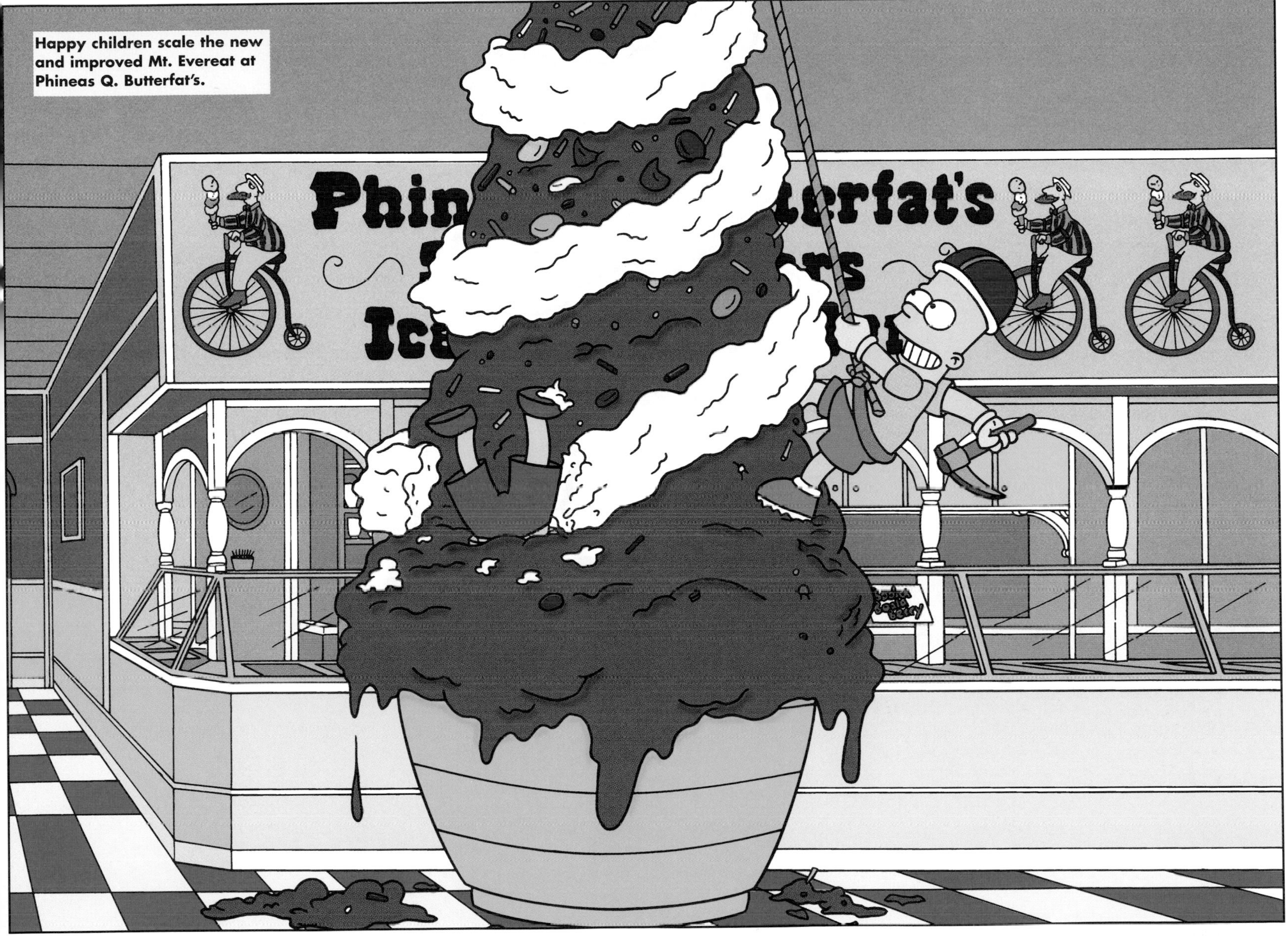

Happy children scale the new and improved Mt. Evereat at Phineas Q. Butterfat's.

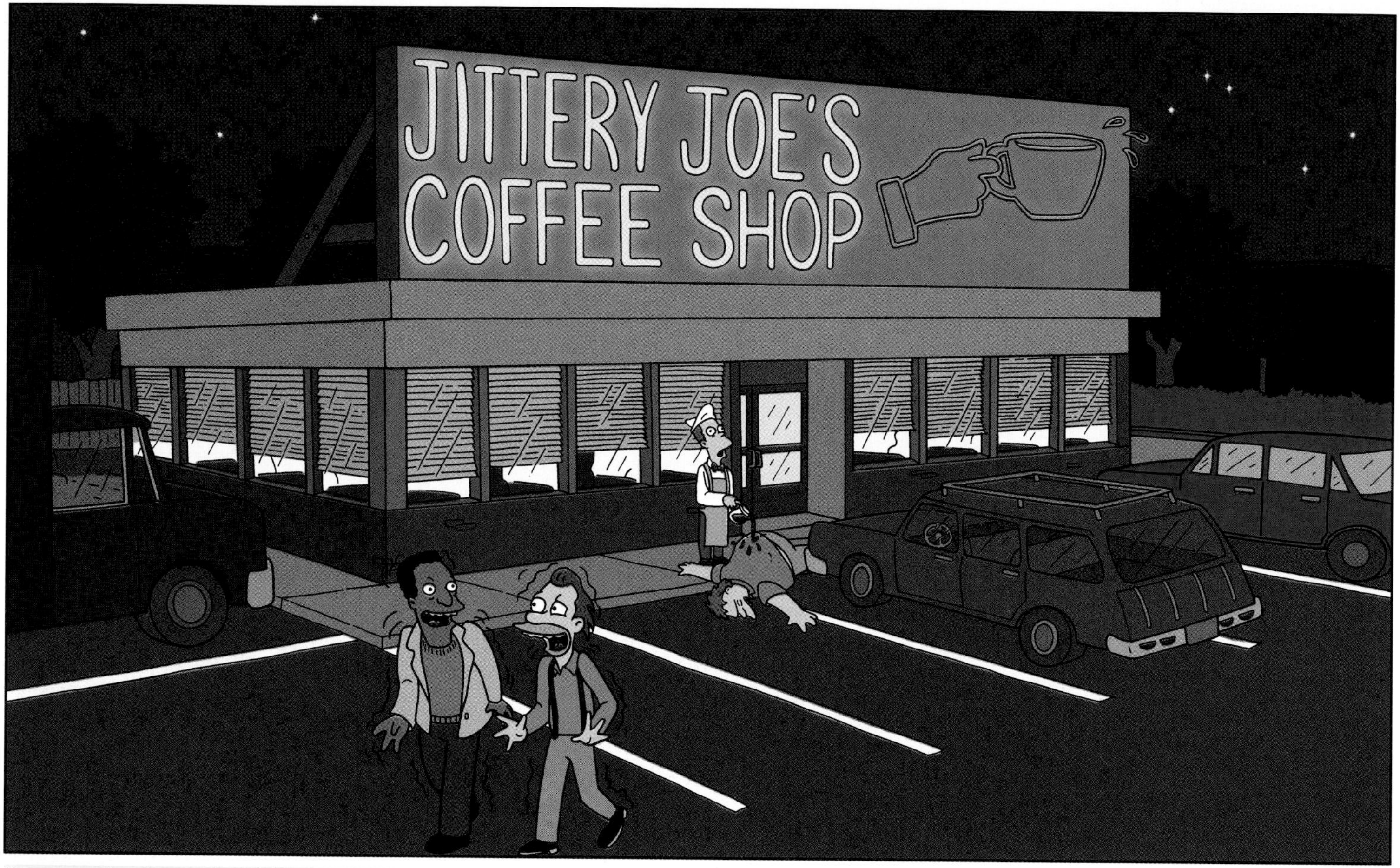
JITTERY JOE'S
COFFEE SHOP

Patrons enjoy the results of dessert while a dazed employee pours a pot of coffee on an unidentified lush at Jittery Joe's.

and poorly maintained animatronics." All things considered, the pizza, although octopus-shaped, is relatively good. And although his tail occasionally catches fire during the final stanza, Señor Beaverotti's "The Impizzable Dream" from *The Man of La Muncha* is surprisingly stirring.

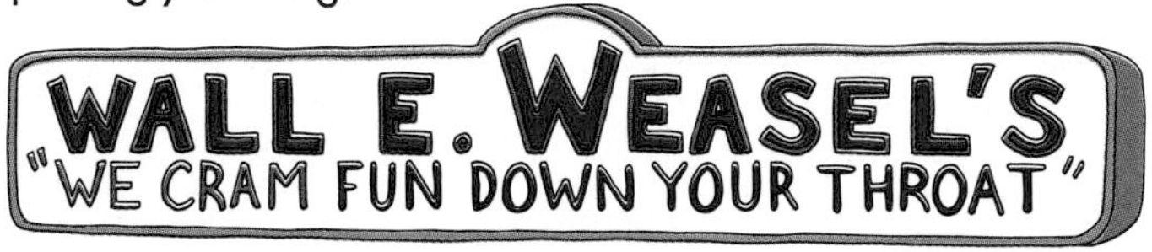
WALL E. WEASEL'S
"WE CRAM FUN DOWN YOUR THROAT"

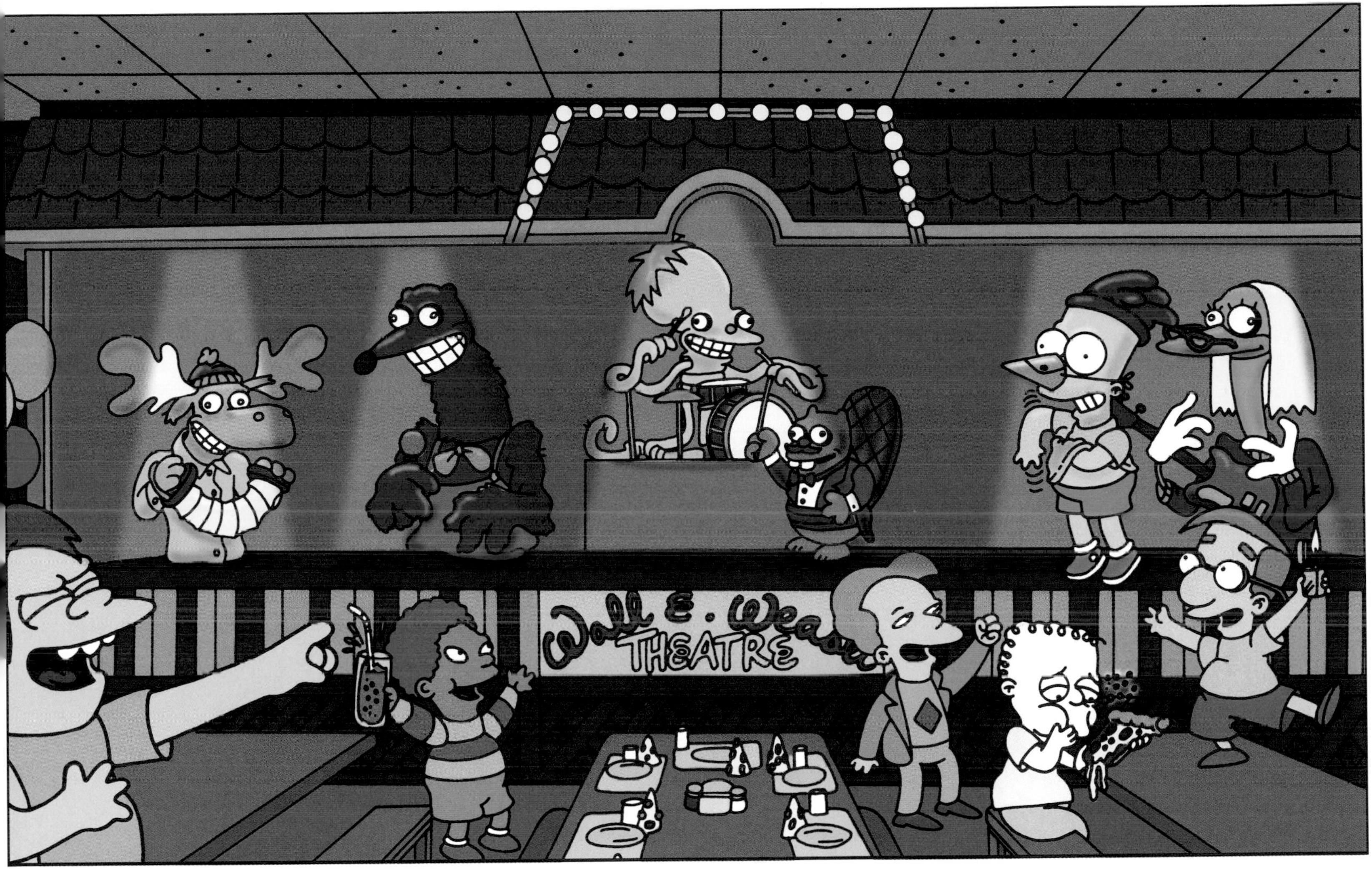
Wall E. Weasel
THEATRE

An aspiring young musician joins the band at Wall E. Weasel's.

WHAT'S RIGHT WITH SPRINGFIELD?

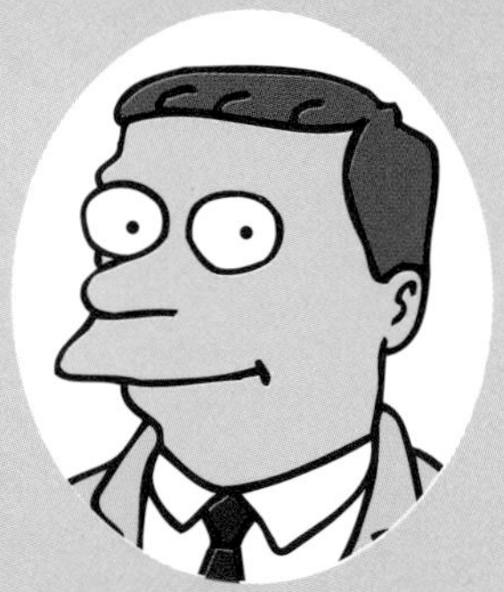

"Cell 46 at the Springfield Police Station Drunk Tank. It's clean, a good place to sleep it off, and I get most of my clients from the advertisement I carved into the wall using the top of my zipper."

—Lionel Hutz, attorney

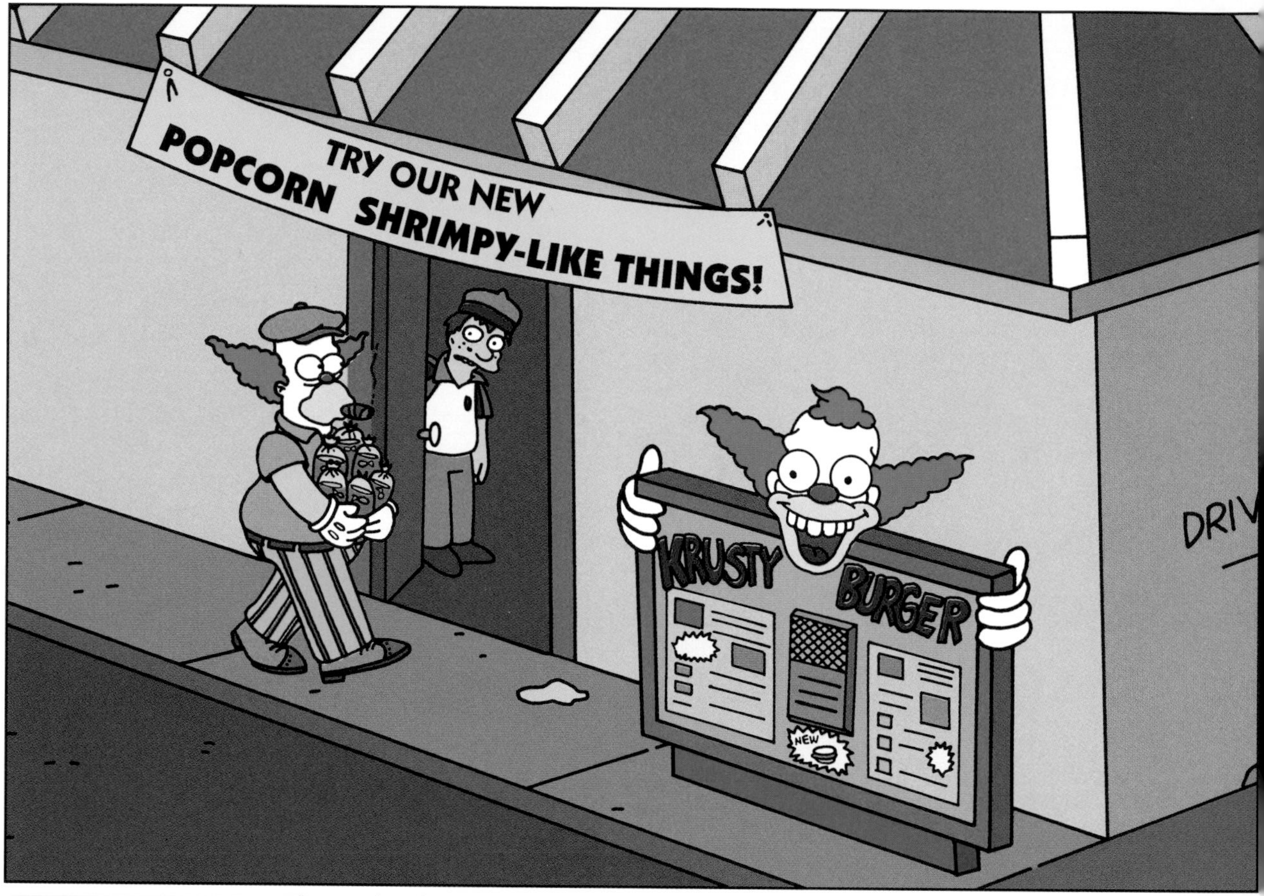
TRY OUR NEW
POPCORN SHRIMPY-LIKE THINGS!
KRUSTY BURGER
NEW

Fresh goldfish delivery time at Krustyburger.

The Singing Sirloin: Serving steaks "rare, medium, or well-sung," this meat-eatery employs dozens of struggling actor-vocalists to serenade you as you dine. Do order the Jerry Lewis Lamb/Dean Martin Mignon Combo. Don't ask the waiters to sing "American Pie"; you'll be there all night.

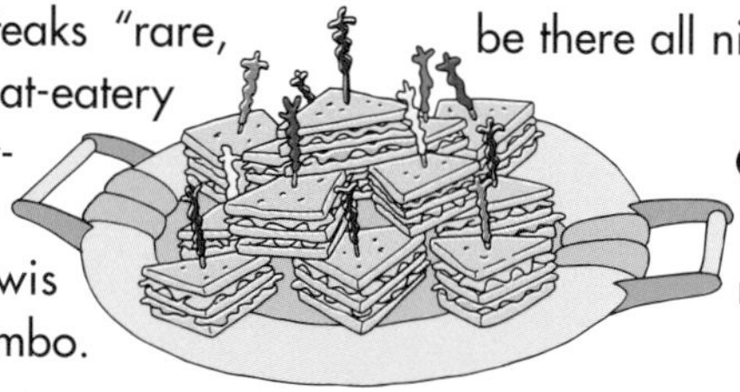

Chez Paree: Elegant French food served by middle-aged men in tuxedos, many of whom have mustaches.

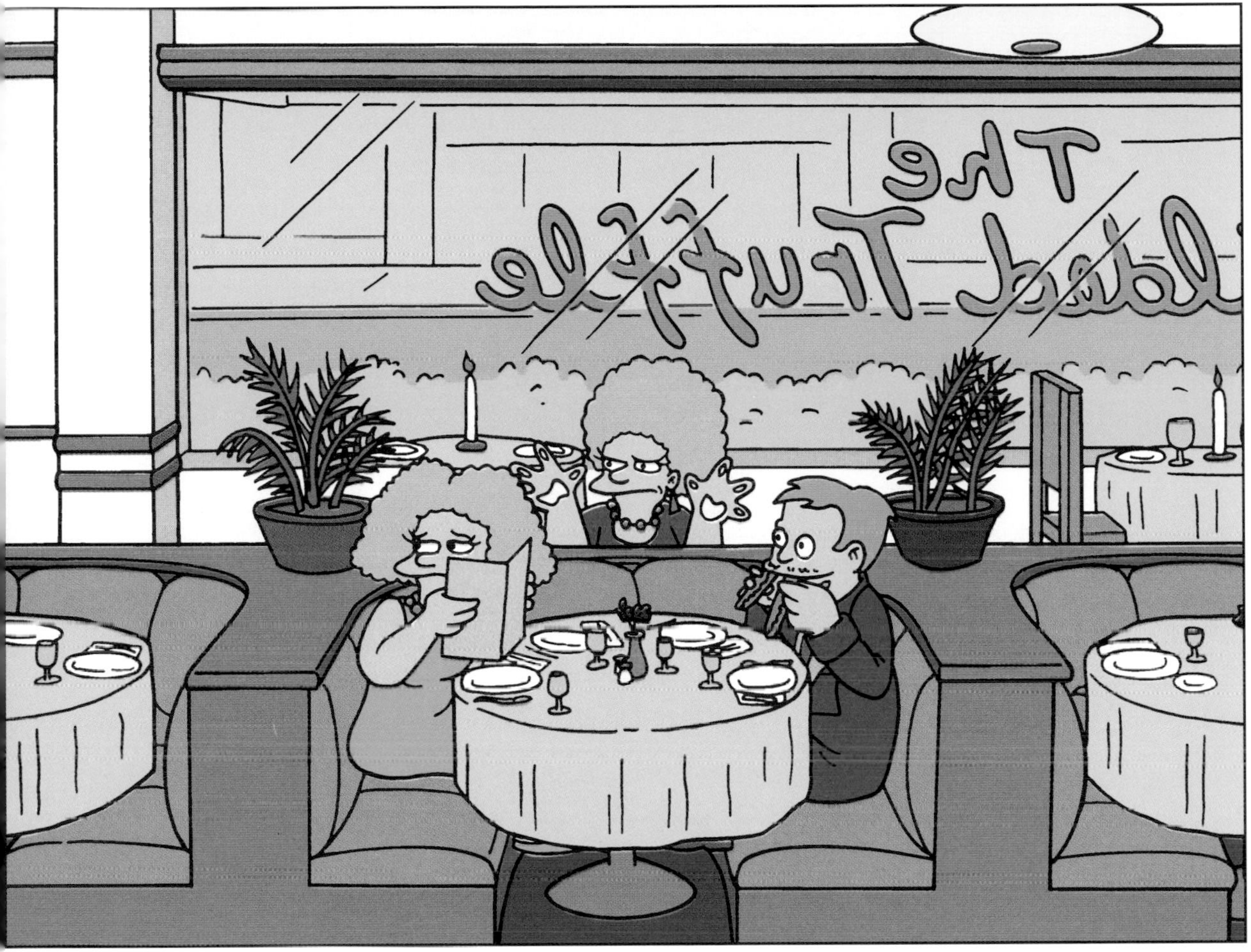

A guilty pleasure; dining at the Gilded Truffle.

Mort's Deli: Formerly the home of the world's largest pickle, Mort's suffered a terrible blow when its prized vinegared cuke was stolen in 1995. Now, the stench of defeat hangs in the air, and Mort slides your fatty pastrami sandwich across the counter with a sullen expression, saying nary a word. Mort's also makes the best kugel in the city.

WHAT'S RIGHT WITH SPRINGFIELD?

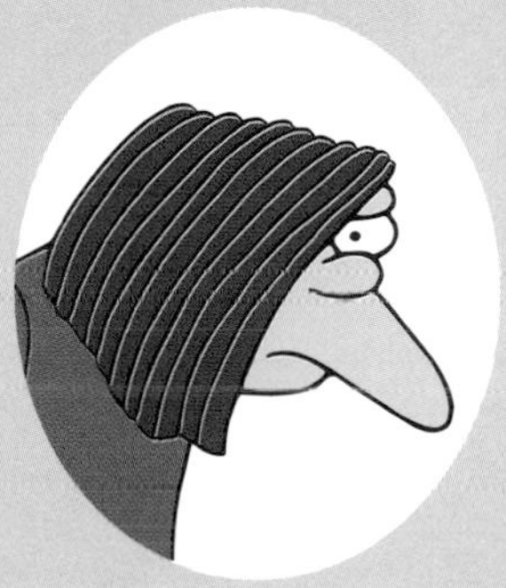

"Egg-hucking is what makes me me. And what better place to huck eggs at people than from the belltower of the **Springfield Church?**"

—Dolph,
age unknown

WELCOME TO KRUSTY BURGER

KRUSTY BREAKFASTS:		KRUSTY BURGER	.59
-SERVED TIL NOON:		KRUSTY CHEESE BURGER	.59
KRUSTY EGG BISCUIT	.59	KRUSTY BACON CHEESE BURGER	.59
KRUSTY EGG & SAUSAGE BISCUIT	.69	KRUSTY PORK SANDWICH	1.29
KRUSTY EGG, SAUSAGE & BACON BISCUIT	.89	KRUSTY GROUND SAUSAGE BURGER	1.29
KRUSTY SAUSAGE & BACON BISCUIT		KRUSTY NUGGETS	.99
DEEP FRIED SALAD ♥	NEW!	6, 12, 24 PIECES:	1.69/2.99
W/ HOUSE DRESSING 1.29		KRUSTY DOGS	.59

KRUSTY FRIES	.59/.99	KRUSTY BRAND CHILI	1.29
KRUSTY CURLY FRIES	.99	KRUSTY DEHYDRATED—	
W/CHEESE	1.19	MILKSHAKES .99/1.29	
KRUSTY KIDS MEAL	1.99	BUZZ COLA	
		DIET BUZZ	
KRUSTY MEAL		KRUSTY ORANGE DRINK	.79
FREE SLIDE WHISTLE!		KRUSTY ICE CREAM	.79
		KRUSTY COOKIES	.59

NOW WITH 5% LESS FAT

Sushi Yes: A horribly misled eatery that likes to be known as "the proud home of bottomfeeder sushi." Brave and stupid epicureans can dine on catfish sashimi, carp rolls, or sunomono with suckerfish. Please heed this warning: It's just not worth it.

Springfield Revolving Restaurant: Recently voted "Most Improved" by *Revolving Restaurant Magazine*, the SRR was completely rebuilt last year after a horrifying accident due to a computer error that resulted in the restaurant reaching an unsafe revolving speed. As the circular structure began to break free from its foundation, sweethearts shot out through the windows, in many cases landing more than three blocks away. Witnesses described the sound of the accident as being akin to "Florida being thrown through a chipper-shredder." Truth be told, it was the worst revolving restaurant mishap in United States history. Do not leave before trying their Baked Alaska.

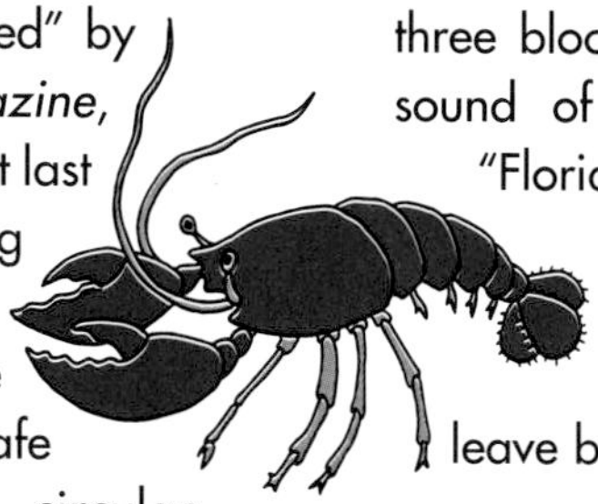

Krustyburger: With dozens and dozens of locations in the Springfield metropolitan

THE STONECUTTERS' SACRED PARCHMENT:

What It Was:
For 1500 years, this simple piece of parchment served as the heart and soul of several world-wide branches of the super-secret brotherhood known as the Stonecutters. Its last place of honor was in the Stonecutters' Springfield branch.

What Happened to It:
Homer J. Simpson, a new initiate to the Stonecutters, used it as a bib while eating ribs. He then blew his nose into it and used it to clean his ears.

Its Worth:
Nothing. People would probably pay you to keep it away from them.

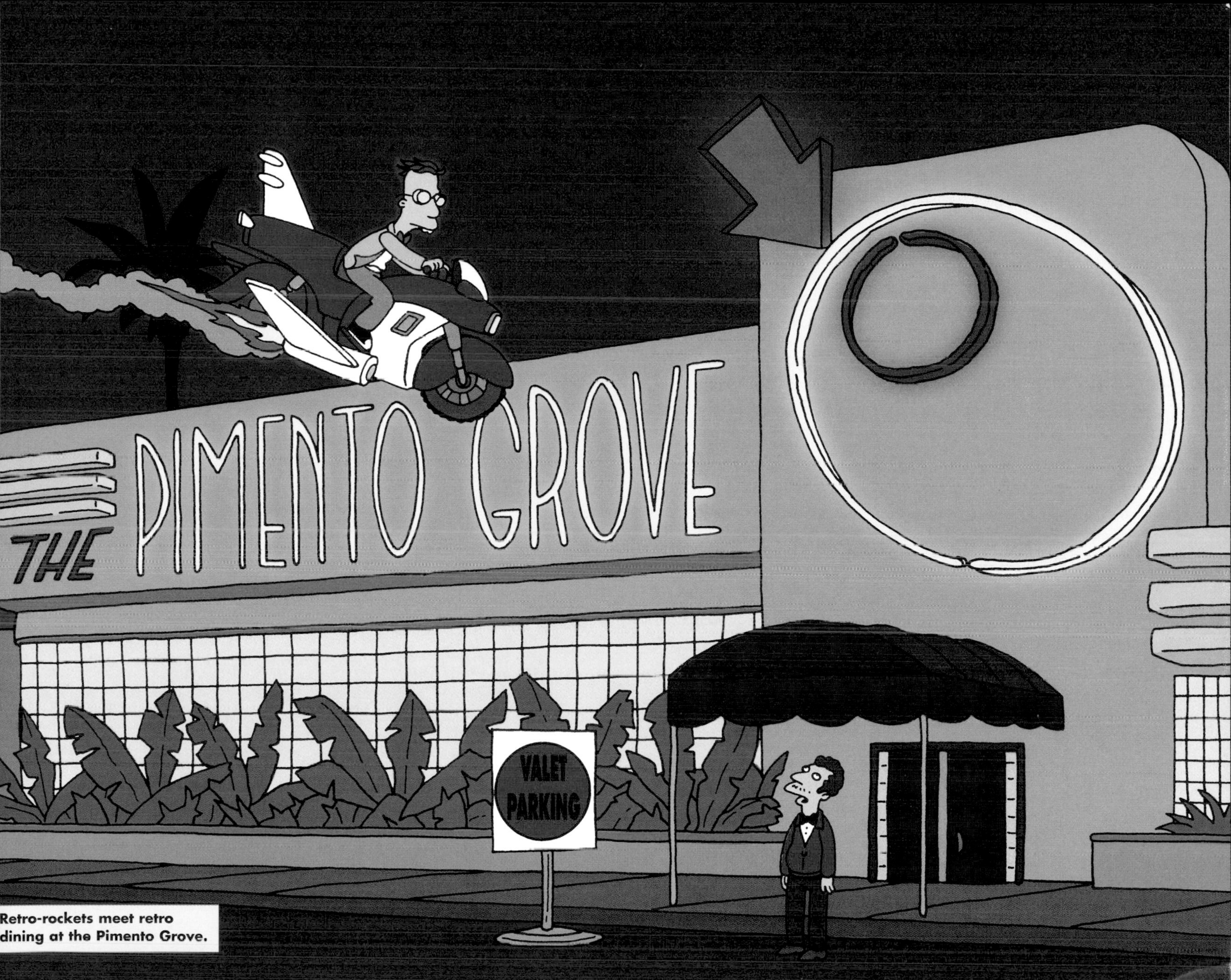
THE PIMENTO GROVE
VALET PARKING

Retro-rockets meet retro dining at the Pimento Grove.

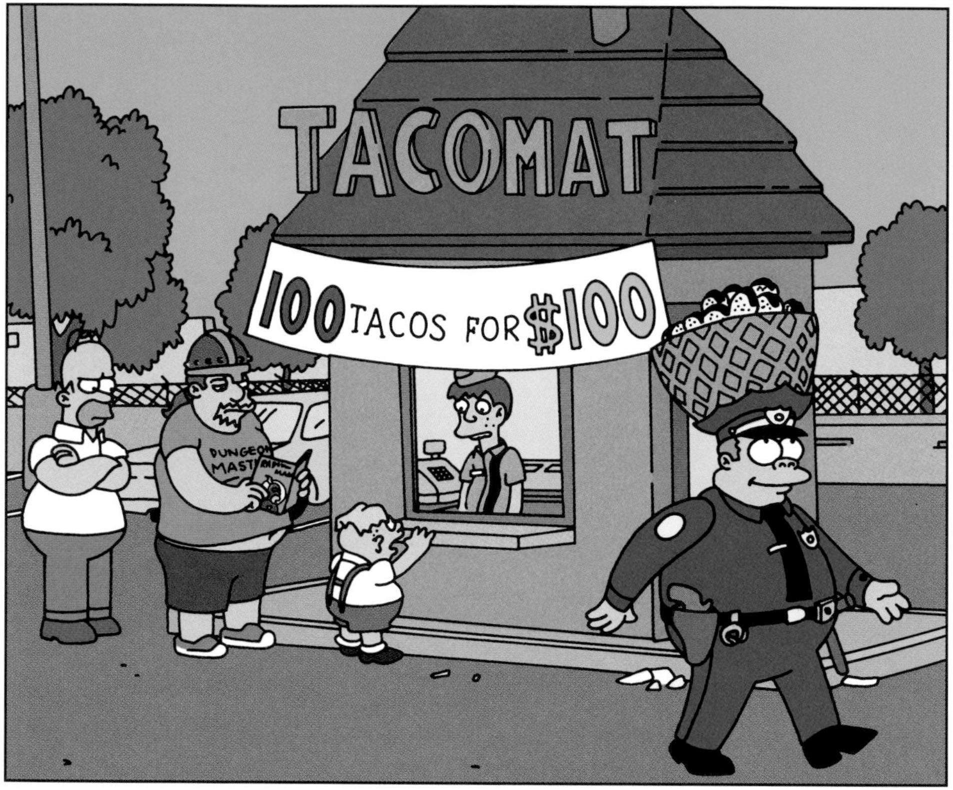
TACOMAT
100 TACOS FOR $100

Obese residents of Springfield take advantage of a bulk taco promotion at the TacoMat.

area, Krustyburgers are the most widely available nonbucket food in the city. Although reputed to be "100 percent real meat" by Krustyburger's founder, Krusty the Clown, scientific tests on the burgers' composition have proven inconclusive. The government encourages non-locals to avoid eating the burgers, stating that the "local populace has seemingly developed a resistance to the burger's inherent bacteria and spirochetes."

Berger's Burgers: Chewy and greasy and with fresh toppings aplenty, Berger's Burgers harkens back to a simpler time in America, when Eisenhower was in office and doctors in magazine ads encouraged you to smoke.

Gulp 'n' Blow: Is the restaurant's name a prediction? A threat? A suggestion? In a word, yes. Always eager to innovate, the Gulp 'n' Blow brought Springfield such limited-time treats as the "Creamycrunch Chugger" (a milkshake in cup made of deep-fried batter), "Pepperoniest Pizza" (sausage pizza with a crust made out of a giant, three-inch thick pepperoni), and the "Proud Texan Sandwich" (a 1/3 lb. burger topped with mustard, pickles, lettuce, and special sauce, shaped into a silhouette of President Lyndon Johnson).

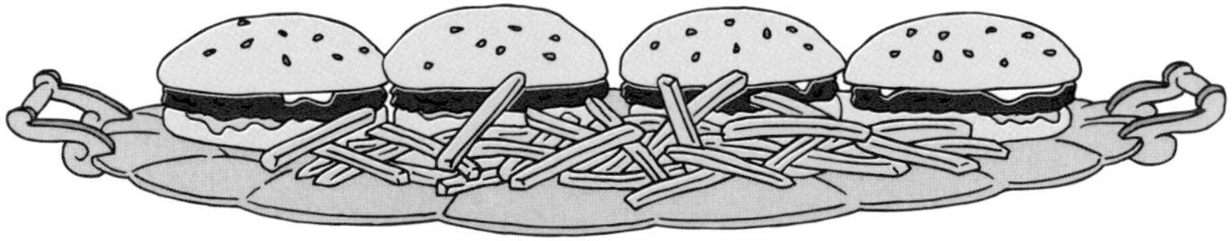

Chez Guevara: Originally an Argentine restaurant, CG switched to Cuban cuisine in the late 1980s. The greatest mambo acts in the country come to CG to play, eat, and set souls afire. CG has hosted such famous mambo-eers as Tito Puente and the touring company of *Ricky Ricardo-mania!*

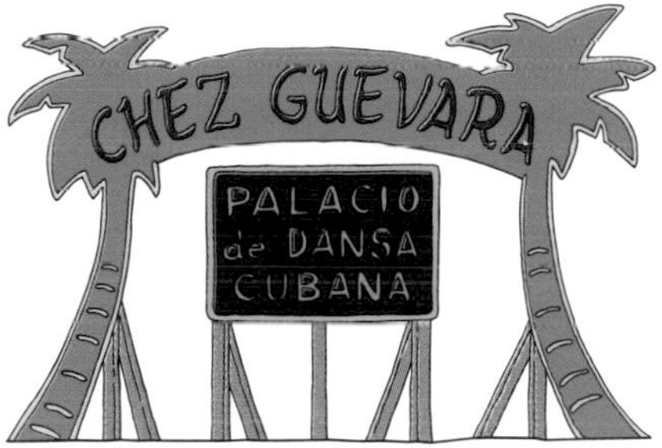
CHEZ GUEVARA
PALACIO de DANSA CUBANA

FaceStuffers: No silverware, no plates just mounds of Facestuff™ (ground beef, eggs, peppers, mushrooms, and cheese, smothered with tomato sauce) on wax paper. Unfortunately, the management cannot accept the reality that this tasty, piping-hot concoction was never meant to be a finger food. Our recommendation: Sneak in a really deep spoon. To-go orders are given out in plastic mopping buckets.

Professor V.J. Cornucopia's Fantastic Foodmagorium and Great American Steakery: A lot can be said for a restaurant with a menu so long that it cannot be read in one sitting. For one thing, its thirty-plus-page bill-of-fare features every bar food known to mankind, from the usual (buffalo wings, mozzarella sticks) to the unusual (Chateaubriand poppers, matzo baseballs with capellini stitching). The steaks are obnoxiously large, and in a move to placate animal-rights groups, patrons are encouraged to publicly apologize to the slaughtered cow via the dining room's PA system. Bon appetit!

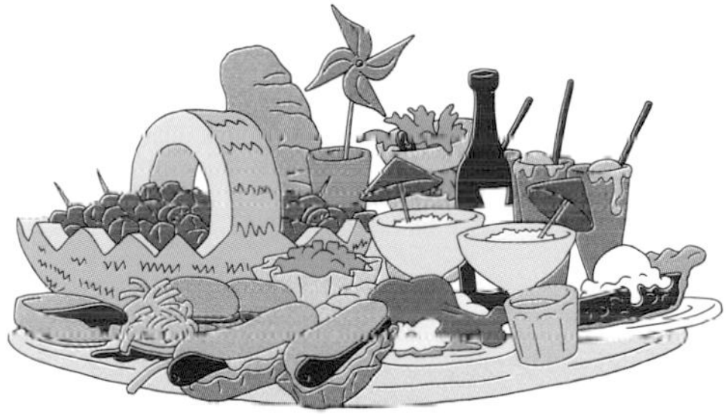

The Texas Cheesecake Depository: Home of the "thirty-pound cheesecake," this eatery unapologetically boasts high-calorie, high-fat, high-cholesterol desserts for "people who just don't give a damn." The devil's food cheesecake is so good that priests have actually been brought in to exorcise it.

The Gilded Truffle: Where the elite meet to talk quietly behind each other's backs. Old-school snootiness and mediocre fois de gras abound, but don't count this place out yet: the violin player is truly gifted. If you tip well, he may play you a rousing rendition of "The Devil Went Down to Georgia."

INANIMATE CARBON ROD:

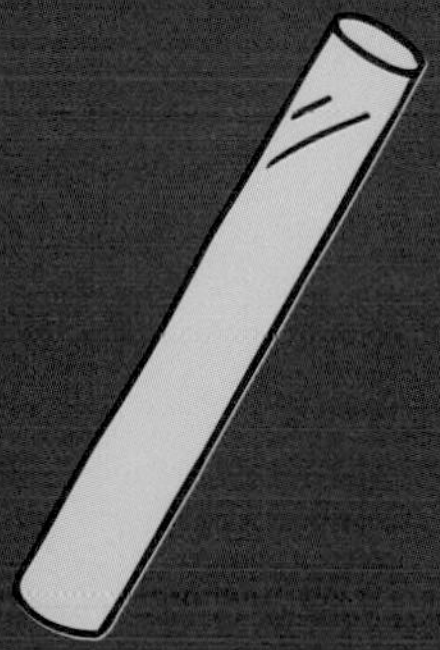

What It Is:
Perhaps the greatest inanimate carbon rod to ever come from Springfield. It was the first rod ever to be named "Worker of the Week" at the Springfield Nuclear Power Plant and it later found its way onto a NASA space mission, going on to save the lives of Springfield "everyman" astronaut Homer J. Simpson and real astronauts Buzz Aldrin and Race Banyon.

Where to See It:
Special appearances by the carbon rod are subject to fees negotiated by the rod's management. The rod often appears on television, endorsing watches, motor oils, and breakfast cereals.

What It's Most Often Called:
"Springfield's Favorite Rod-Son."

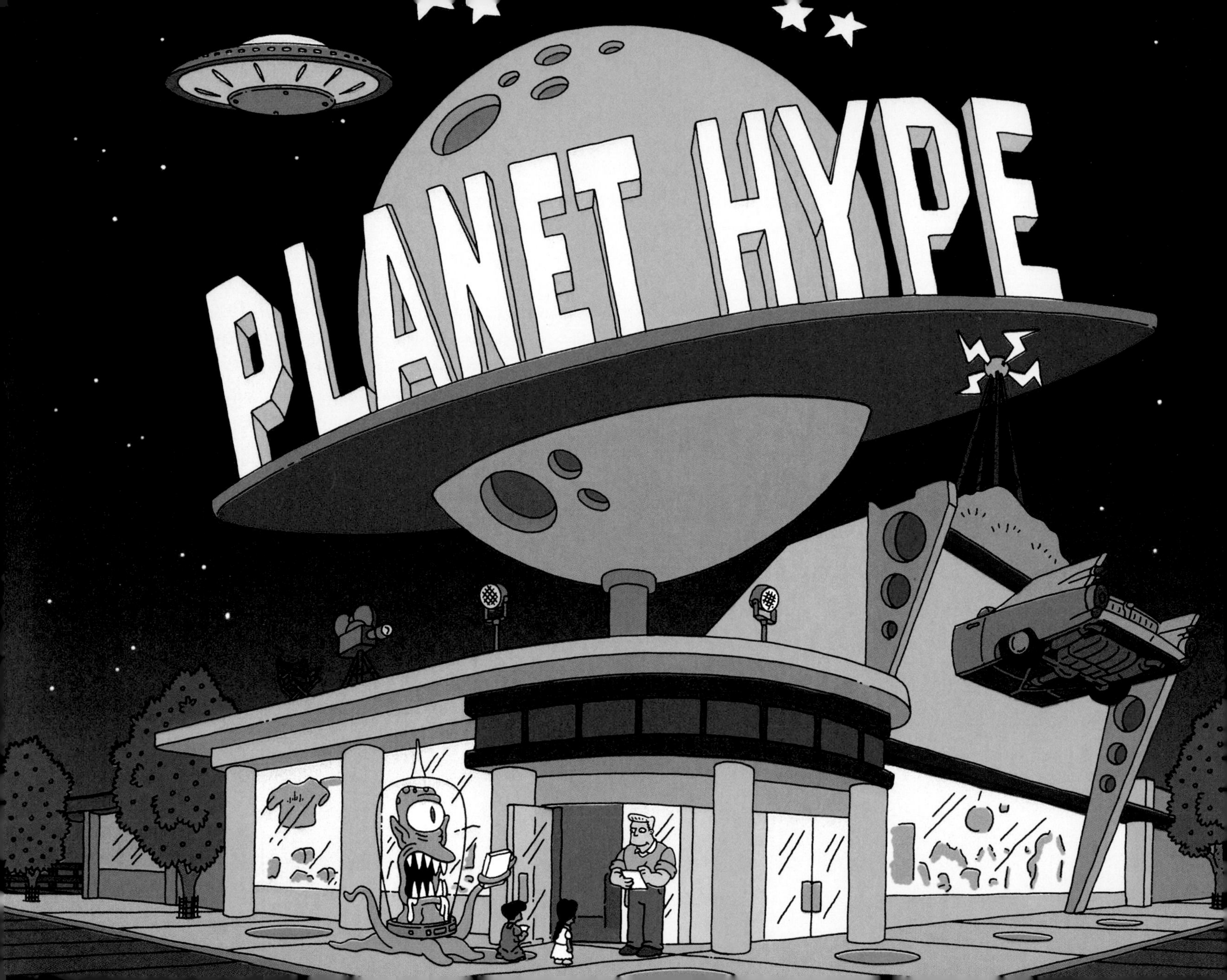
PLANET HYPE

(At left) Lucky movie fans get Rainier Wolfcastle's John Hancock at Planet Hype!

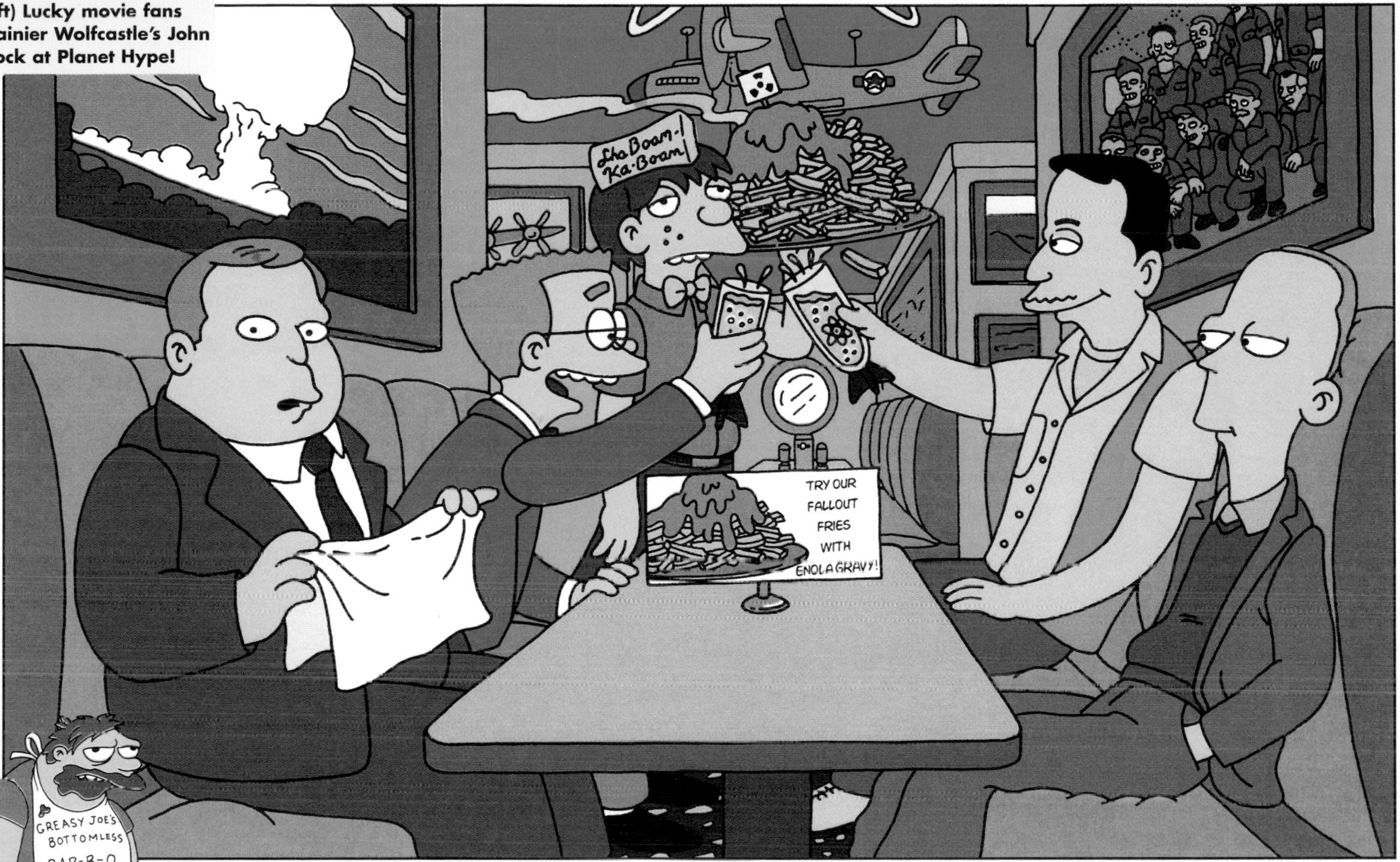
Sha-Boom! Ka-Boom
TRY OUR FALLOUT FRIES WITH ENOLA GRAVY!

Arch radio-talkshow conservative Birch Barlow enjoys a festive meal with a group of close personal friends at the Sha-Boom Ka-Boom Cafe.

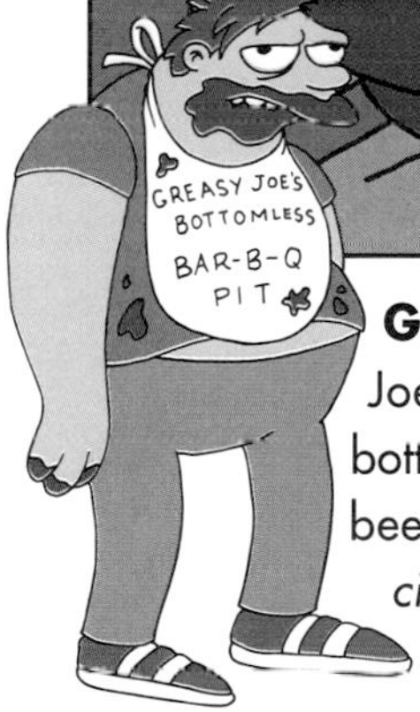
GREASY JOE'S BOTTOMLESS BAR-B-Q PIT

Greasy Joe's Bottomless Bar-B-Q Pit: Joe is truly greasy, the Bar-B-Q is truly bottomless, and, alas, the word "pit" has never been more aptly used. *Do not, under any circumstances, let your bare skin come into contact with any of the surfaces of this establishment.*

Lard Lad Donuts: Here's the trick that made Lard Lads famous: take a freshly fried donut, put it on a napkin held taught

WHAT'S RIGHT WITH SPRINGFIELD?

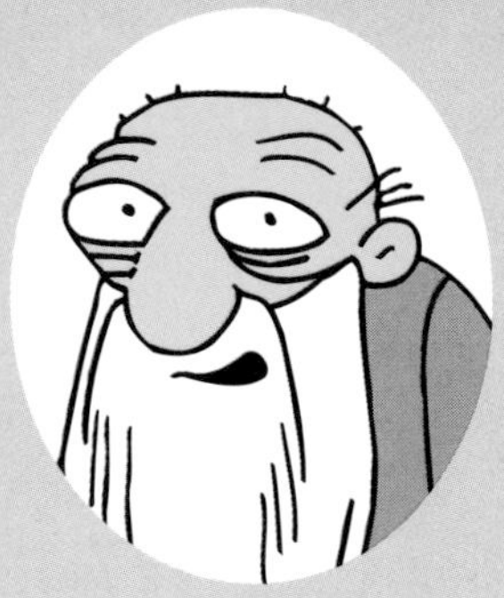

"The Mt. Swartzwelder Cider Mill in autumn captures all the beauty of God's wondrous creation. Also, the free cider helps me flush out the pipes, if you know what I mean."

—Jasper, retiree

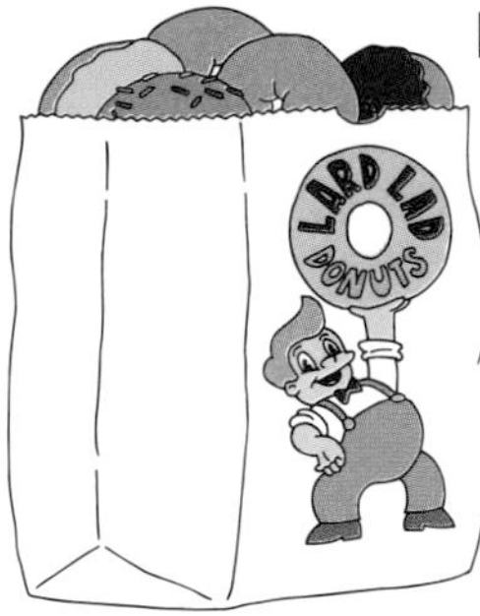
LARD LAD
DONUTS

between your hands, and watch the oil and weight of the donut cause the napkin to collapse. It's the same trick that led the company to be roundly condemned by the American Medical Association. Our advice: Savor one donut and wait until next year to have another.

Much Ado about Muffins! This muffin stand features summer-stock Shakespeareans singing the praises of their so-so product. Get thee to a bakery!

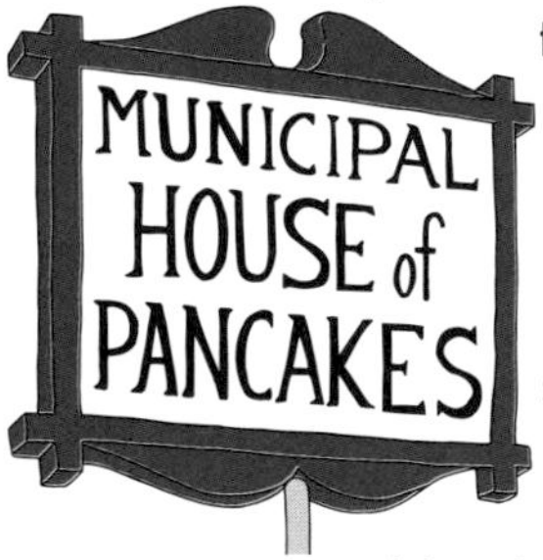
MUNICIPAL
HOUSE of
PANCAKES

Municipal House of Pancakes: Pancakes, schmancakes—it's the syrups that are the stars here. Choose from four lukewarm varieties sitting on your table the moment you step in: Marionberry, Chocayummiful, Blue, and Imported Flavourless. Order your requisite flapjacks and plan to take them home to your dog, then pour yourself a bowl of MHoP's wonderful syrup—easily the best sugar-delivery system on Elm Street!

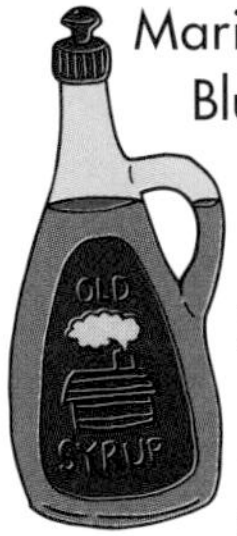
OLD
SYRUP

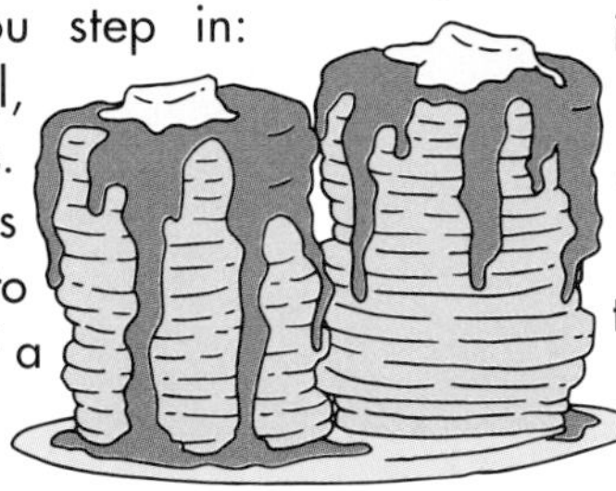

The Pimento Grove: To this very day, the late 1940s and early 1950s are still being diced up, fried, and served with a dusting of paprika at this historic downtown eatery. Often called "a Chasen's without bathrooms," this restaurant has been the dining choice for stars passing through Springfield on promotional tours or after getting horribly, horribly lost. Look for two —count 'em —two pictures of Barry White on the wall.

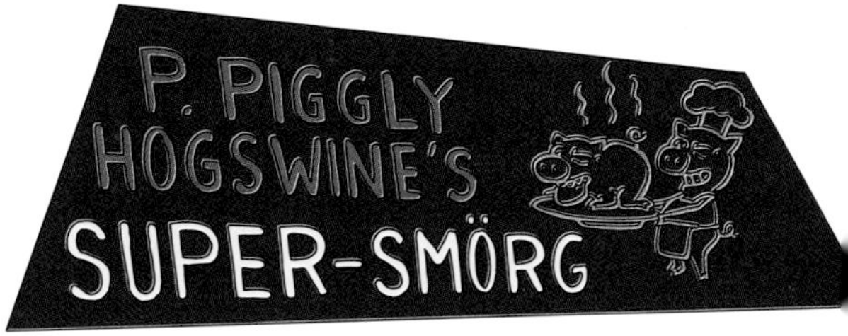
P. PIGGLY
HOGSWINE'S
SUPER-SMÖRG

P. Piggly Hogswine's Super-Smörg: Four out of five Springfield seniors make P. Piggly's their smörg-of-choice; the fifth would probably agree but is most likely laid up in bed after eating too much sugar-cured ham. Though the all-you-can-eat policy is still in place, patrons are no longer allowed to remain eating longer than eight hours. Also: P. Piggly's is the only restaurant in town to give out loaner dentures to

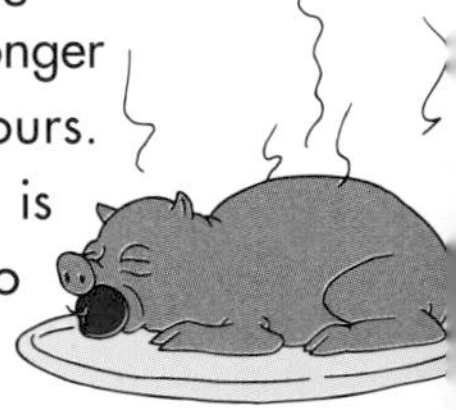

seniors who break theirs on the jawbreakers or the strudel.

The Spaghetti Laboratory:
A holdover from the 1980s fun-restaurant boom, the Spaglab (as regulars call it) features bizarre, Italian science-fiction food, such as Penne from Planet X and Manicottimal. *Everything about this place is strange and unsettling, and we strongly suggest you avoid it.*

TacoMat: Billed as "Taco convenience incarnate," this converted parking-lot photography kiosk is also the smallest four-walled taco-dispensing structure

in the world. Remarkably, upwards of twenty-seven employees can be found working inside, serving up tacos and hooking up fresh tanks to the tiny building's oxygen supply. Twice a year, the 'Mat has a special "100 Tacos for $100" promotion, offering the consumer five dollars in savings for buying in bulk.

Tannen's Fatty Meats:
A remnant of Springfield's Lower East Side, Tannen's serves up nonlean pastramis and corned beef. One of their knishes was recently analyzed by a Springfield lab as containing 89 grams of fat and only 1/ grams of knish. Oy!

Bloaters at the Squidport: Specializing in alcoholic drinks that bounce, Bloaters is the preferred tavern of college kids who want to chew their shots. Bloaters also serves standard bar fare, but with a twist: all of their food has liquor in it. Rummy pizza fingers and beer-soaked mashed potatoes are two menu favorites.

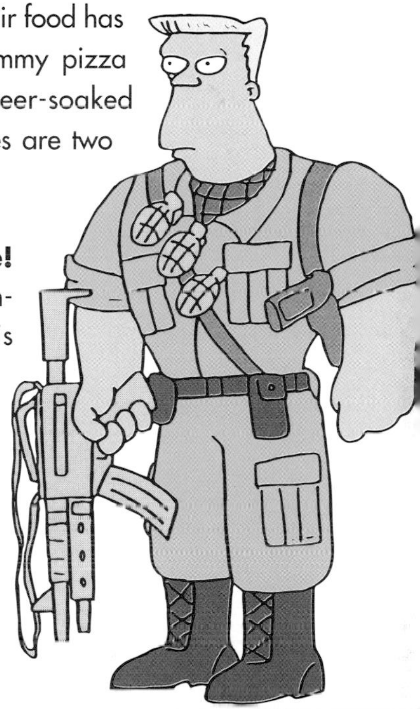

Planet Hype!
A principal investor in this restaurant is Rainier Wolfcastle, star of such McBain classics as *McBain IV: Big Flamin' Payback* and

PORTRAIT OF BURNS:

How It Came to Be:
After several unsuccessful commissions (which systematically alienated the entire Springfield art community), C. Montgomery Burns asked Springfield Art Fair's first-prize winner, Marge Simpson, to paint his portrait. Burns's intrusion upon the Simpson's home did little to endear him to Marge, and the portrait reflected her feelings toward him: It showed Burns as a frail, vulnerable —and thus, human —naked old man.

Where To See It:
The Burns Wing of the Springfield Palace of Fine Arts.

How Long the Average Person Can Handle Looking at It:
45 seconds.

ARTIFACTS

WHAT'S RIGHT WITH SPRINGFIELD?

"Ah, Fudge! is the name of the factory that creates my favorite confections. I go on their factory tour at least once a week. They no longer allow me to have any free chocolate, but they do let me lick the cocoa dust off of the cogs."

—Uter, age 10

McBain XII: Simon Says Die. Apparently, his questionable taste in storytelling pales in comparison with his taste in food. Inexplicably, the restaurant specializes in breakfast-cereal-encrusted meats, such as the Krusty-O chicken. In addition, the only star ever sighted in the restaurant (other than Wolfcastle) was one of the less important Coreys. Planet Hype, indeed.

Sha-Boom Ka-Boom!
cafe
LITTLE BOY-$3.95
FAT MAN-$12.95

Sha-Boom Ka-Boom Cafe: Atomic kitsch is alive and well and living in this pink, mushroom cloud-shaped eatery. Packed with tons of faux souvenirs from the birth of the bomb (such as replica toilet seats from the *Enola Gay)*, this restaurant is a must-see for fans of insensitive, heartless camp. That said, the Oppenheimerburger is quite tasty.

Springfield Elementary School Cafeteria: Remarkably, the most exotic kitchen in all of Springfield resides in its grade school commissary. Where else can the bold gourmet sample such dishes as Jerk Hooves and Legal Meat-Product Curry? And yes, the rumors are true: they serve the best tater tots money can buy.

Buzzing Sign Diner: Famous for its custom mashed potatoes (patrons can choose from extra lumpy to liquid form), this diner features standard American fare and a constantly buzzing sign. As if this weren't enough, it also has a buzzing insect zapper, a buzzing door alert, and a barber who gives free buzzcuts in the corner booth. The combined noise is so loud that the vibrations often make eating soup impossible.

Big
BURGERS & FRIES

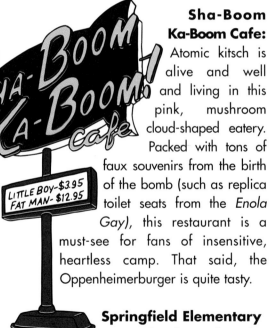

Big T Burgers and Fries: Big T capitalizes on the primal need of human beings to have food served to them out of a giant red letter. Due to ongoing litigation with Mr. T, Big T no longer features its

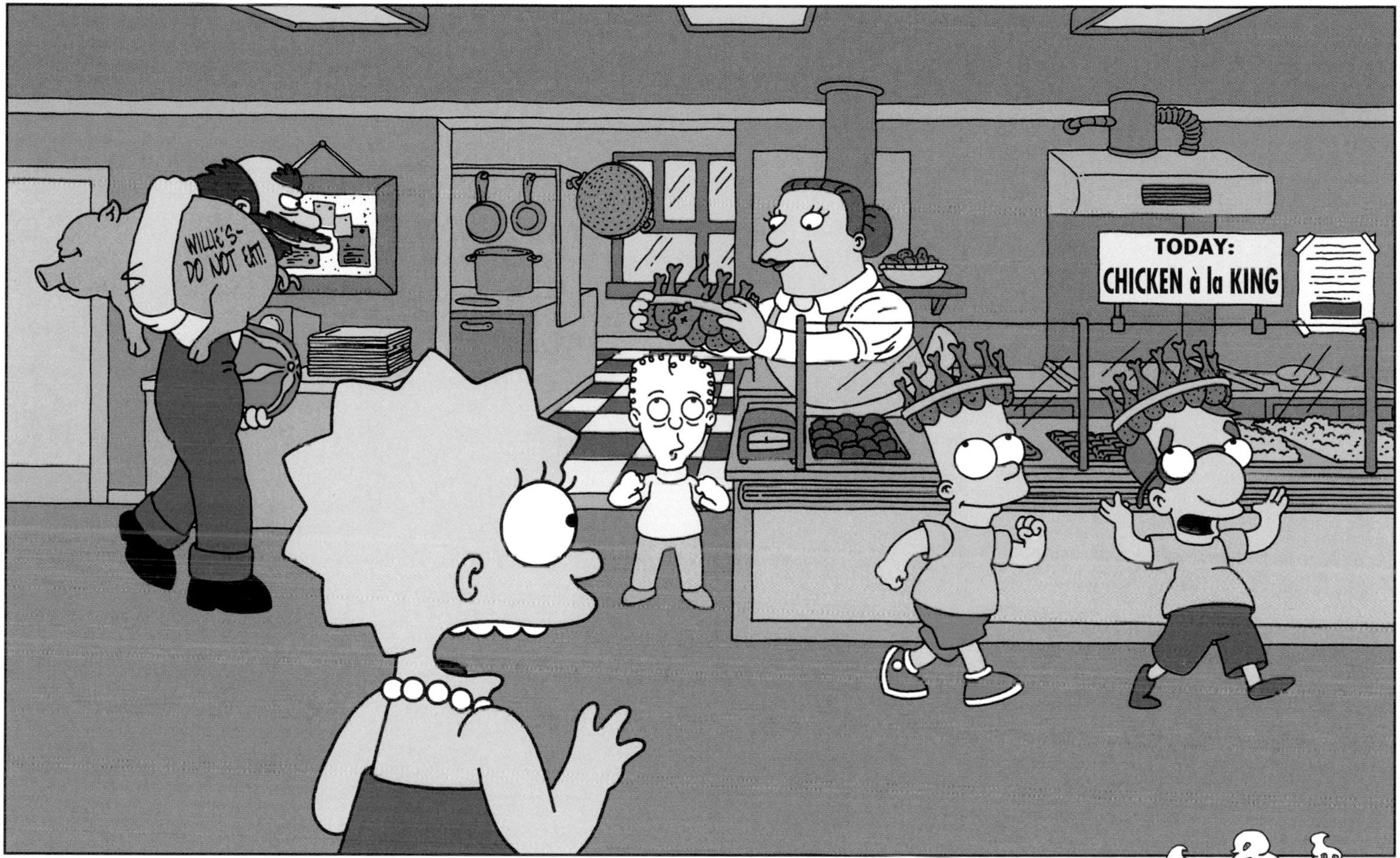
WILLIE'S-
DO NOT EAT!
TODAY:
CHICKEN à la KING

Children wear C-grade poultry at the vegetarian's nightmare known as lunchtime at the Springfield Elementary School Cafeteria.

mascot, a nondescript English fellow shaped like their favorite letter. It does, however, continue to serve the best T-shaped food in the city.

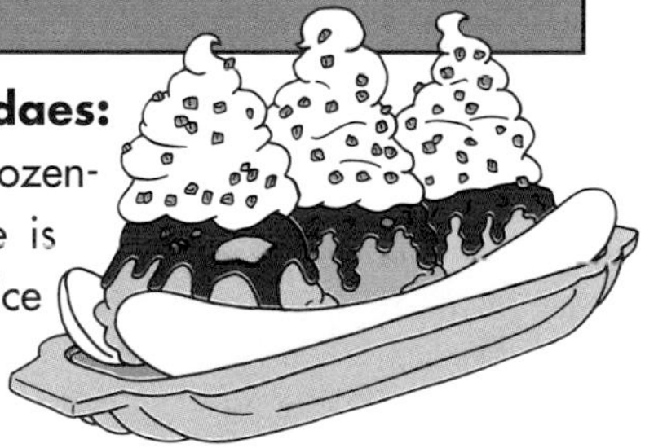

Splitsville Ice Cream Sundaes: With its relentless pursuit of frozen-confection innovation, Splitsville is single-handedly bringing the ice cream split into the twenty-first

WHAT'S RIGHT WITH SPRINGFIELD?

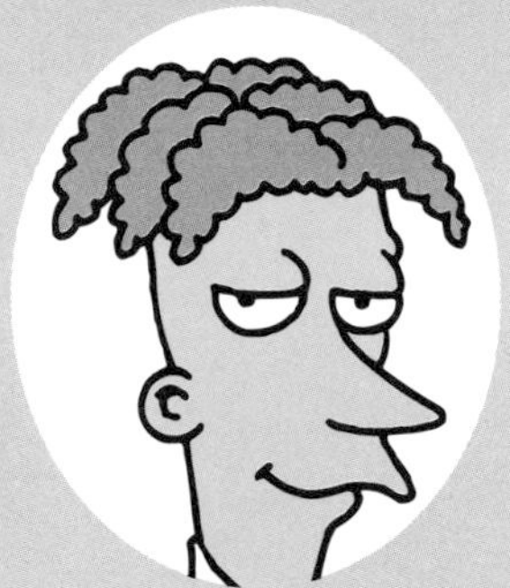

"Ironically, **Springfield Dam**—the site of my greatest failure and most painful defeat—still holds a great deal of allure to me. If I were there today, why I'd stand upon its lofty observation deck and consider how I would go about making that horrible little burg pay for stripping me of my freedom. I'd imagine the city in flames, its residents scurrying around like rodents as their lives were literally engulfed in the just fire of my awful retribution. By the way, if anyone from Springfield is reading this and is interested in the substandard treatment of prisoners in its jails, I'll have you know that we are not allowed to keep our own wine cellars. Yes, it's true. You can help possibly correct this grave injustice by contacting Mayor Quimby's office and complaining. Thank you."

—Cecil,
former hydroengineer

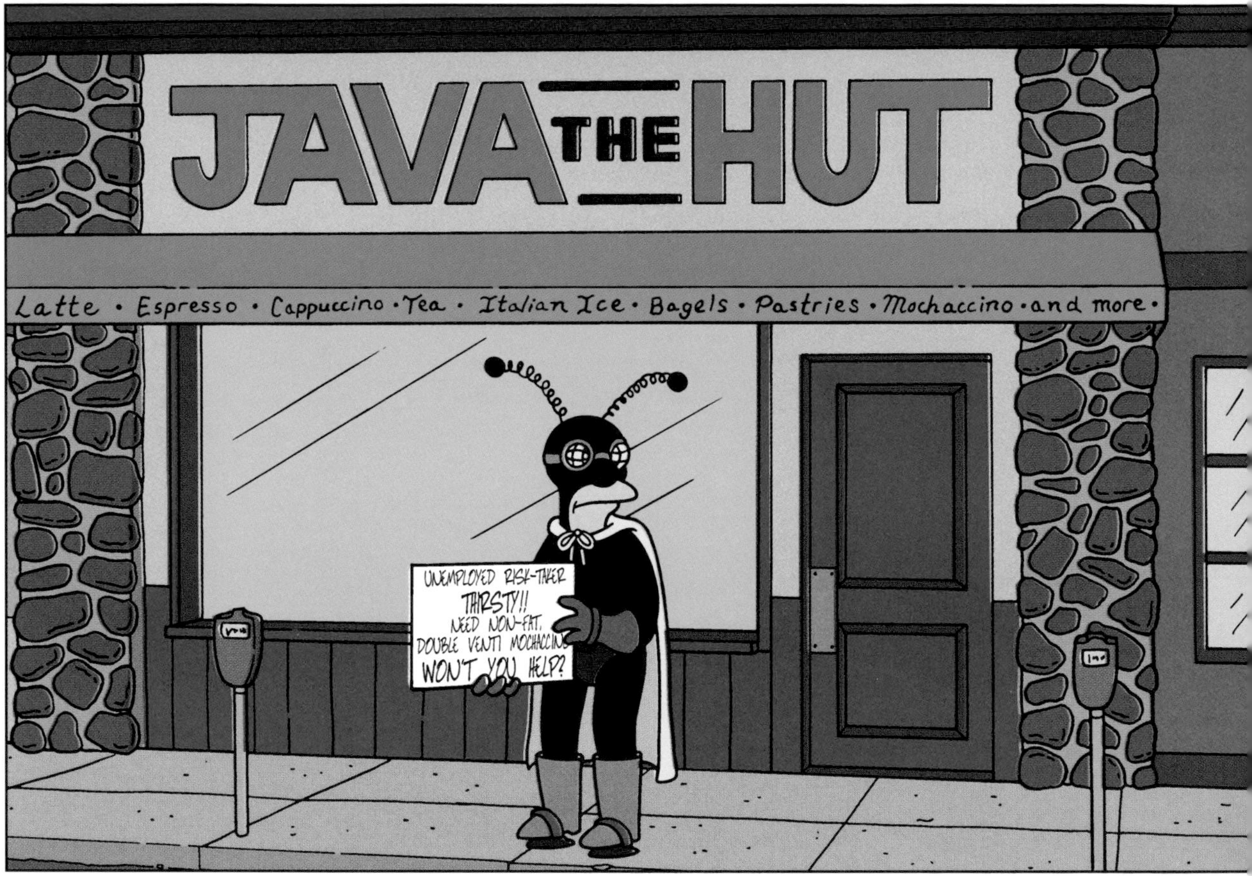
JAVA THE HUT
Latte • Espresso • Cappuccino • Tea • Italian Ice • Bagels • Pastries • Mochaccino • and more •
UNEMPLOYED RISK-TAKER
THIRSTY!!
NEED NON-FAT,
DOUBLE VENTI MOCHACCIN
WON'T YOU HELP?

Publicity hound and coffee lover, The Human Fly.

century. Featuring such variations as the Mango Split, the Plantain Split, the Pretzel Log Split, the Giant Gummi Bear Split, and the Sugar-Sprinkle Crunch Split, the banana appears to be going the way of the club-footed kangaroo mouse.

Skip's Diner: A remarkably unexciting dining experience. Neither good nor really bad, Skip's specializes in making homestyle food that bores. Basically, it's not

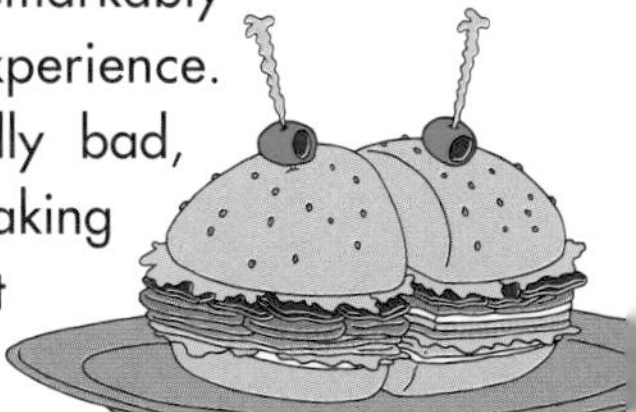

a bad choice in a pinch, provided the diner is not out of condiments.

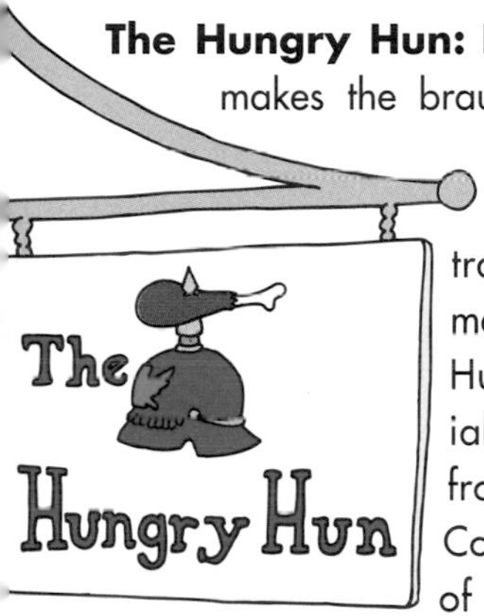
The
Hungry Hun

The Hungry Hun: It's the place that makes the brautbest brautwurst in Springfield. Apart from traditional German favorites, the Hun also specializes in cuisine from the former Communist nation of East Germany. Such former Iron Curtain favorites as "Old, Long-Awaited Kaiser Roll" and "Mock Dehydrated Sauerbraten" are offered but rarely served, as they taste really, really bad.

Shorty's Coffee Shop: A fine place for a tuna melt, but the real star here is Helen Lovejoy, the gossipy wife of Springfield's most prominent pastor. Here, Helen Lovejoy holds court, loudly relating her latest bits of small-town scandal to her tittering cronies. Though visitors likely will not know who she's talking about, her tales of indiscretion are delivered with an irresistible mix of shock, delight, and moral outrage.

Donuts: A little donut stand with an unimaginative name, awful bear claws, and very little parking, this place has but one thing going for it: a really cool-looking monster donut resting on top of the structure. Skip the donuts, grab a cup of the tolerable coffee, and climb up to the top of the billboard-sized pastry. The minimum wage employees won't lift a finger to stop you.

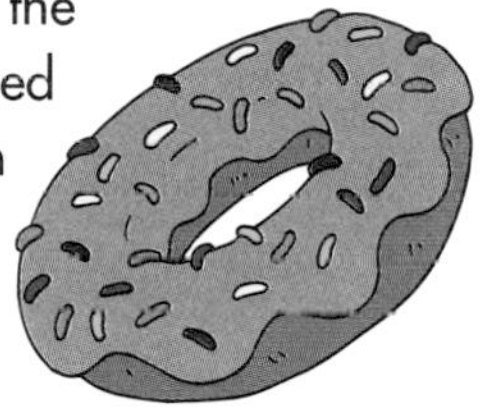

Java the Hut: This coffeehouse offers both the complicated (a double-blended decaffeinated soy mocha-malted espresso with cinnamon and Italian mint syrup) and the simple (iced caffeine), served quickly and with a stimulant-generated smile. Customers who sit out front and try to look like they're having a good time receive a 10 percent discount.

Zesty's Pizza + Sub: Zesty's is a solid pizzeria, offering the standard array of pies and subs plus one remarkable dish: the world's first crustless pizza. Served in a flat bowl, this dish is mainly comprised of two inches of sauce, covered by cheese and toppings. Customers can opt to have their crustless pie blended or regular, and to-go orders are served in oversized novelty Frisbees, with plastic soup spoons and lobster bibs.

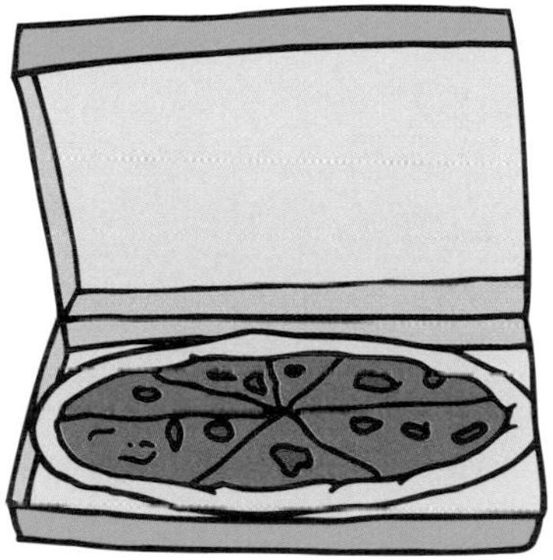

Yogurt Nook: The big tribute to the quality of this yogurt stand is that they've managed to stay in business for many years despite the fact that they only offer one flavor, vanilla, with no available toppings. Locals will tell you: that's one damn good vanilla.

Luigi's: With service so rude you'll swear you're eating at a French restaurant, this Italian eatery features fresh pasta, pizza, and Chef Luigi, a man who will greet you with a smile and then loudly belittle you in the kitchen. Still, their marinara can't be beat and they use those plastic take-out pizza protectors, so that must mean they care.

Swingin' Springfield:
A Bachelor's Guide to My Favorite Town
by Kirk Van Houten, Springfield Resident

Just about the time the sun goes down, I hear the night call to me, "Kirk, come out and trip the light Springtastic." I take a shower, listen to some Manilow, put on my vest-and-slacks combo, use my nose drops, clean my glasses, slip on my gold chain, and step out the door of my pad at the Casa Nova Apartments: A Transitional Place for Singles. I'm ready to answer that call.

Springfield's nightlife burns like the tire yard—red hot and with brain-addling vapors, 365 days a year. It swings all night long to the loopy rhythm of the busted shake machine down at the Krustyburger on Main Street, and like that shake machine, it mixes up a stone-cold, lumpy treat for all who dare to chug it down.

Chug with me, won't you? First stop: Moe's Tavern, for beers with the guys. Since splitting up with my wife of several years, I've been coming here to start the night off right. It's a place where guys go to drown their troubles and then pass out. Moe's a real character, and, occasionally, there's a knife fight to watch.

Where to next? Home, for a can of Chef Lonelyhearts's No-Regrets Rigatoni. Then, I put on my dancin' boots, use my bronchial inhaler, and hit Shotkickers, my favorite country-westernish bar. I enjoy line hoofin' because it's an easy way to dance near women without having to actually ask them to. People down there call me Alba-Kirky. Well, the guy who cleans the bathroom does (in front of other people if I give him a dollar).

If it's my turn, I stop back at Moe's to turn Barney the lush on his side so that he doesn't swallow his tongue.

Next, I drop by Lard Lad for a donut. Being a swingin' bachelor takes plenty of energy, what with the dancing, the talking over loud music, and the running away from larger bachelors who don't like me. I really can't think of any better energy source than icing-filled, carmelized, double-fried crullers.

If I'm feeling bold, I have a drink at the She-She Lounge. I know, I know. You're thinking, "What's a swingin' bachelor lookin' for love doing in a lesbian bar?" Well, to be honest, I like the odds. I'm only the guy in the whole place, and it's possible that one of the regulars may have brought a heterosexual relative or coworker. Plus, they make the best Mai Tais in town.

(At right) Moe's Tavern: A place to drown your sorrows and develop new ones.

74

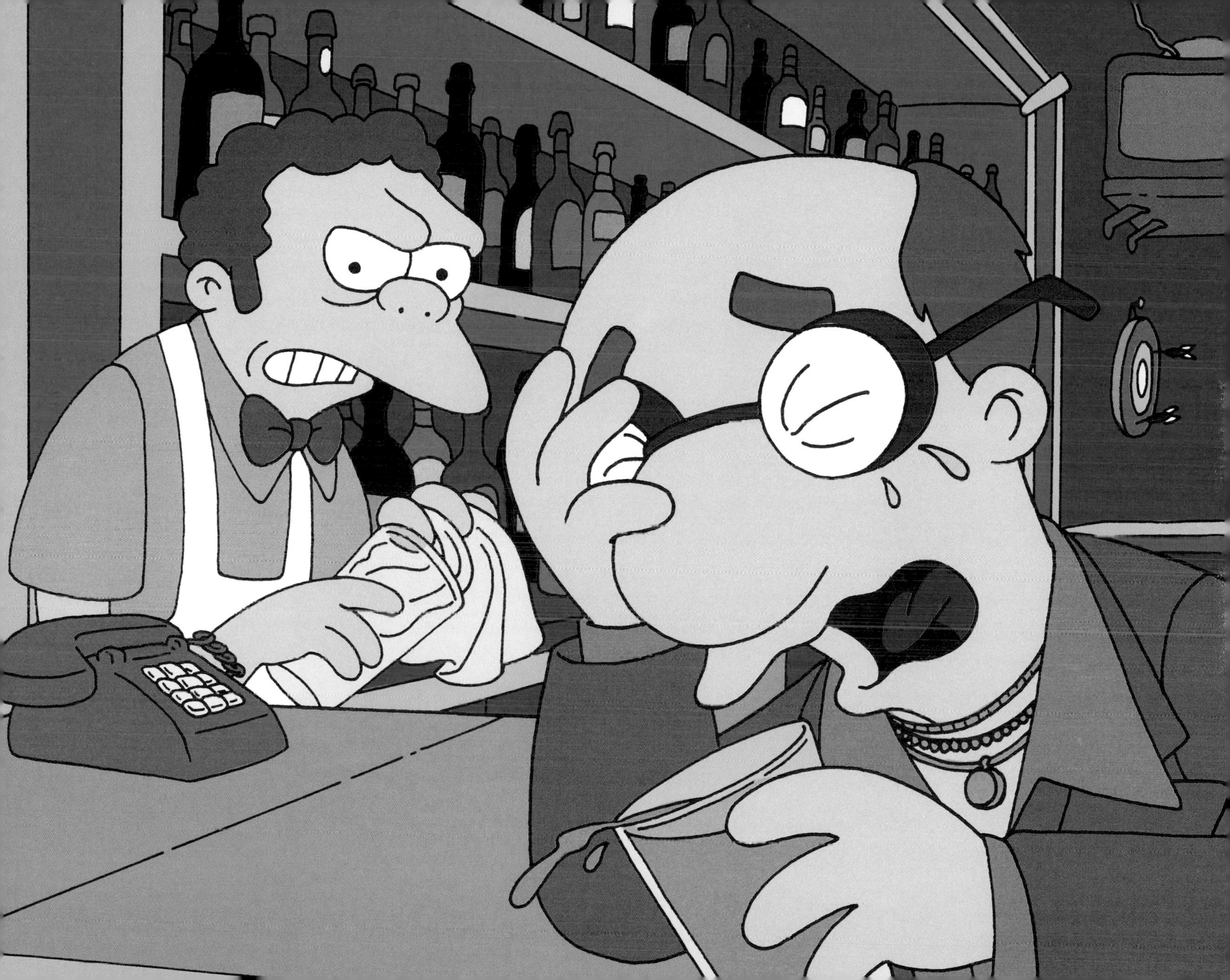

I've also stopped by once or twice at a swell little dinner theater known as the Maison Derriere. A lot of untruths have been passed along about the place, like they don't validate parking and that it's a strip club. Those are just rumors. Of course they validate parking. And the charge that the Maison is a strip club couldn't be further from the truth—the women aren't actually naked; they wear skimpy, occasionally see-through outfits that force you to use your imagination when the spotlight isn't bright enough! There's singing and dancing and they have a frequent-dining program that's amazing. Buy five meals and get one free! I must have had like a dozen free steaks there.... But don't get the wrong idea. I'm not obsessed with the place. I only go there on weekdays or weekends, during business hours. It's not like I've ever been caught lurking around after closing time, trying to peek at the girls through those freakin' windows.

Sometimes, late, late at night, I go to the bus stop to sit in the plastic chairs and watch the coin-operated television sets. I pretend that I'm a secret agent, about to leave on a top-secret mission, and I'm getting my instructions through the program I'm watching. It's hard to explain, but this can be really fun if you're a very, very lonely man.

After that, it's back to Moe's for a few nightcaps. Then, when I've ingested enough liquid courage, I go to the Kwik-E-Mart for a carton of overpriced eggs, which I would never buy while sober. I take the eggs over to the Southern Cracker Company factory, where I used to work, and egg their sign until it's covered with yolk. Then I usually (well, always) wash the sign off with some dish soap, a squeeze of lemon, and three buckets of water. It's a good way to vent my aggression while not burning any bridges. In fact, after one egging and cleaning, I told one of the security guards I was kinda hungry and he gave me a very flavorsome dog biscuit.

Finally, if I'm still feeling the effects of Moe's, I stop by Berger's Burgers to weep and eat a double cheeseburger. I sometimes stumble home after that, my shirt covered in special sauce and tears, crying out my ex-wife's name, hoping that somehow, by screaming "Luann!" loudly enough, the cruel universe will return her to me and stitch together my hopelessly tattered heart.

Well, that's my Springfield! A topsy-turvy swinger's paradise full of nightlife adventure, romantic possibilities, laughs, and fun, fun, fun!

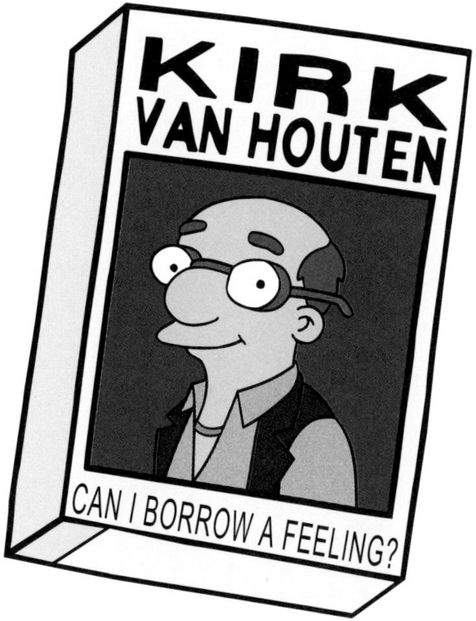
KIRK
VAN HOUTEN
CAN I BORROW A FEELING?

This essay was also recorded as a spoken word piece on Kirk Van Houten's recent self-released album, "Can I Borrow A Feeling?"

NIGHTLIFE

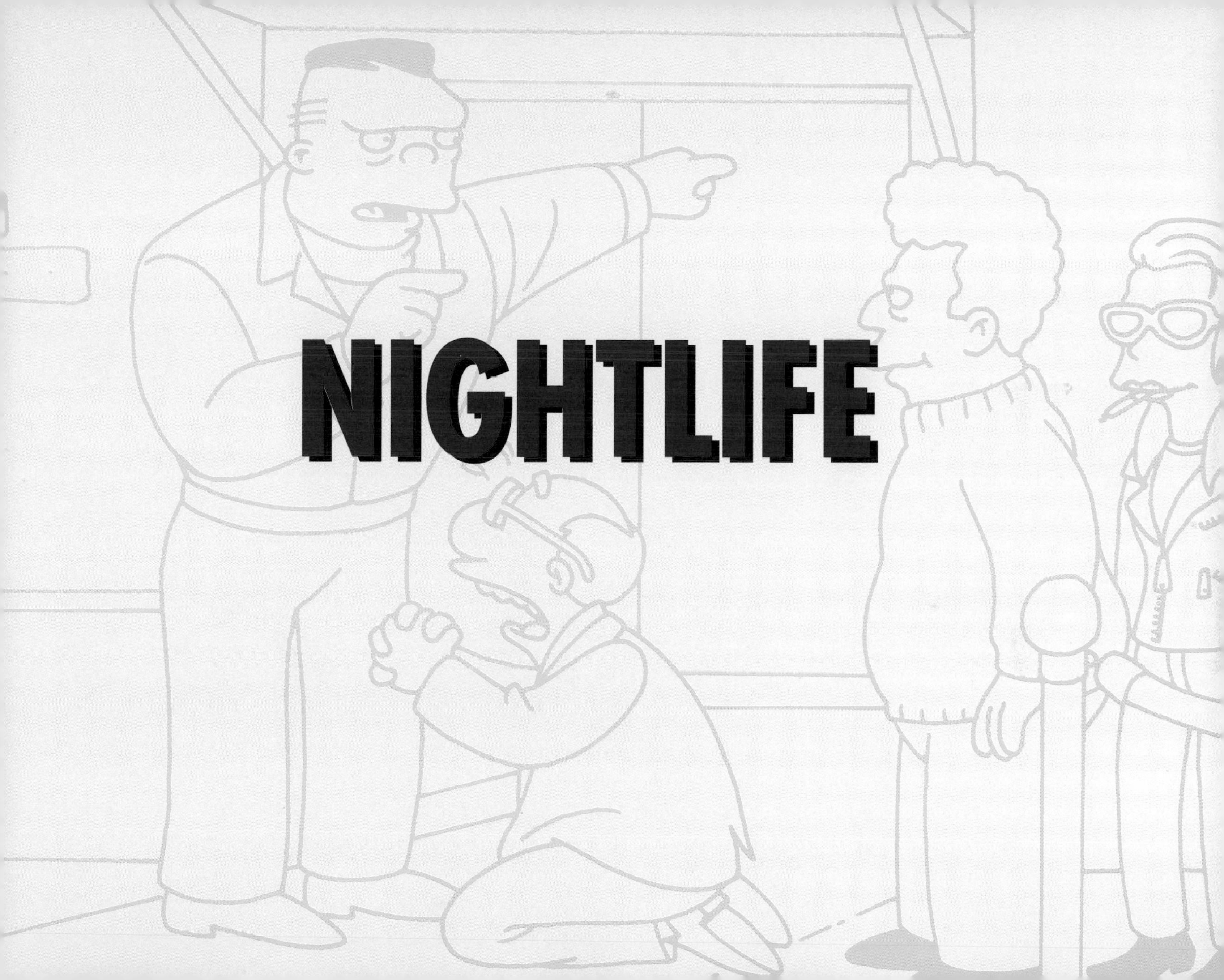

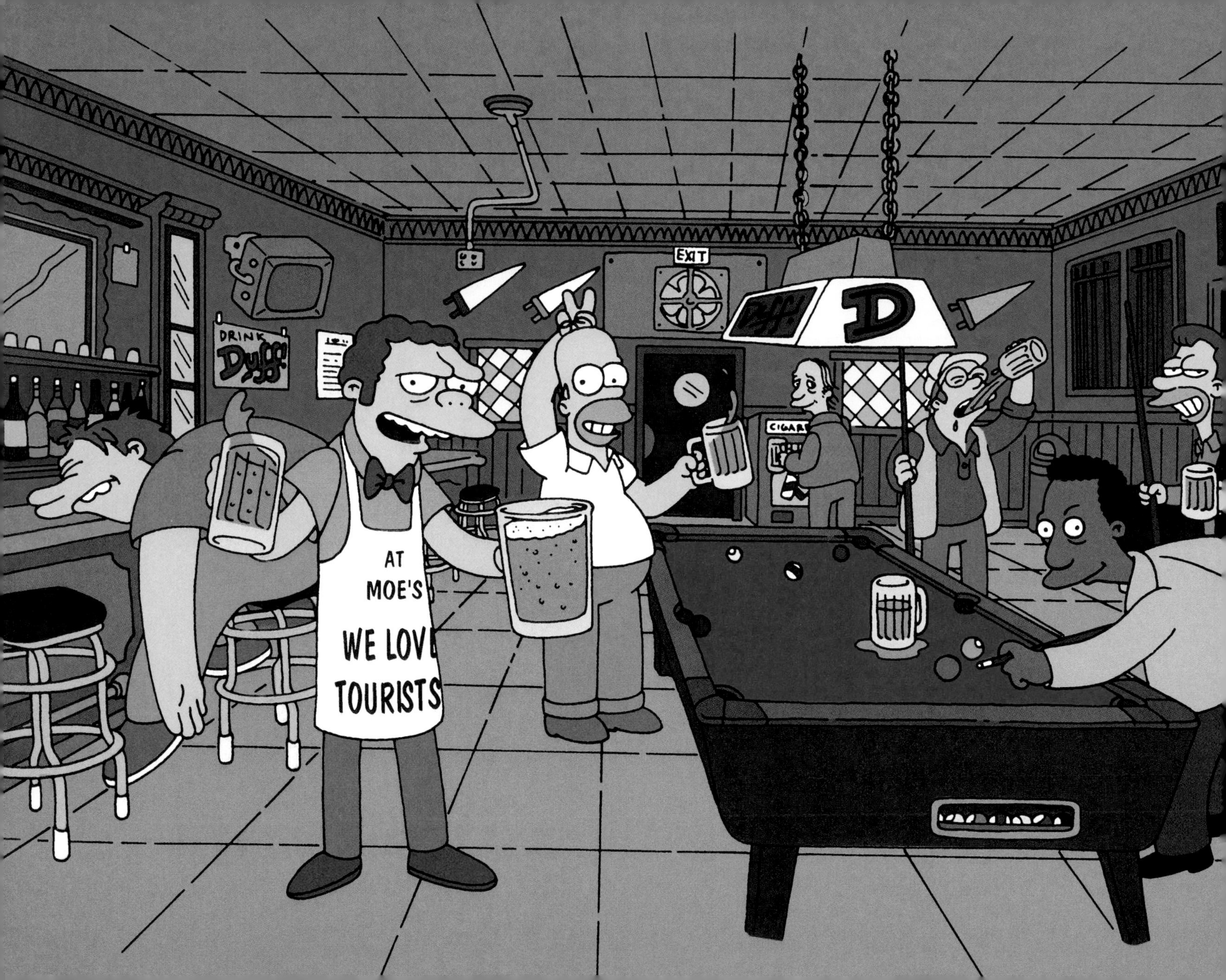
EXIT
DRINK Duff
CIGARS
AT MOE'S WE LOVE TOURISTS

HOMER
BARNEY
SAM
Lenny
LARRY
CARL

On the wall at Moe's, local booze-hounds are enshrined in "Mt. Lushmore."

Take one part smoky haze, one part glowing neon, throw in a jigger of extremely liberal open-container laws, shake well, and pour over very, very nice. What have you got? One tall, cool glass of Springfield nightlife, that's what! And what better way to get a sense of the SpringScene than to take it all in with one gluttonous night of debauchery down the danforth in a swingin' Springfield Pub Crawl?!?

(At left) Drunkards pose for a picture at Moe's Tavern.

Deep into the seedy part of Springfield is a sign featuring two neon martini glasses clinking back and forth. If there is a God in heaven, this glowing glassware signage of **The Aristocrat** will continue its martini mambo until the end of time. With its red door, pay phone, jukebox, ashtrays, and multipurpose seltzer gun, The Aristocrat isn't much; yet, it has an indisputable, grimy charm that former kiddie-TV cohost, maniac, and former Springfield mayor Sideshow Bob Terwilliger called "a tolerable alternative for those of us who cannot afford to drink in a decent bar." For his semi-kind words (spoken during a recent interview with *Four-Time Loser Quarterly*), The Aristocrat named a drink after Terwilliger. The Spo-Dee-O-Dee Sideshow is two parts Tawny Port, two parts Nighttrain, and one part Perrier, with a lime twist.

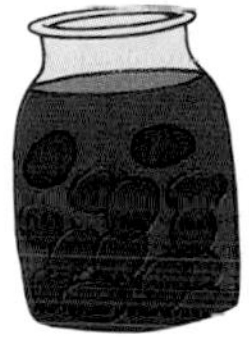

Perhaps the quintessential Springfield bar is **Moe's Tavern**, with its classic novelty signs ("You don't buy beer—you rent it!" and "Everyone believes in something, I believe I'll have another drink!"), arbitrary love-tester

THE TRILLION DOLLAR BILL:

Its Origin:
President Truman authorized the one-time printing of this official United States currency to use as funding for the post-World War II reconstruction of Europe. The president then entrusted the bill to C. Montgomery Burns—one of the richest and, thus, most trustworthy, men—to transport the bill to Europe. The bill never made it to the Continent; Burns kept it, thinking the aid to Europe was wasteful and unnecessary. The bill remained in his possession until the United States government put together a mission to retrieve it. In the ensuing debacle, the bill fell into the hands of Fidel Castro.

1,000,000,000,000
ONE
TRILLION

Its Worth:
A trillion dollars (even more to coin collectors—it was printed in 1945).

Its Featured President:
A smiling Harry S. Truman, simultaneously giving the thumbs-up and A-OK signs.

WHAT'S RIGHT WITH SPRINGFIELD?

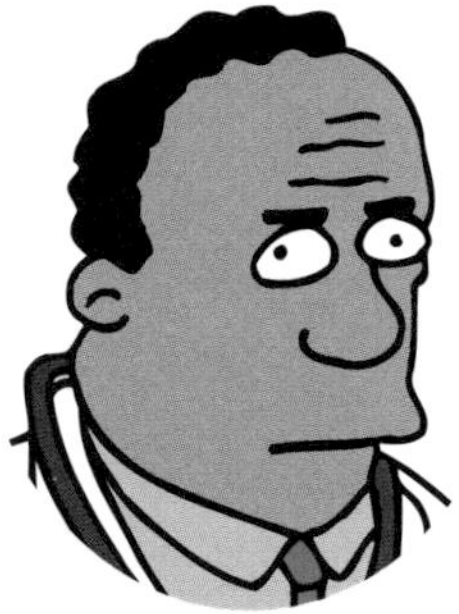

"I like the Springfield Auction House. Fine art, fine wine, and no annoying riffraff accosting you for change or emergency medical assistance—ah, hee, hee, hee!"

—Dr. Julius Hibbert, physician

machine, and free Spanish peanuts. Although for a brief period this neighborhood tavern was serving a drink called the Flaming Moe and attracting a glittering throng of international hipsters, Moe's is currently a bar that harkens back to the mediocre days of President Jimmy Carter's administration, when it sometimes felt like the country was captured in amber during a particularly dreary PBS special. If you're lucky, you may get to watch as Moe receives a prank phone call. If so, be sure to get in on the fast-paced wagering as the regulars bet on which of Moe's many facial veins will be the first to pop out.

For real entertainment value, put on your dancin' boots and head on over to **Shotkickers**, Springfield's only country-western, Tex-Mex, non-politically correct tattoo bar. Here, clapping and walking side to side is considered dancing, you can get alcohol with worms in it (worms served on the side by request only), and you can give your spine some permanent vacation memories on an automatic bull ride. Be sure to speak in a slow, midwestern drawl or risk a severe beating or possibly a long debate on who was a more important literary character, the city mouse or the country mouse (you may want to bring notecards outlining some key points on this issue, just in case).

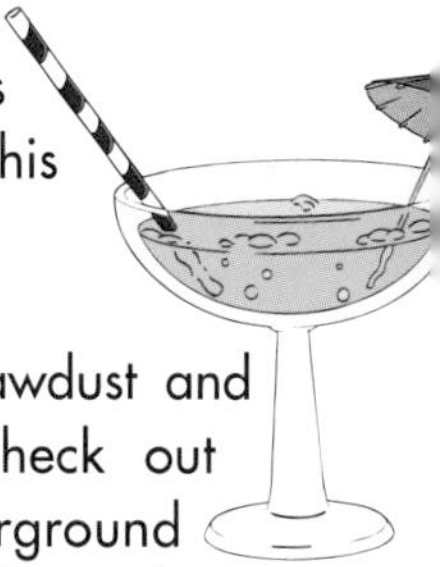

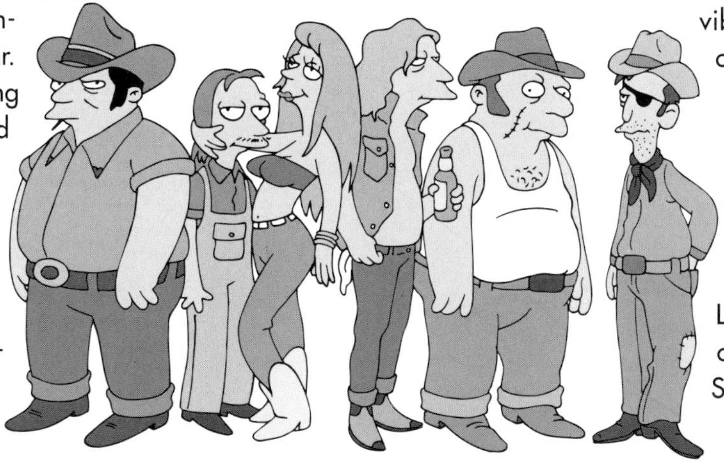

When you've had your fill of sawdust and Merle Haggard, it's time to check out Springfield's premier underground nightclub, **The Hate Box**—where the habitually pierced meet to consume smart drinks and get tattooed in the restroom. This is the nightclub for people-watching; one fun activity is to try to distinguish the men from the women and the anarchists from the nihilists. One word of warning, though: people with weak spleens should avoid the Hate Box—its dance floor delivers enough vibrating bass to cause tin cans to spontaneously implode.

Next on the crawl is the **She-She Lounge**. Lesbian bars have come and gone in Springfield, but the She-She remains a source of pride, sisterhood, and the best damn margaritas in the city (called the Lovely Margarita Meter Maid, to be

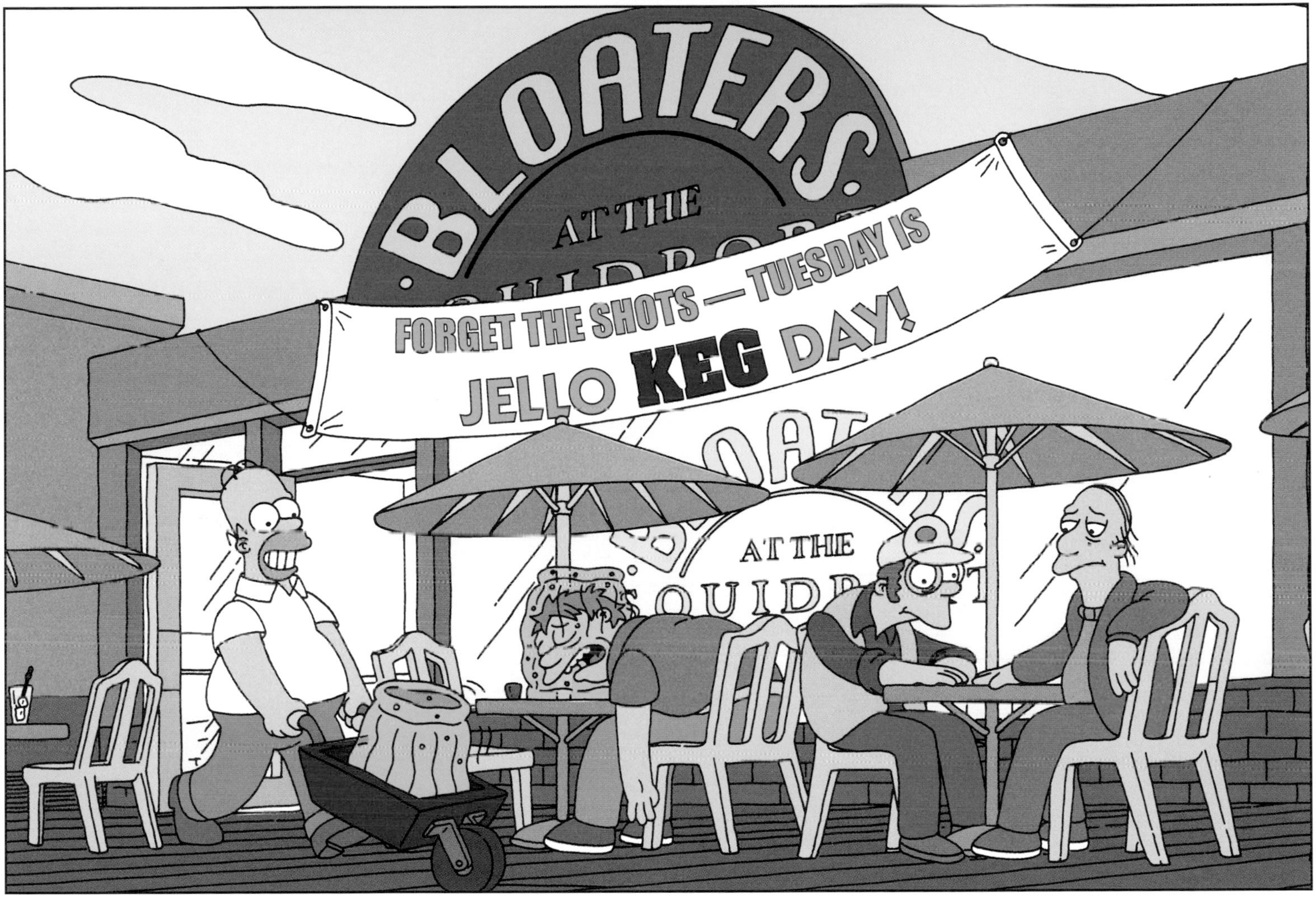
BLOATERS
AT THE
FORGET THE SHOTS—TUESDAY IS
JELLO KEG DAY!
AT THE

Springfielders enjoy jiggly alcohol at Bloaters at the Squidport.

precise). Providing a friendly, laid-back atmosphere, the She-She is one of the finest watering holes in town. However, keep an eye out for that one lone, pathetic guy-loser who frequents the place hoping to have an easy shot at one of the patrons' heterosexual friends or relatives.

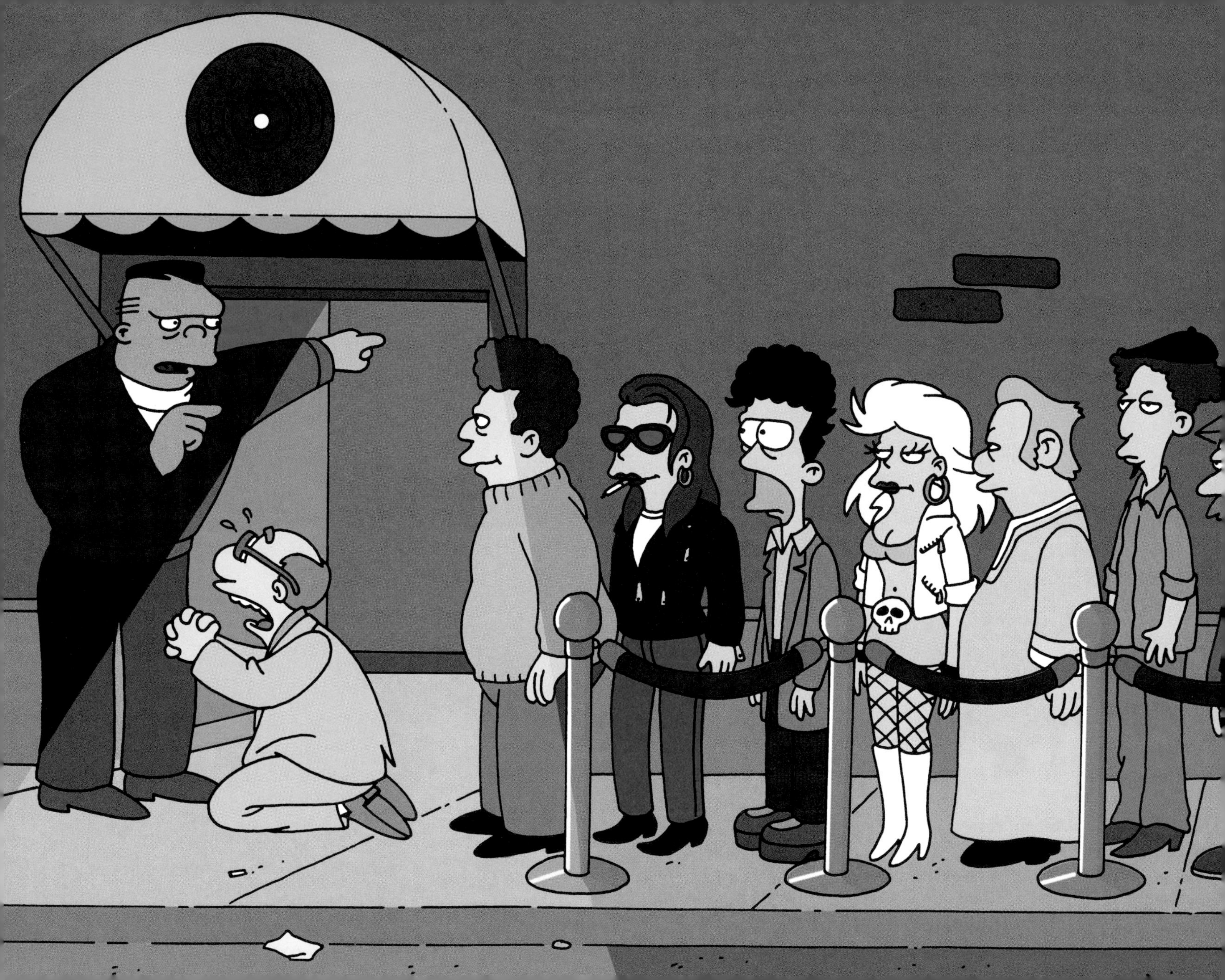

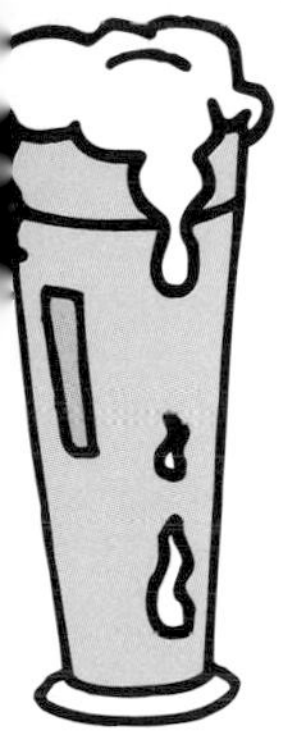

The Little Black Box at the Springfield Airport is much less inclusive, allowing entry only to pilots, copilots, and people who have played either on TV. However, nonpilots aren't missing anything: serving swillish drinks with little bags of honey roasted peanuts, this hole-in-the-wall makes Moe's Tavern look like a much, much nicer tavern. "The Li'l Black Boksh" (as the pilots call it) was recently knocked over by a 747 that overshot a runway, but plans are being made to put it back in full uptight and crocked position very soon.

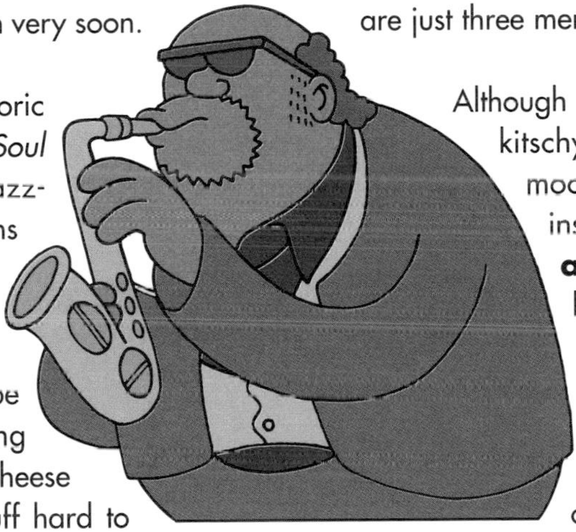

In the liner notes to his historic 1969 album, *Saxreligious Soul Massa #9*, Springfield jazz-blues legend Bleeding Gums Murphy called **The Jazz Hole** "...a great place to play, a groovy place to dig jazz, but a lousy place to be a dishwasher—everything they serve is baked with cheese on top and boy, is that stuff hard to get off." The traditions continue at The Jazz Hole—especially the baked cheese (in fact, try the French Onion Shooter for a heady rush of hot, tequila-laden soup and bubbly fromage). For great musicians, The Jazz Hole poses the ultimate challenge: playing to unsophisticated audiences (often armed with rotten produce) that have little, if any, appreciation for jazz or cheesy food.

(At left) The process of natural selection can be experienced nightly at the entrance to Stu's Disco.

Next up, for a uniquely vacuous bar experience, **Bloaters at the Squidport** is the obvious choice. Specializing in alcoholic drinks that bounce, Bloaters is the preferred tavern of college students who would rather chew their liquor than drink it. Bloaters also serves standard bar fare, but with a twist: all of the food has liquor in it. Rummy pizza fingers, beer-soaked mashed potatoes, and Bloody Mary poppers are just three menu favorites.

Although it's in the same hotel that has such kitschy accoutrements as tiki torches, moonshine stills, vines, and robots installed in its themed rooms, the **Bar at the Aphrodite Inn** is merely a bar, nothing less than a mundane cocktaillery, nothing more than a place that makes an okay Lemondrop. There are none of the flights of fancy that are contained within the guest quarters mere feet away; the only interesting moments that occur here are when the occasional hotel guests walk in, still wearing their room-supplied costumes. Spotted recently: Mayor Quimby and guest in wet suits and scuba gear.

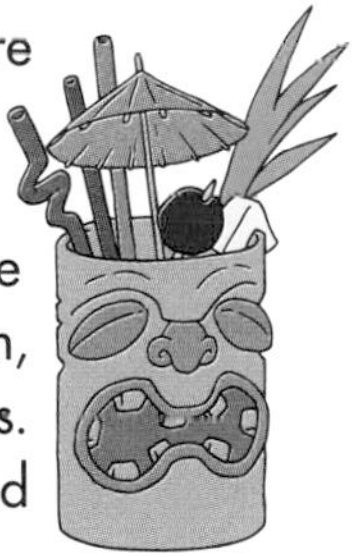

WHAT'S RIGHT WITH SPRINGFIELD?

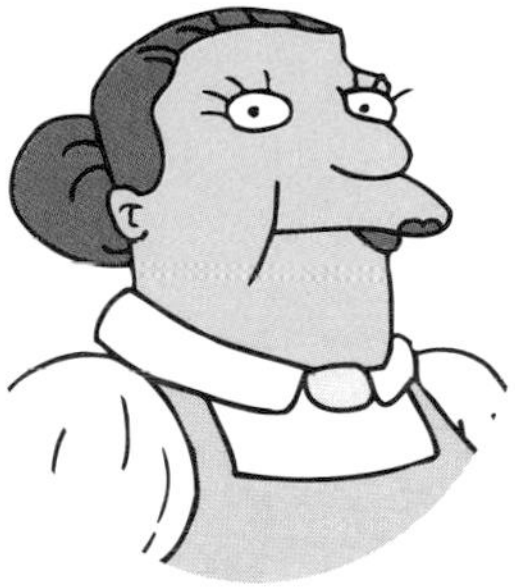

"The Springfield Mystery Spot. For some reason it's the only place that takes the stink of sloppy joe off my skin."

—Doris, lunchlady

A stark contrast to the Bar at the Aphrodite Inn is the **Maison Derriere**, which is far, far more than just a tavern—it features a fully choreographed floorshow populated by scantily-clad ladies every night of the week. The Maison delivers far more entertainment for the buck than every other bar in town, provided you're a heterosexual male between the ages of eighteen and eighty, with no shame and plenty of one-dollar bills in your pocket. (Similar, if not more "up-front," Springfield clubs for these men include **Florence of Arabia**, **Girlesque**, **Foxy Boxing**, **Mud City**, and the **Sapphire Lounge**.)

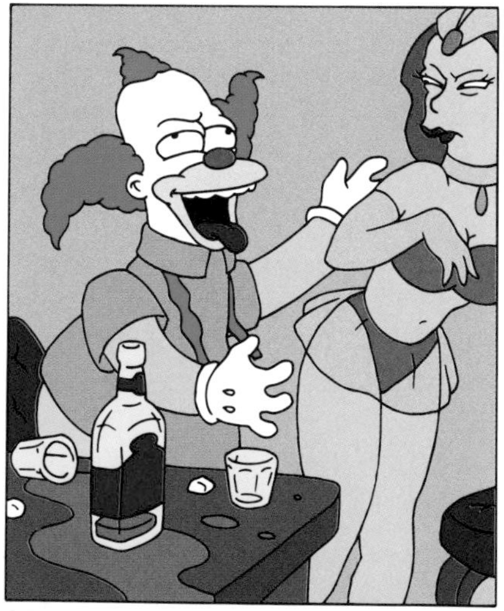

But what of the self-destructive bender? Where does one go to drown their sorrows in 100 proof swill, smoke cigarettes until the throat is raw and sore, and encounter the cackling scum of the night, all in a swirling montage of music, clinking glasses, and undertipped bartenders? Try such Springfield slosh-spots as **The Gutter Room**, **Blottos**, **Spinners**, **D.T. McShakes**, and **The Bloated Liver**. Pick up an AlcoCard at the Springfield Chamber of Commerce which entitles you to an extra olive in any martini at no additional cost. Also, if you get the card punched at the three aforementioned establishments in the same night, you'll receive a free colorized copy of *The Lost Weekend*.

Finally, we end our pub crawl at **Stu's Disco** for stone cold, retro-chic boogie-oogie-oogie and watered-down Fuzzy Navels (from concentrate). If you're too old to remember how ugly the seventies were, or too young, stupid, and pathetically trendy to notice, then Stu's Disco is for you. Hustle on down and don't forget your dancin' shoes! By the way, Stu's partner, Disco Yehoodi, has a platform repair shop in an alcove next to the men's room for your convenience.

ARTIFACTS

THE HOMER:

What It Is:
The car designed by "average American" and Springfield resident Homer J. Simpson. Complete with extra-large drink holder, tailfins, two bubble domes, shag carpeting, and a horn that plays "La Cucaracha," it's the model that drove the once-mighty Powell Motors out of business.

Where It Can Be Seen:
Right now, nowhere. No one is quite sure of the whereabouts of the Homer prototype. Some say that the Petersen Automotive Museum in Los Angeles, California, purchased it to be the centerpiece of a planned Really Stupid Cars exhibit.

Its Worth:
Hundreds of thousands of dollars. For the serious automotive collector, the Homer represents one of the rarest, ugliest, most poorly thought-out cars in history.

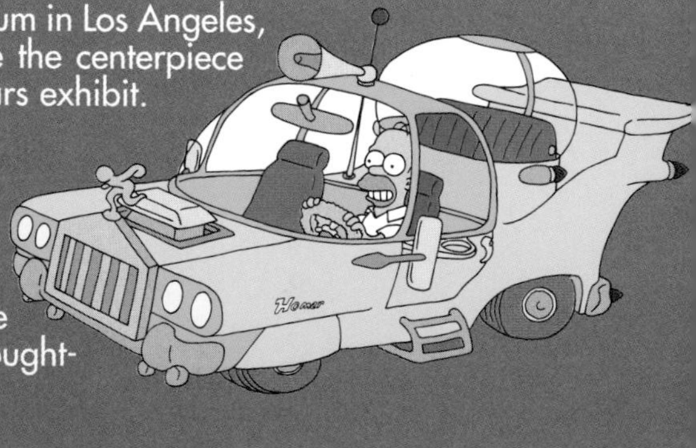
Homer

SHOPPING

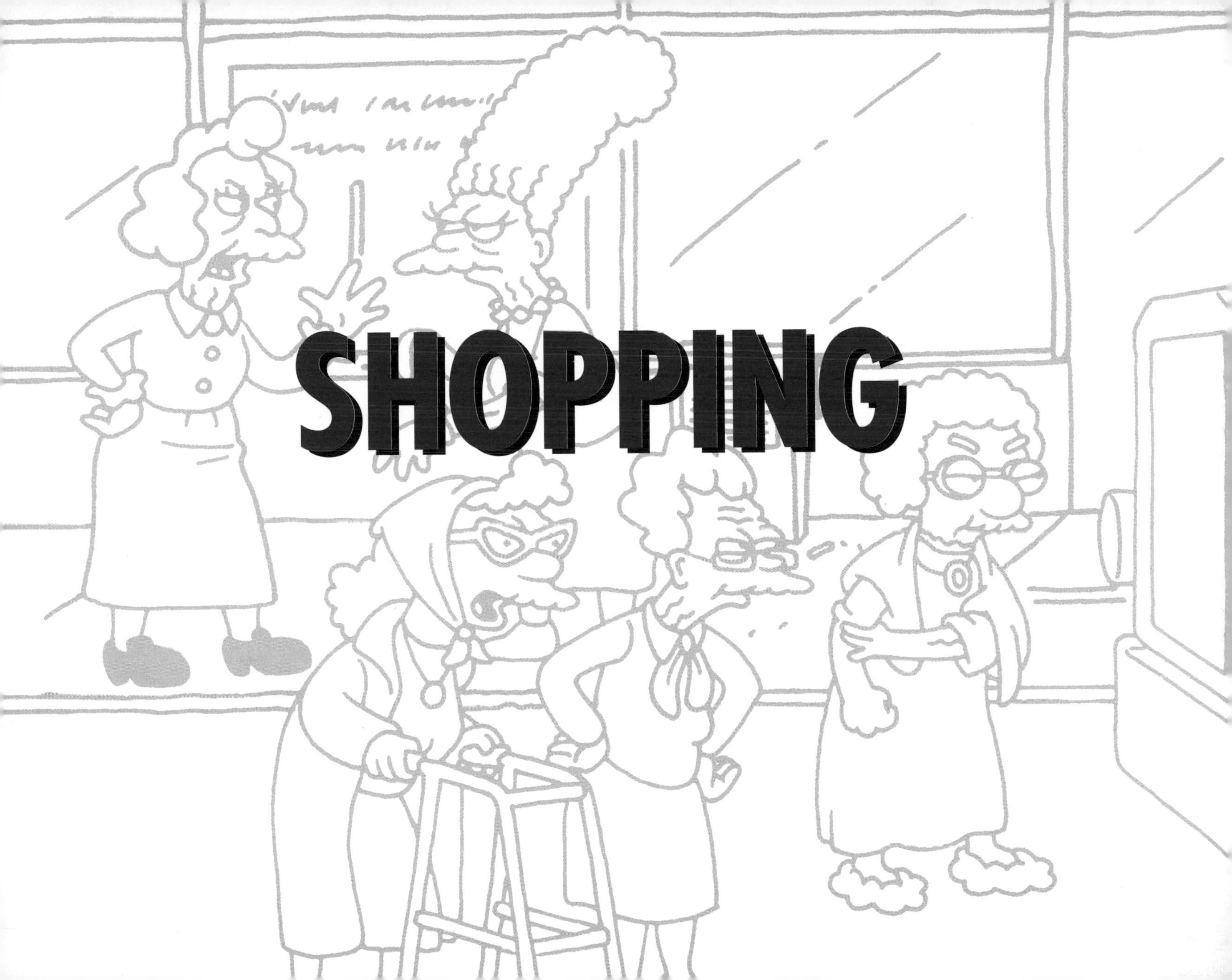

WHAT'S RIGHT WITH SPRINGFIELD?

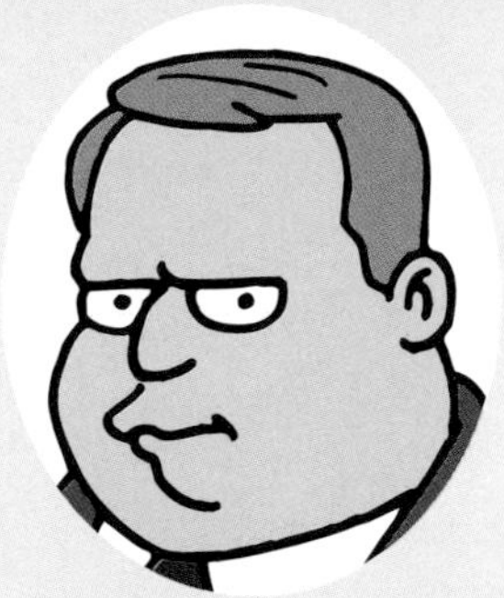

"Springfield Park. The site of the first and only visit of the late, great, President Richard Milhous Nixon to the rolling gables of Springfield. He came to whack snakes; if only he could have whacked the bloated, pot-smoking, libation-filled liberal floozyphile Diamond Joe Quimby out of office. Oh, what could have been..."

—Birch Barlow, radio personality

In the 1962 Springfield Chamber of Commerce promotional film, *Some Came Shopping*, Troy McClure calls the city, "a paradise on Earth for those souls who love exchanging money for goods." Those words have never been truer than right now. Springfield is practically choked with stores offering everything from the chintzy to the ritzy—with prices to match. Bring an empty trunk on your visit because you will most certainly fill it with trinkets, whosamabobs, and durable goods that are yours for the taking—we mean buying—from the following establishments (and please remember, no fruits or vegetables are legally allowed to leave the city).

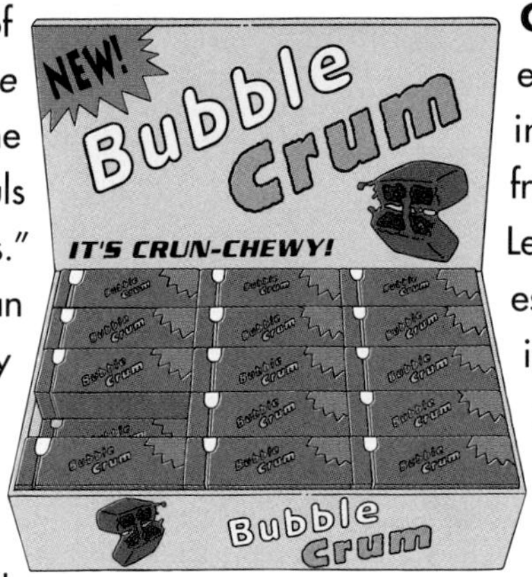
NEW!
Bubble Crum
IT'S CRUN-CHEWY!
Bubble Crum

All Creatures Great and Cheap: Specializing in freeze-dried pets that come to life when watered (brine shrimp, frogs, locusts), this pet store also carries dogs, hamsters, cats, and lizards. Perhaps its most unique offering is the amoeba farm, a petri dish complete with pet amoebas, amoeba food, microscope, and amusing cartoon amoeba logos.

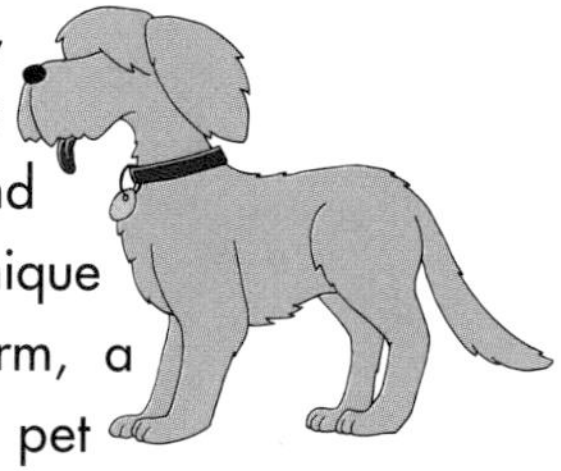

Gum for Less: Springfield's pre-eminent discount gummery. With its immense flavor selection and freshness-ensuring gumidor, Gum for Less is the place to buy gum in the city, especially if you prefer to pay less for it. Rumors abound that the owners might open a sister taffy store; happy gum shoppers can only hope the story will be substantiated.

International House of Answering Machines: IHAM doesn't merely offer answering machines; they offer answering machines *from all over the world.* Available for purchase are a fifty-pound, vacuum-tube-laden phone answerer from Soviet-era Russia, a tiny combination bottle-opener-and-answering-machine from Japan, and a crank-operated message recorder from Canada.

The Jerky Hut: Upon entering this store, patrons are met with the pungent odor of a wide array of the dried meats that cover every wall of the establishment, much like pliable shingles. This is part of a calculated move by the proprietors—due to rapidly declining jerky consumption in

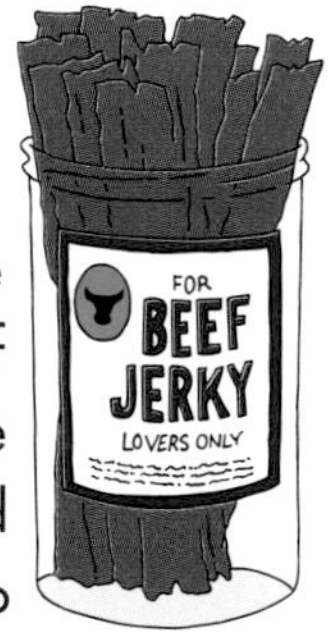
FOR
BEEF
JERKY
LOVERS ONLY

the United States, jerky-jerks are looking to sell dehydrated steaks not only as food, but as home decor. To wit, the Jerky Hut offers such domestic accessories and apparel as jerky throws, jerky placemats, and jerky jackets. A very, very frightening concept.

The Ear Piercery: Don't let the name fool you—this store pierces far more than ears. Noses, eyebrows, cheeks, tongues, belly-buttons, webbed toes, other body parts that aren't discussed in public—you name it, this place pierces it. And now, the Ear Piercery features twelve state-of-the-art self-piercing stations, allowing those too young to get pierced legally by a licensed technician to join the fun by piercing themselves.

Girdles N' Such: For those Rubenesque souls who want to look their best as they go back for seconds, Girdles N' Such offers easy alternatives to eating a healthy diet and exercising. Their best-selling, custom-made man-girdle—the Shatner—has sold over 25,000 units and was named the "Official Undergarment of the United States Senate." A better man-girdle you cannot buy.

One-Size-Fits-All Lingerie: This store was one of those ideas hatched after some daring entrepreneur ingested bad shellfish or was hit on the head by a pickle jar. Avoid, avoid, avoid.

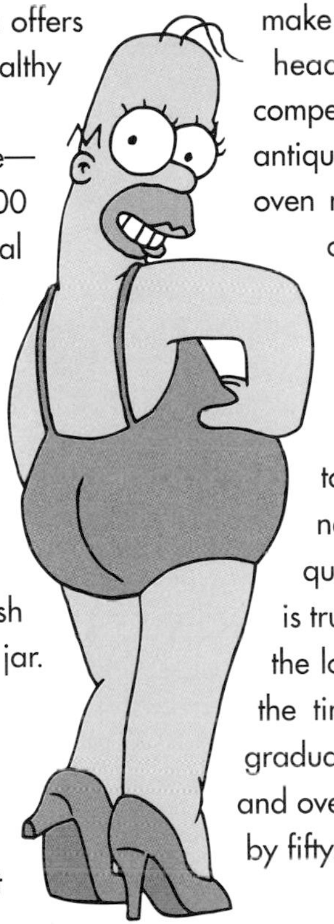

Potholder Barn: Exotic fabrics, innovative designs, and remarkable features are what make this establishment's potholders head and shoulders above the competition. Stocking everything from antique potholders to bulletproof-kevlar oven mitts to energy-matrix potholders of the future, the Potholder Barn has everything you would ever need to hold pots.

Just Rainsticks: If you decide to enter this store just to see if its name is to be believed, don't. You'll quickly find out not only that the sign is true, but that the store itself is one of the lower levels of Sonic Hell. Imagine the tinny drumming of two rainsticks, gradually beginning and ending over and over again. Now multiply that sound by fifty. Three store managers have gone

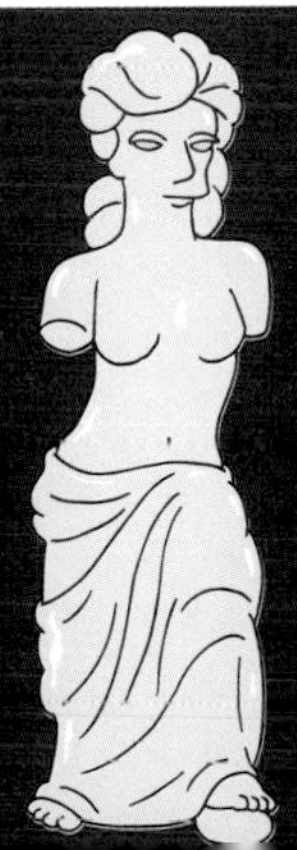

GUMMI VENUS DE MILO:

What It Was:
The rarest gummi in the world. It was carved by several master gummi artisans working together over more than a year to produce this masterpiece of candy. The Gummi Venus de Milo was intended to be an everlasting tribute to those brave confectioners who brought gummi to the United States in the early 1980s. Instead, the gummi statue was stolen from its owners at the Candy Industry Trade Show and eaten without compunction by Springfield resident Homer J. Simpson.

Its Composition:
90 percent gummi, 5 percent ascorbic acid, 5 percent flavor.

What It's Been Called:
The chewiest piece of beauty this side of "The Taffy Creation of Man."

WHAT'S RIGHT WITH SPRINGFIELD?

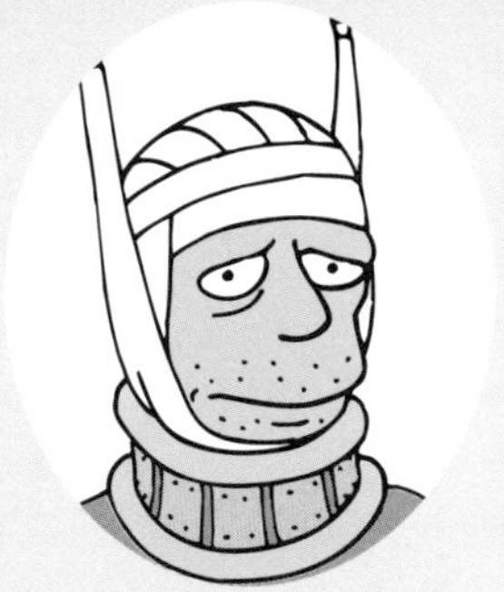

"Marvin Monroe Memorial Hospital. I just had two vertebrae fused there and those folks did a bang-up job. That place serves the best pudding cup, has the finest adjustable beds, and they administer painkillers in a timely, consistent fashion. Take it from a guy who's spent two-thirds of his life laid up in hospitals: MMMH is the best."

—Captain Lance Murdock, professional daredevil

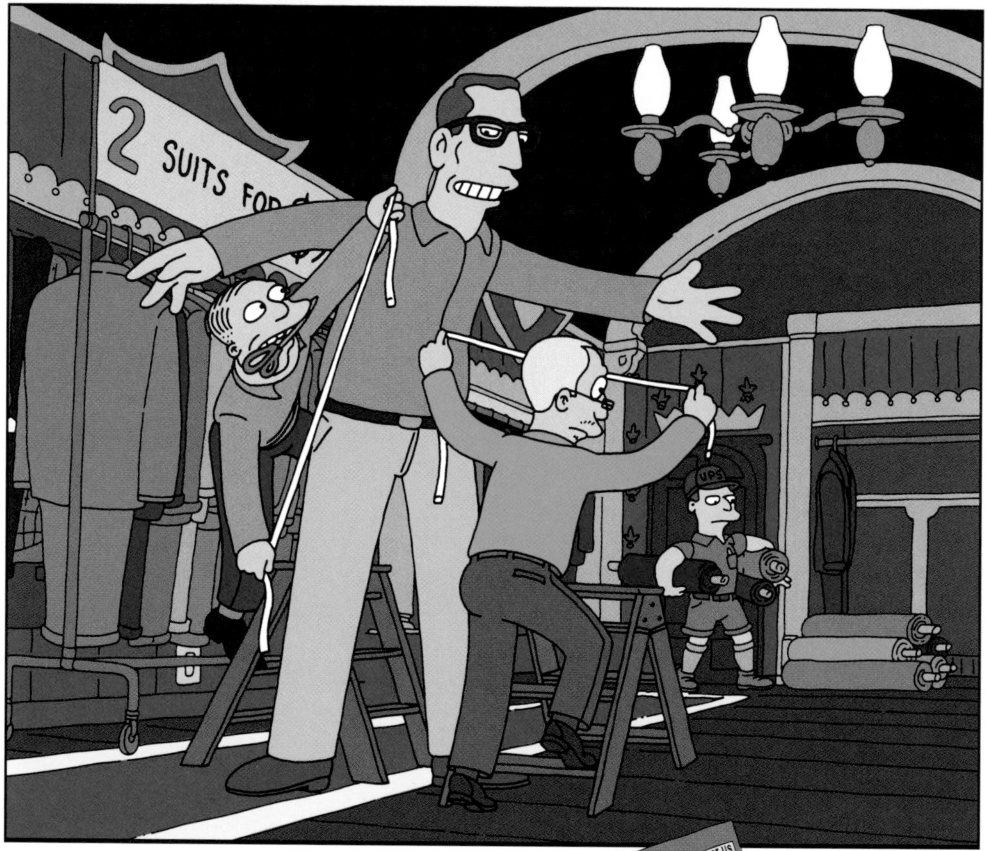
2 SUITS FO
UPS

One of Springfield's taller inhabitants puts Royal Majesty tailors on red alert.

insane inside three weeks, and at least two customers stuck waiting in line during the Christmas rush started hallucinating that they were in a coffee bar in Seattle.

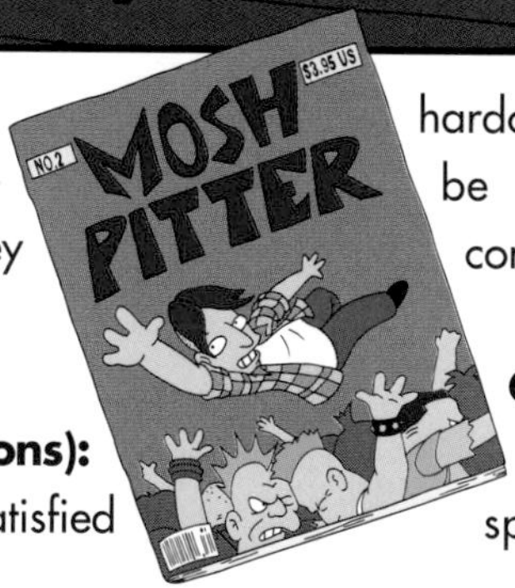
$3.95 US
NO.2
MOSH PITTER

Suicide Notes (formerly **Good Vibrations):** Looking for disenfranchised, hopelessly unsatisfied people to look down upon your musical tastes and hairstyle? Well, you've come to the right place. Even the hippest of the hip will get the cold shoulder from the underpaid, under-whelmed staff of this mediocre CD and poster shop. To make the condescending experience complete, ask one of the surly young employees if he or she can make a recommendation for a hardcore Kenny G fan. Invariably, you'll be directed back to the hospital to complete your lobotomy.

Crypto Barn: This store offers customers an interesting product: special codes that make ordinary electronic devices do extraordinary things. Want to sound like James Earl Jones to everyone who calls your house? The Crypto Barn will sell you a series of numbers that, once entered into your telephone, will activate a special, secret chip inside, enabling your receiver to make your voice sound like Darth Vader. Other examples are: a code that allows your VCR to tape sitcoms without the laughtrack; one that makes your clock radio ask you if you really meant A.M. or P.M.; another that turns your desktop computer into a sentient electronic being that'll love you no matter how big a jerk you are.

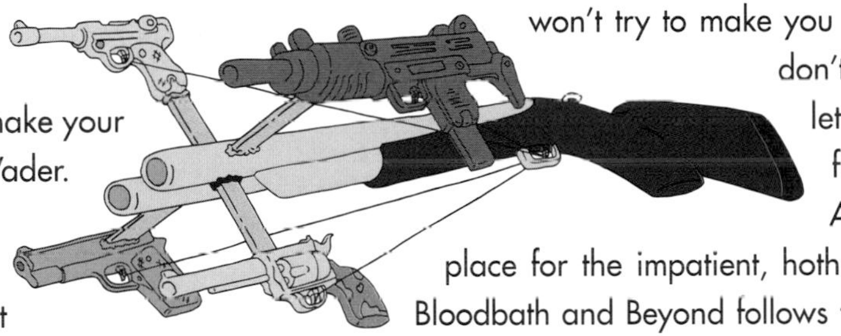

The Brushes Are Coming, The Brushes Are Coming: Whatever type of brush you need, this store has it: toothbrushes, grill brushes, paintbrushes, butter brushes, industrial-use cog-and-piston brushes, and home-plate brushes, just to name a few. Curiously, the store does not carry hair brushes, as the management believes they are nothing more than "glorified combs."

Bloodbath and Beyond Gun Shop: For those who take the Second Amendment way too literally, Bloodbath and Beyond represents a fun, pressure-free way to buy guns, low-to-high-grade munitions, grenades, and hand-held surface-to-air missiles. The employees don't work on commission, so they won't try to make you buy a gun that you don't *need*; instead, they let you discover the firepower you *want*. Alas, this is not the place for the impatient, hotheaded or psychotic: Bloodbath and Beyond follows the guidelines of the Brady Bill and thus makes patrons sit out the required waiting period before getting their new firearms. As a way to help overanxious customers get through this time—and to make them feel like somewhat of a "big man" before they get their new weapons—the store does give out loaner BB guns.

Wicked Excess: *The* place to shop for platinum lobster traps, mahogany vests, and VCRs that set their own time using signals from the U.S. Atomic Clock in Boulder, Colorado. Those looking for a bargain would do well to try someplace else, as Wicked Excess does not offer sales. In fact, twice a year they mark up prices 30 percent to get a break from all of the "upper-middle-class riffraff" and concentrate on their truly rich customers.

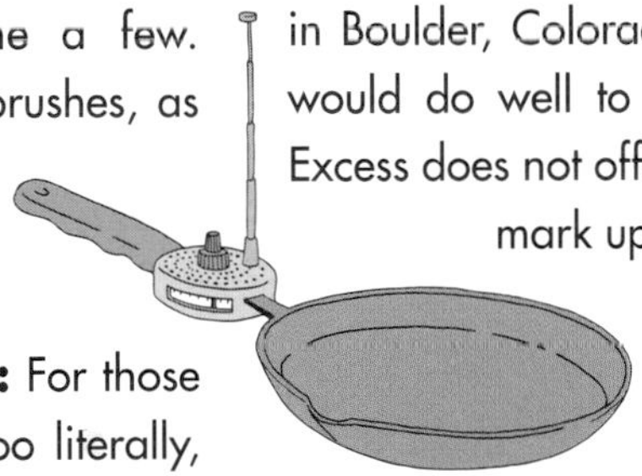

WHAT'S RIGHT WITH SPRINGFIELD?

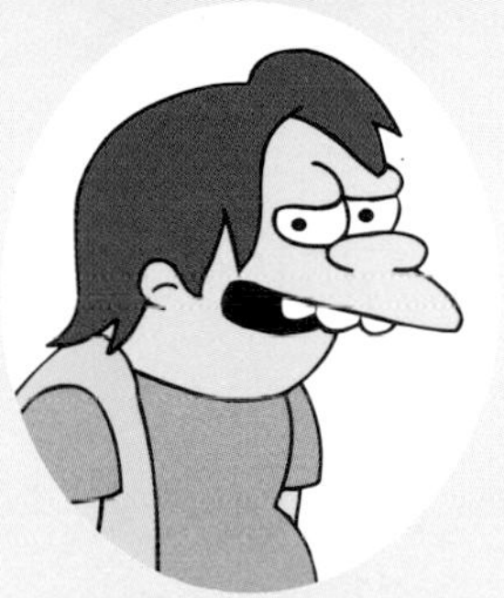

"Springfield Gorge. Whenever I look at it, I remember the day this kid's dad tried to jump it on skateboard. He bounced down the side, and by the time he reached the bottom, you could barely recognize his face. Man, it was a bloody mess! Ha, ha!"

—Nelson Muntz, age 10

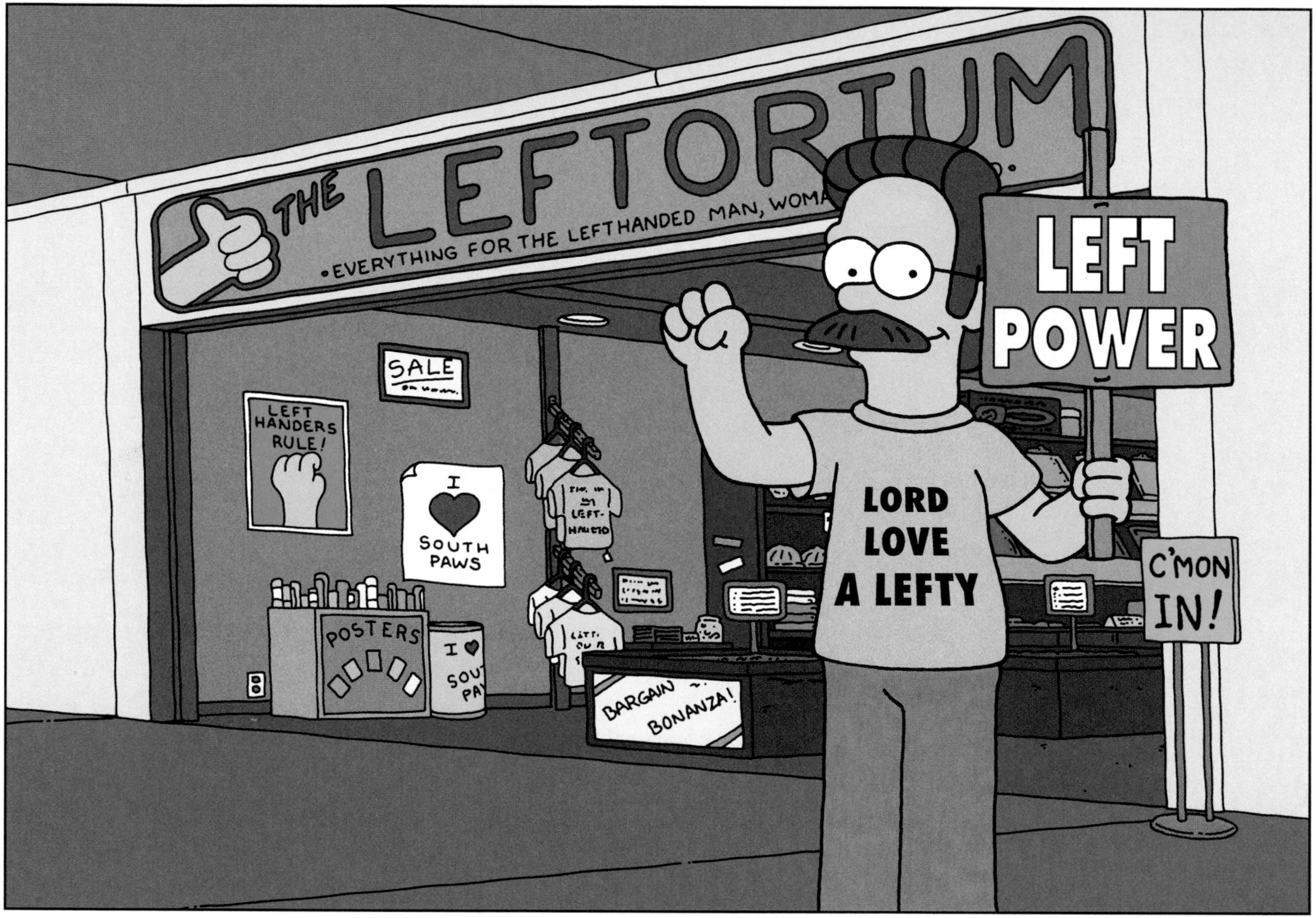
THE LEFTORIUM
•EVERYTHING FOR THE LEFTHANDED MAN, WOMA
SALE
LEFT HANDERS RULE!
I ♥ SOUTH PAWS
POSTERS
BARGAIN BONANZA!
LEFT POWER
LORD LOVE A LEFTY
C'MON IN!

Leftorium proprietor Ned Flanders uses both hands to drum up business outside his store.

Kidstown, U.S.A.: It's not a state, city, or municipality, but Kidstown, U.S.A. has become a number-one children's destination. Why? It has one of the best giant floor pianos in the city and Springfield's best selection of Malibu Stacy dolls and accessories, located in their Valley of the Dolls aisle. For boys (and modern girls who have managed to evade the soul-crushing gender stereotyping of our patriarchal society),

Kidstown offers Kidstown's Foamtown, an aisle of every foam sporting goods item on the planet—from foam cricket bats to foam shotputs. The store also has toys for preschoolers, from the basic (My First Yarn Ball) to the advanced (the "Let's Take Apart the Air Conditioner While Mommy Is Gone" game).

Royal Majesty for the Obese or Gangly Gentleman: For the well-dressed yet abnormally tall and/or morbidly obese, the Royal Majesty represents a quantum leap forward in the arena of challenge-tailoring. Very high and very wide men come from all over the country to clothe themselves in high-volume-fabric duds fashioned at this world-famous Springfield haberdashery. Past accomplishments include a custom purple crushed-velvet tuxedo for a 400-pound man, a traditional African dashiki for a seven-foot ten-inch man, and six pairs of Bermuda shorts for a 178-pound man. That last one sound unimpressive? Keep in mind, that man was only *three feet tall*.

GRANDMA'S WORLD
"FOR THE OLD LADY IN ALL OF US"
FEELING SPRY DENTURE PASTE INC.

A wait for late freight.

Circus of Values: Selling nothing over five dollars, the Circus of Values is a bastion of bargain scrunchies, multi-pack air fresheners, and minor-brand candies. To combat the store's sense of desperation and dissatisfaction, managers now require all employees to wear clown noses. Needless to say, things have gotten worse.

Bob's RV Round-Up: For those affluent travelers who bought a one-way ticket to Springfield with the intent of leaving town in a large, recently purchased recreational vehicle, Bob's RV Round-Up is a must. The Round-Up's most notable offering is the Supreme Behemoth—Millennium Edition, the world's first three-story RV. Featuring such amenities as a whirlpool bath, racquetball court, surgical theater, escape pod, and personal indentured sushi chef, the

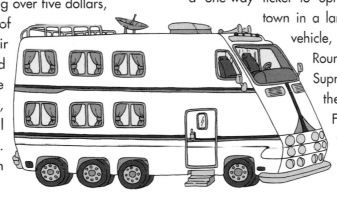

Supreme Behemoth is the ultimate in recreational vehicle-ing. Tell Bob that you read about him in this guide and he'll throw in a happy-face air freshener and extra bathroom with every Supreme Behemoth purchase.

The Leftorium: For left-handed visitors, the Leftorium offers an opportunity to pick up useful items that are unavailable in most parts of the country (left-handed hedge clippers, left-handed nutcrackers, left-handed surgery-quality scalpels) and chintzy knickknacks to announce to the world your unfortunate condition ("Lord Love a Lefty" needlepoints, "God Left the Best 'Til Last" beer steins). No purchase required for parking validation.

Grandma's World: Featuring aisles and aisles filled with hats, clown paintings, video collections of the *Merv Griffin* and *Mike Douglas* shows, bulk ginger ale, and purses with special compartments to hold restaurant sugar packets and wet naps, Grandma's World is a shopping experience for—as the sign says—"the Old Lady in All of Us." Those allergic to the smell of mothballs should avoid this store completely.

Simply Shoes and Athletic Equipment and Active Wear: Although this store carries sneakers designed for bocci, kick boxing, arena football, and bullfighting, it doesn't only sell shoes. It also stocks a full line of athletic equipment, with everything from full-contact paintball-croquet sets to harpoon guns and leisure apparel. Come in naked, barefoot, and bored and leave clothed, sneakered, and with a heck of a lot of sporting goods. (The management requests that you do not actually come in naked.)

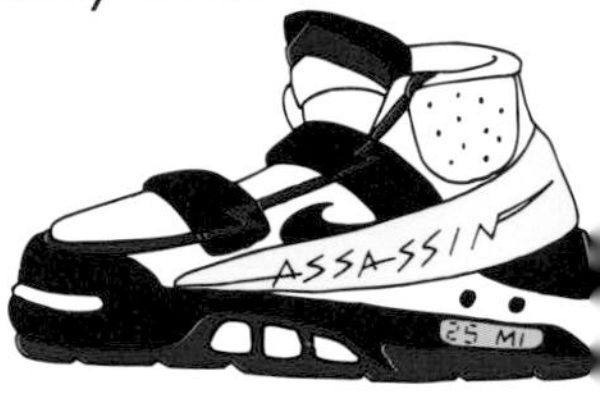
ASSASSIN

Malaria Zone: Would-be jungle adventurers—and those who merely want to look like one—should do quite well at this palace of pith helmets and mosquito netting. Here is one of the only places in the country where patrons can get a designer cologne laced with DDT to lure a date and keep bugs away at the same time. Plus, the store no longer requires employees to greet you by shouting in a ridiculously affected tone, "Dr. Livingston, I presume?" (Over ten employees a day were getting punched in the face.)

ARTIFACTS

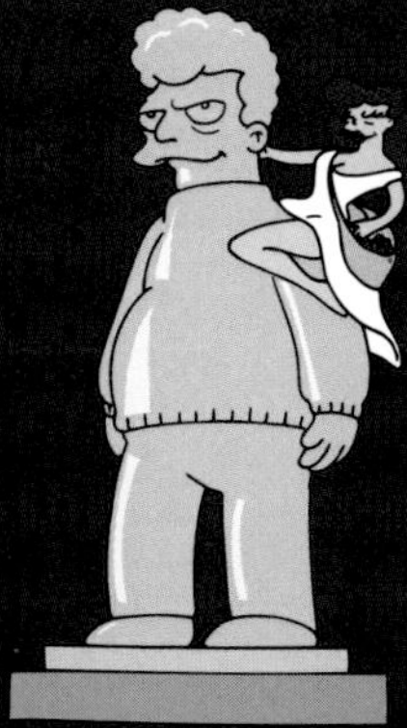

THE GOLDEN BRAD GOODMAN:

What It Is:
A golden statue of self-help guru and sweater wearer Brad Goodman. Goodman briefly transformed the town of Springfield into a city of id, guiding the citizens to follow the lead of a little Springfield boy named Bart Simpson, who said, "I do what I feel like." After the whole town adopted Simpson's credo, things began to deteriorate quickly. It all culminated at a Do- What-You-Feel festival that broke down into a riot. The Golden Brad Goodman was featured at that ill-fated festival.

Special Feature:
A mini-altar in the back for discreet animal sacrifices.

Its Current Use:
The statue was rumored to be purchased by the Propuldyne Defense Systems, owners of the Wall E. Weasel pizza and amusements chain. Supposedly, they plan to convert the statue into giant, golden Wall E. Weasel with a big fun slide down the back.

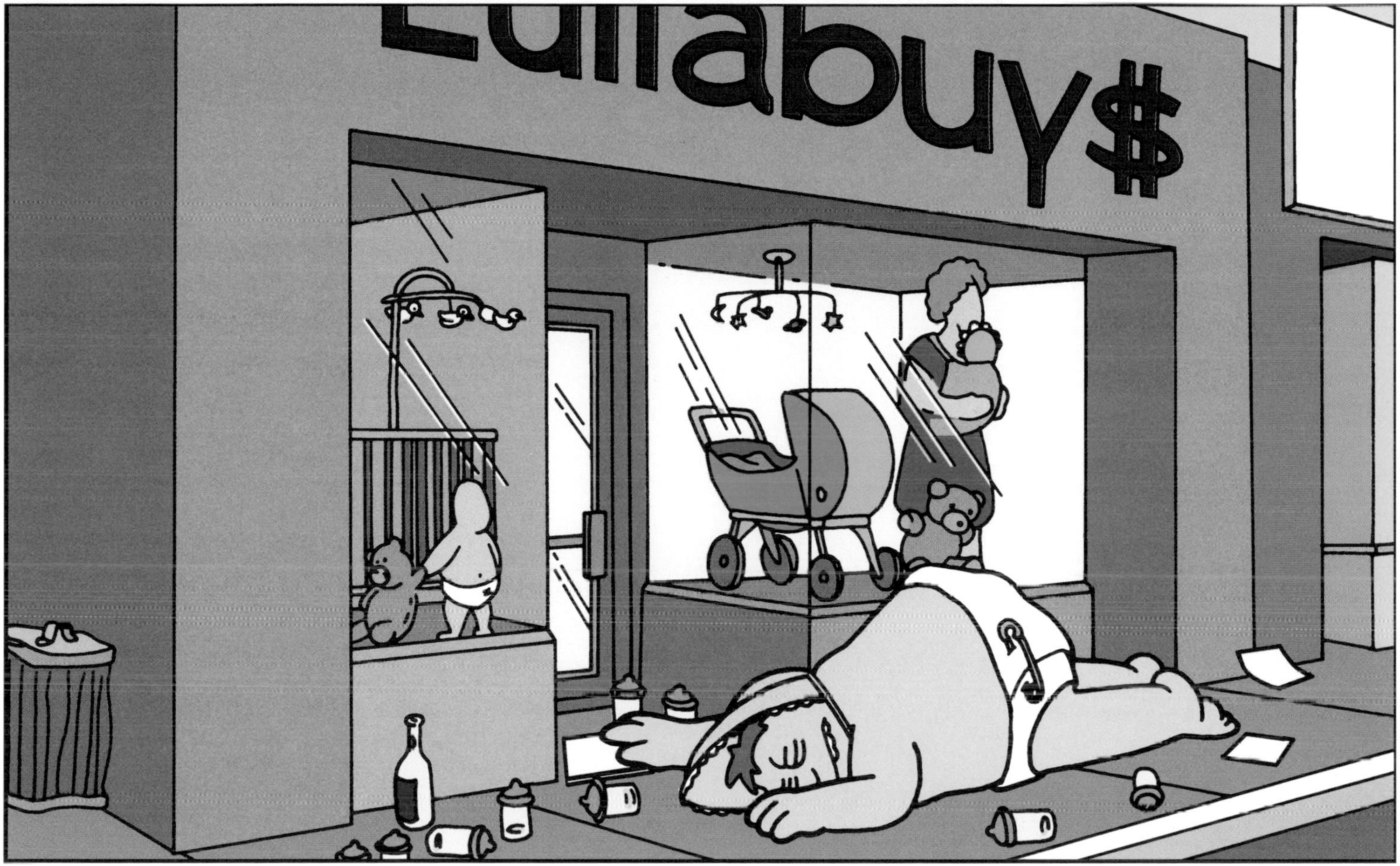
Lullabuy$

The Family Jewels: Springfield's premier jeweler. Actually, Springfield's only major jewelry store—making it less of a store and more of a cartel. Because of the scarcity of competition, the prices are high, the salespeople can be as rude as they like, and engagement rings are sold on a strict, "one-size-fits-all" basis.

Public Relations Specialist Barney Gumble, drunk on the job.

Lullabuy$: If there is one type of product consumers should not take chances on, it's baby furniture and accessories. Yet, every year, hundreds of bargain-hungry Springfielders pay little to nothing for Lullabuy$'s rickety cribs made of bamboo, plastic sheeting,

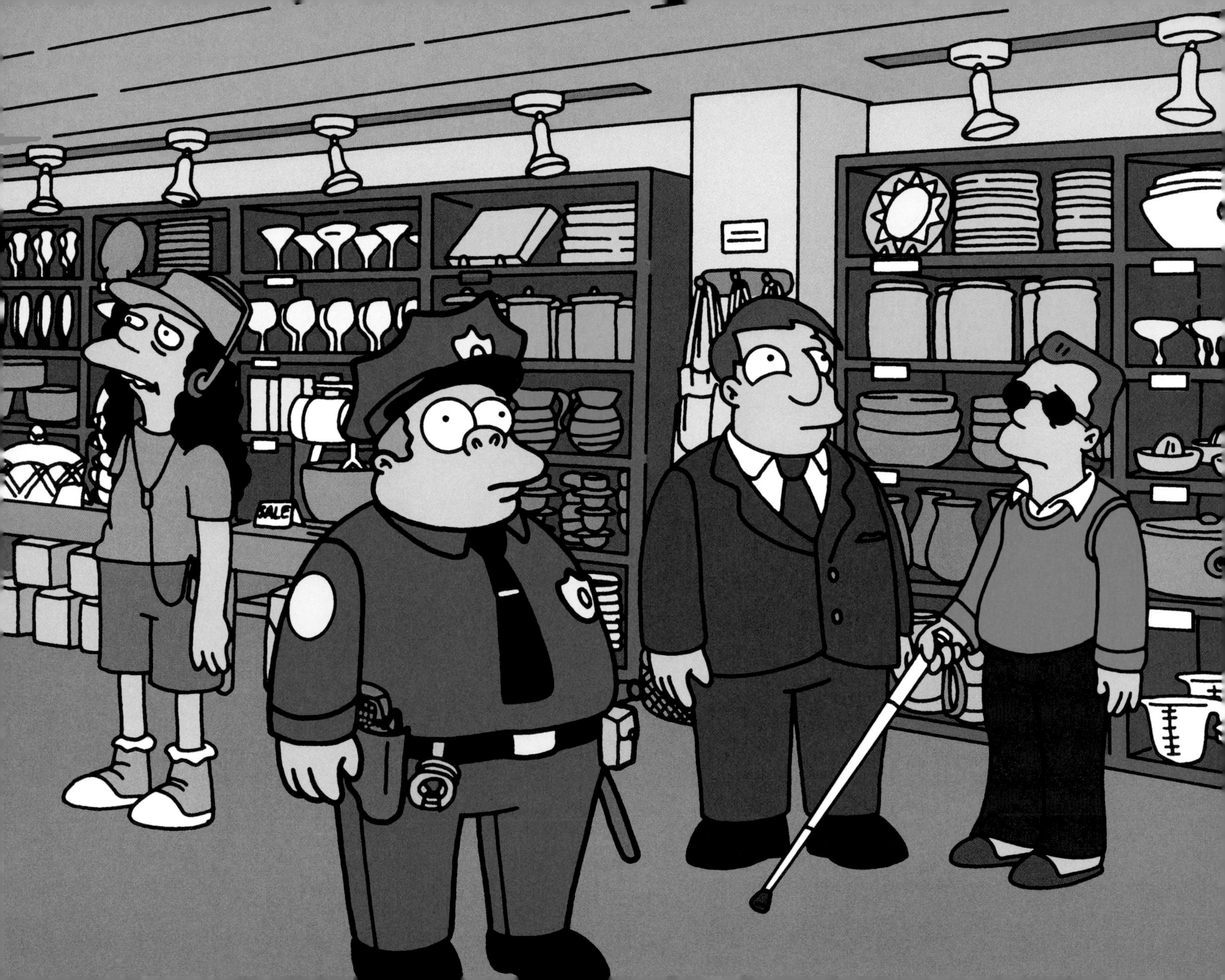
SALE

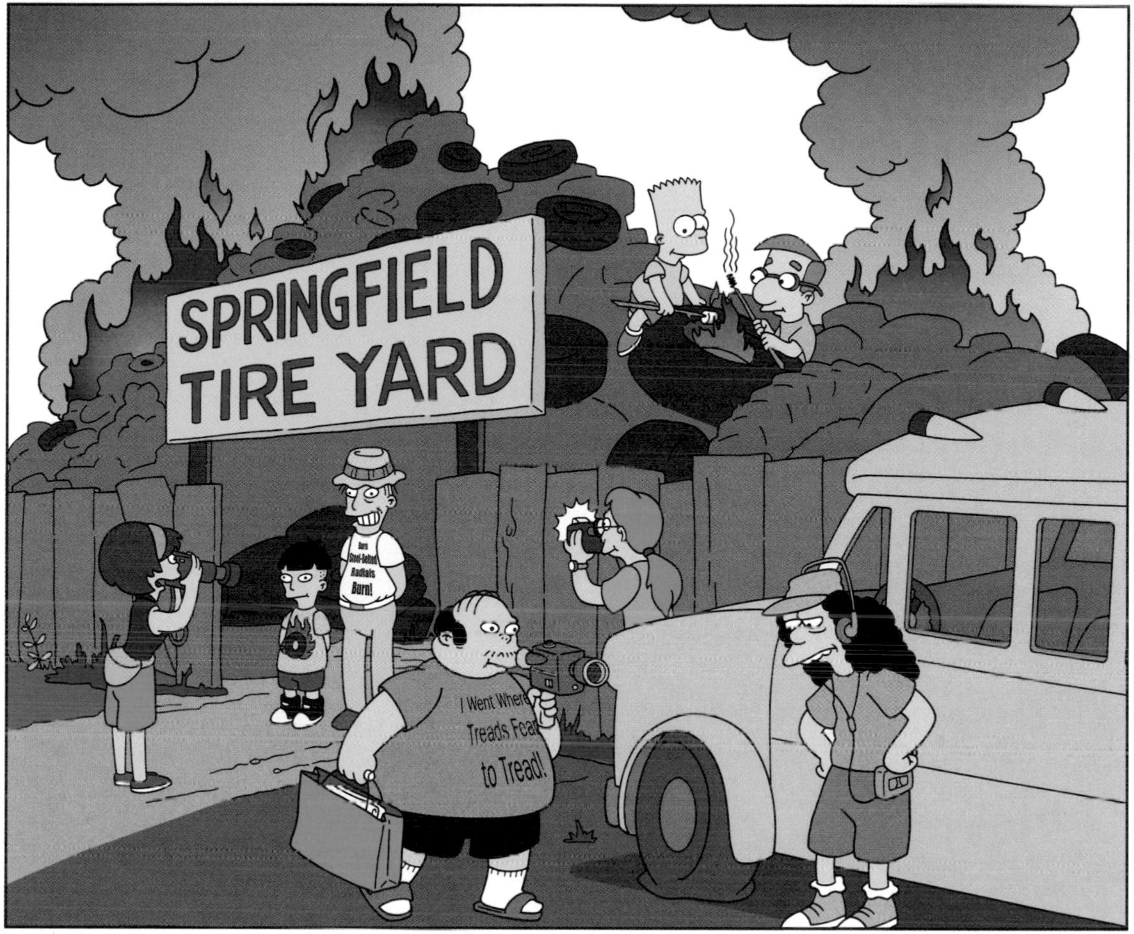
SPRINGFIELD
TIRE YARD
I Went Where
Treads Fea
to Tread!

Tourists enjoy the vaporous beauty of the Springfield Tire Yard.

and duct tape; pacifiers made of army surplus gas caps and rubber bands; and rattles made of roadside gravel and Buzz cola cans. This store is a sickening testament to the lack of thought Springfielders give to even the most important of decisions, *plus they do not validate*. As if all this were not enough, a foul-smelling, obese drunk often stands (or is passed out) in front of the store, handing out

(At left) Confused shoppers look around in disappointed wonder at Stoner's Pot Palace.

WHAT'S RIGHT WITH SPRINGFIELD?

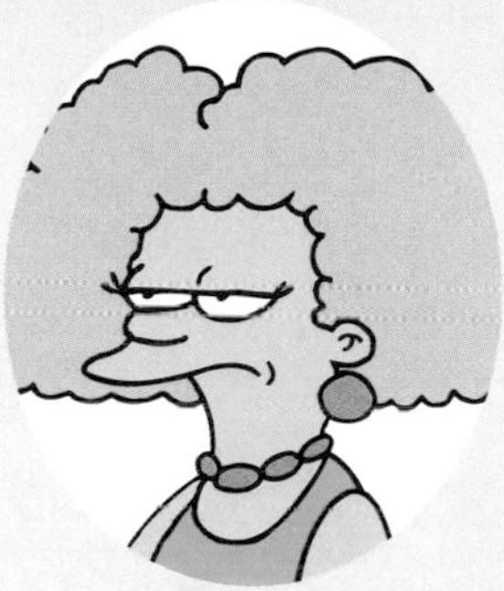

"Well I like pathetic men. You can usually find them at the **Monstromart** in the bulk mustard aisle. If you don't mind guys that smell kinda weird, this place is fulla easy pickins."

—Selma Bouvier, DMV employee

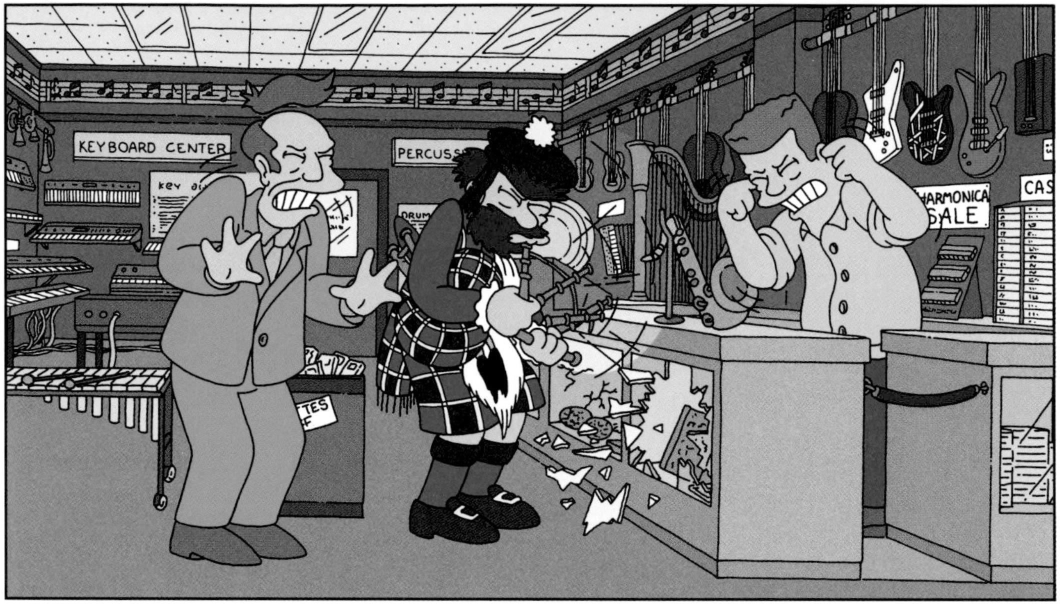
KEYBOARD CENTER
HARMONICA SALE

A local musician tries bagpipes and patience at King Toot's Music Store.

flyers and wearing nothing but a diaper and a bonnet. For shame.

Stoner's Pot Palace: For years (actually, four years), Stoner's has supplied Springfield's six or seven gourmands with high-priced, chef-quality cookware, silverware, dish towels, woks, and corn-cob holders. Among the elegant blenders and spatulas, confused burnouts shuffle around listlessly, disappointed at their discovery of what type of store the Pot Palace really is.

Around the World News: This newsstand has it all: a wide selection of magazines, lottery tickets, cheap cigars, and a sassy cashier who will chide you on your choices. Some of Around the World News' more obscure periodicals include, *Scott Christian's Science Monitor, Illiterate and Loving It Magazine*, and *Fish & Chips Fanatic.*

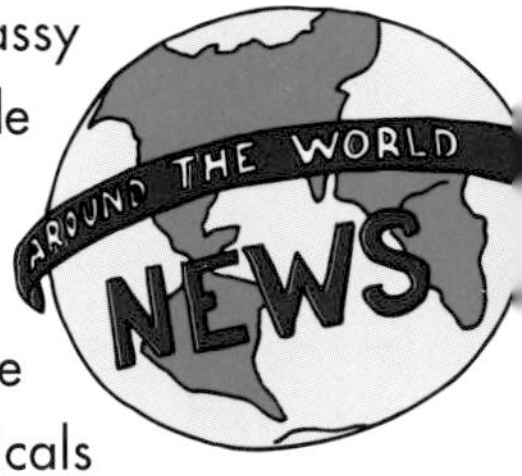
AROUND THE WORLD
NEWS

Springfield Tire Yard: Need a used tire? Why not buy it at one of the most famous burning tire yards in the country? The Springfield Tire Yard has been burning continuously for years and years and that means only two things for the consumer—incredibly low prices and noxious, bad-smelling fumes. There are very few establishments in the world that allow you to purchase goods from them while they are on fire; thus, a visit to the Springfield Tire Yard is a must. Just wear flame retardant clothing and watch out for the flesh-searing melted rubber.

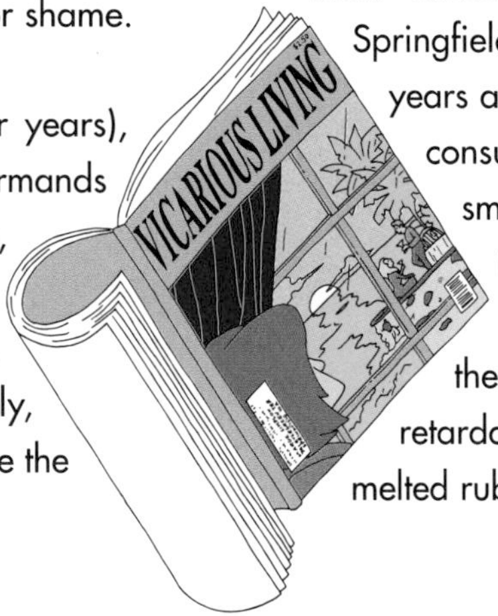
VICARIOUS LIVING

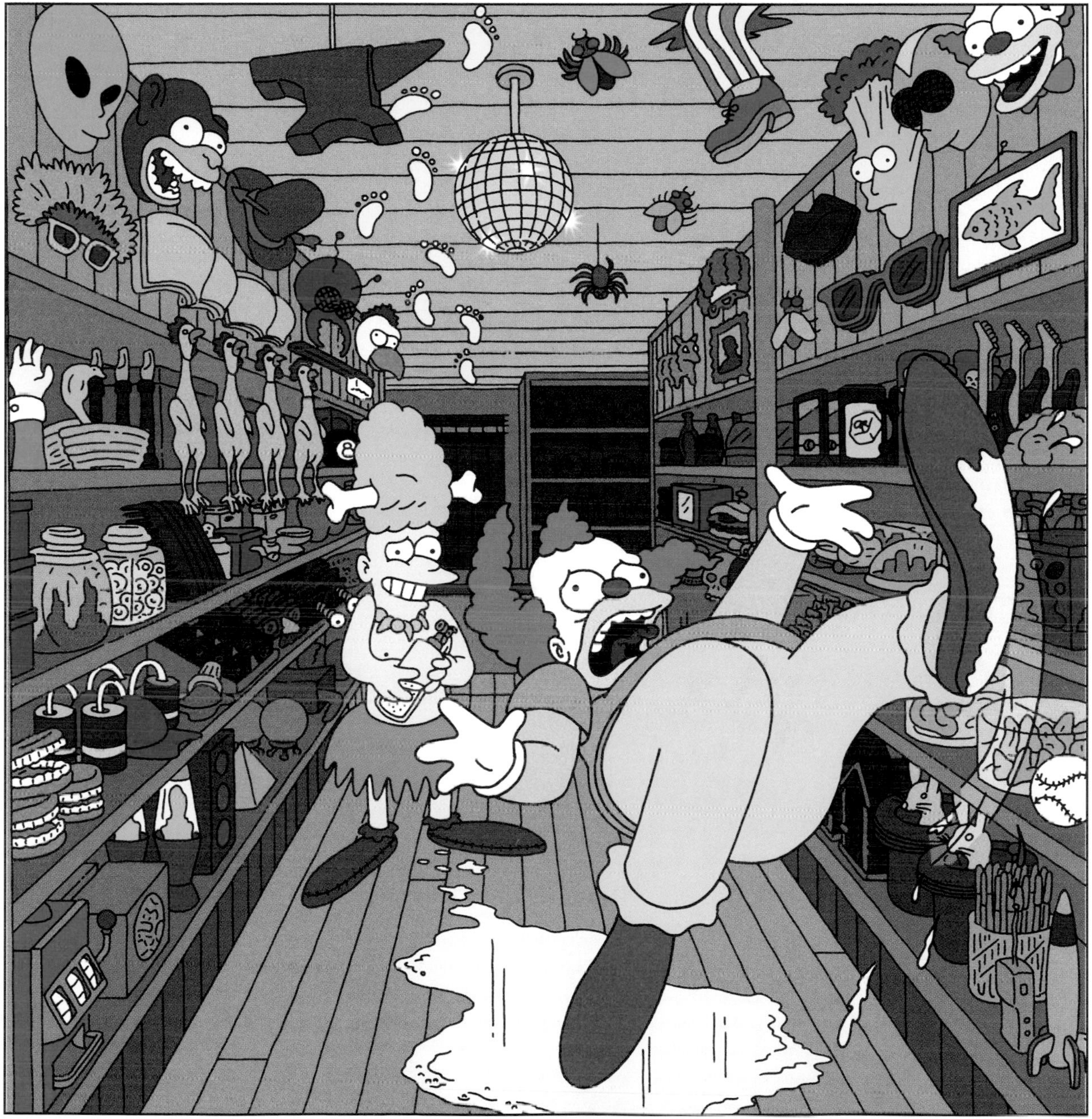

At Yukingham Palace, Krusty the Clown and Sideshow Mel shop for some new gags to enhance their act.

Crazy Vaclav's Place of Automobiles: Need a unique gift for the folks back home? Why not pick up (and we really do mean "pick up") one of the quaint, tiny automobiles offered at this dealership of cars from the Eastern Bloc of the former Iron Curtain? Not only are these small, puttering subcompacts hilarious reminders of the failure of Communism, but they run on kerosene or corn alcohol and can get 300 hectares to the gallon. For the elderly, these slow, cramped semicars are the perfect alternative to dignity-stealing motorized carts; for college students, they're coed conversation starters that are a heck of a lot more alternative and "fly" than mopeds. Plus, if you're returning home by plane, they fit easily and securely in the upper storage compartment.

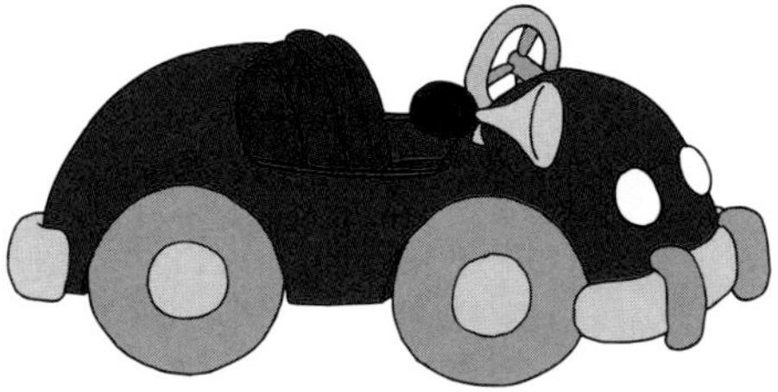

Sweet Home Alabama: Sadly, this establishment, which has always claimed to be "the store with things from Alabama," was recently caught stocking items from the neighboring state of Kentucky. This explosive discovery shocked and saddened the people of Springfield, who, for the past decade, have depended on Sweet Home Alabama for all of their Alabama-product needs. After closing its doors and ousting its CEO, Sweet Home Alabama has reopened. Under intense scrutiny, it now claims to offer only 100 percent Alabama goods. Whether this will be enough to win back Springfield's broken-hearted Alabama aficionados remains to be seen.

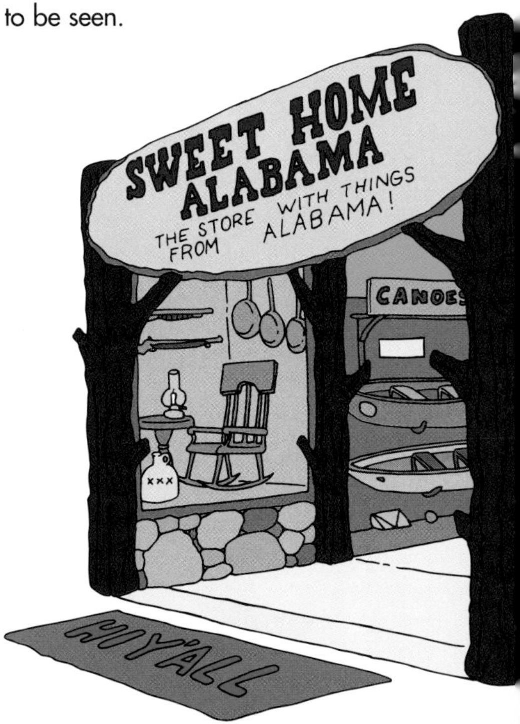
SWEET HOME ALABAMA
THE STORE WITH THINGS FROM ALABAMA!
CANOES
XXX
HI Y'ALL

ARTIFACTS

THE FINAL PANEL OF *RADIOACTIVE MAN* #1:

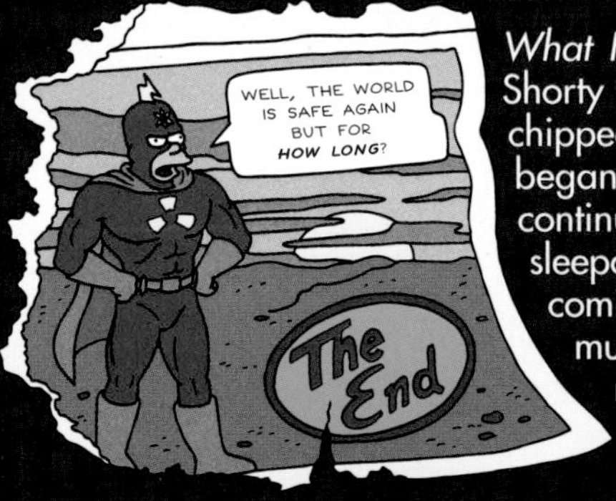
WELL, THE WORLD IS SAFE AGAIN BUT FOR *HOW LONG?*
The End

What Happened to the Rest of the Comic Book: Shorty after three young men from Springfield chipped in to purchase the comic book, they began squabbling over it. The squabbling continued well into the night, as the three held a sleepover in a treehouse. During a struggle, the comic was blown out of the treehouse into a mud puddle. A dog then pounced on the mud-soaked comic, tearing it apart. Finally, the remains of the book were struck by lightning.

Former Value:
(as a part of a mint copy of *Radioactive Man*
$100.00

Current Value:
Not worth the low-grade, sun-yellowed, industria pulp it's printed on.

Current Use:
Part of a Springfield bird nest.

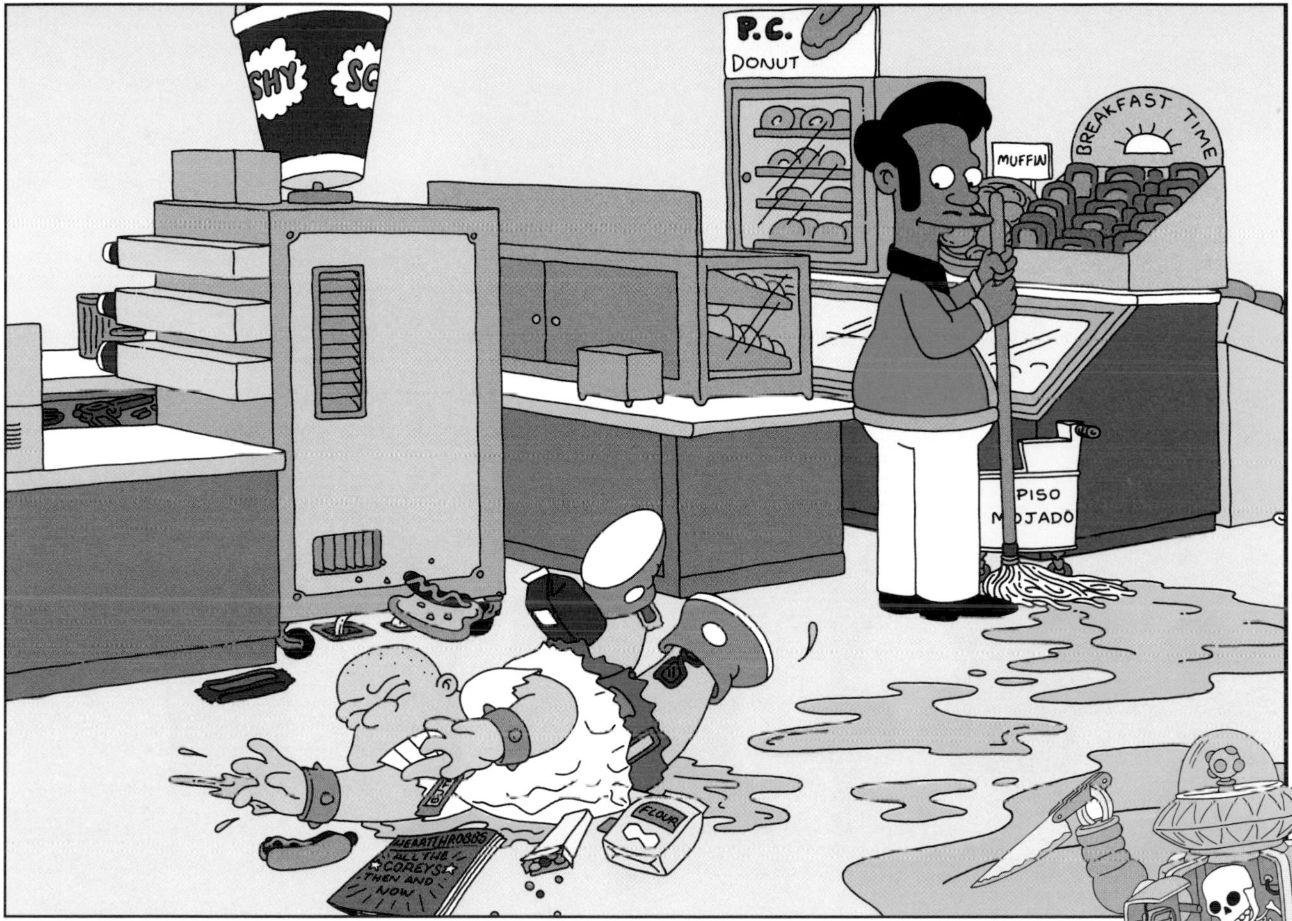
P.C.
DONUT
MUFFIN
BREAKFAST TIME
PISO
FLOUR

Kwik-E-Mart owner-operator Apu Nahasapeemapetilon catching an unidentified (and ambitious) shoplifter.

Cockamamie's: This wonderful little kitsch-en of creamed, chipped culture on toast is the last bastion of camp in Springfield. The store is nearly bursting with one-of-a-kind frivolities, such as mementos of films (like *Cry Gila Monster!* and *It Was All Just a Freakout*); old lunchboxes (some complete with original lunches); campaign buttons; Rex Mars super-commander brain-massager helmets; and *Eight Is Enough*

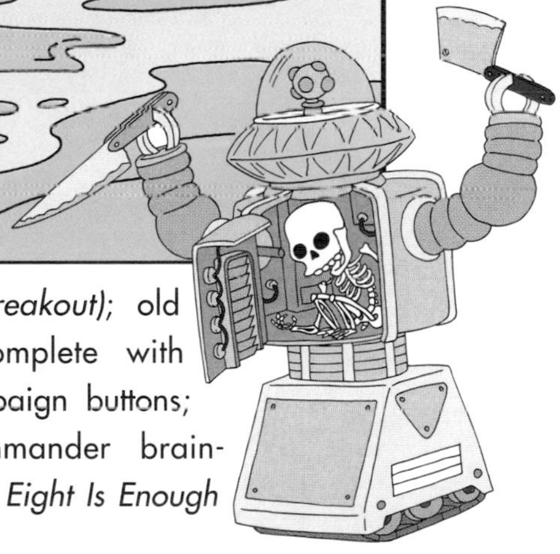

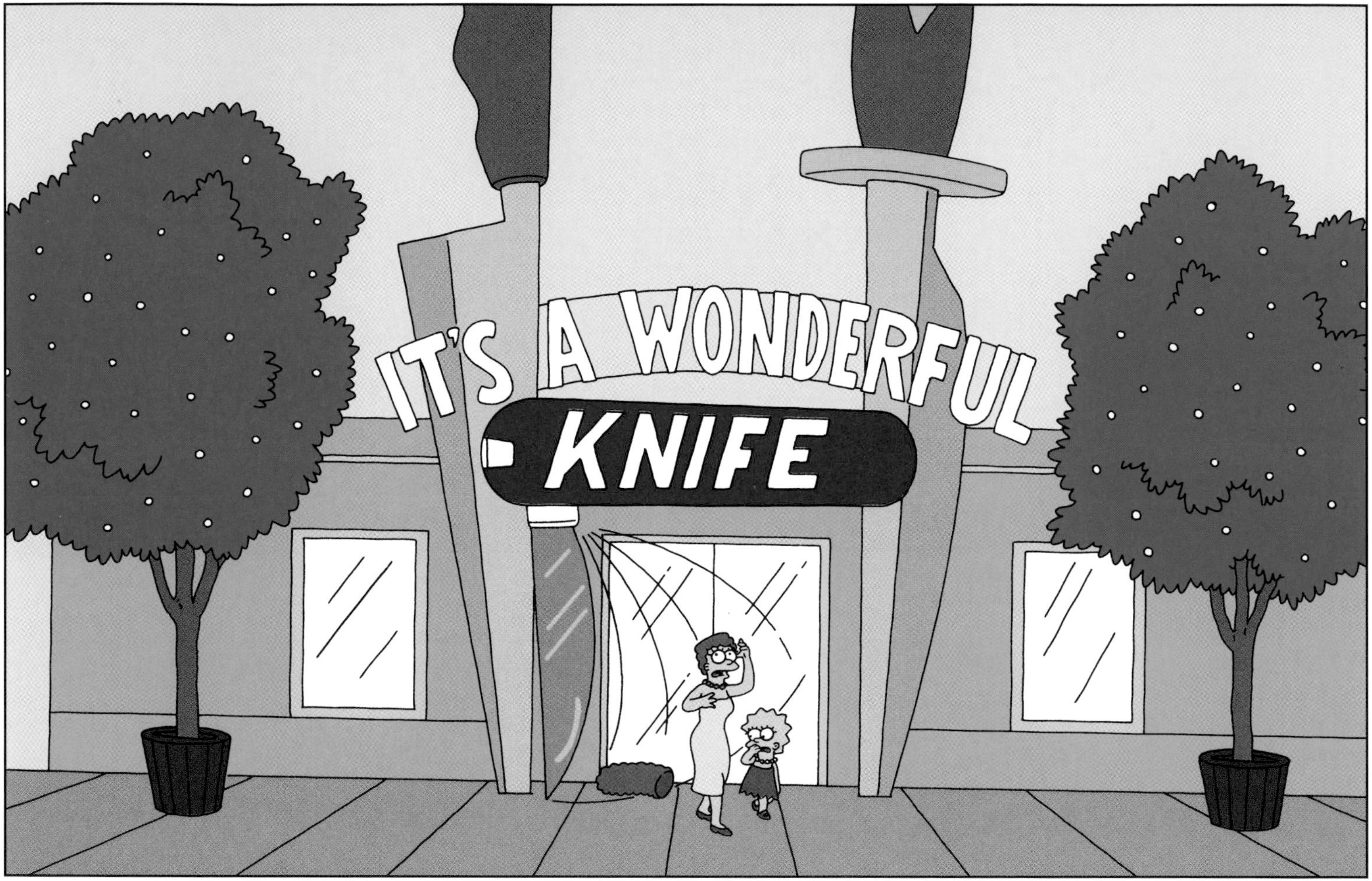
IT'S A WONDERFUL
KNIFE

An unlucky potential cutlery buyer gets an impromptu haircut at the entrance to It's a Wonderful Knife.

marionettes. Set aside at least half a day to tour this kingdom of pop couture, and bring some brightly colored snack cakes to munch on to keep with the mood—the management won't mind.

Spelunker's Paradise: Unless you're a serious cavern hiker, this store is anything but paradise. Thin, pasty "great indoors" aficionados arguing over the best strap-on forehead torch gets unbearable very quickly, so unless you're planning a trip to

Carlsbad Caverns anytime soon, skip this beady-eyed freakshow.

Sportacus: Outside, this store offers a spectacular facade, reminiscent of the Acropolis. Inside, it stocks every sporting good you could ever need, including high-quality pseudo-sports equipment (like graphite hula hoops and a sleek aerodynamic version of that lemon thing that kids swing around their ankles). But the truly unique thing about Sportacus is its employee gladiator matches, in which the store's two worst salespeople battle each other in the parking lot with Wiffleball bats and curling sticks. The winner gets to keep his or her job.

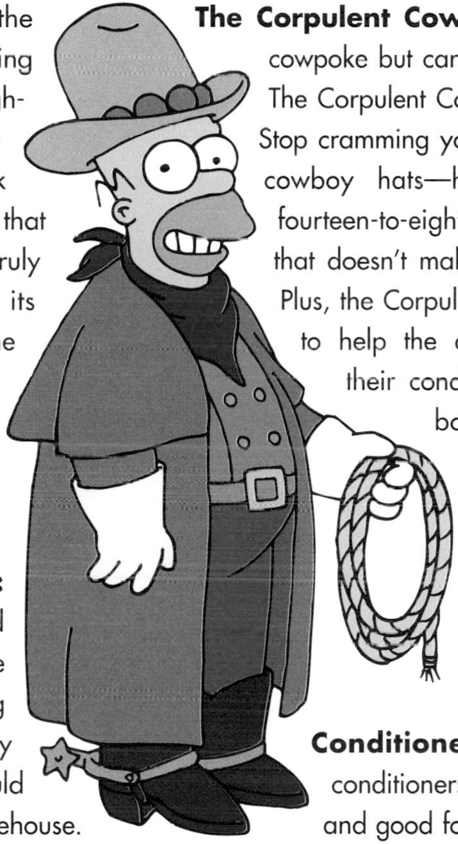

The Caramel Corn Warehouse: With its twenty-foot-high corrugated aluminum ceiling, its unfinished concrete floor, its fluorescent lamps' maddening hum, its forklifts' constant beeping as they back up, there is no way anyone could mistake this place for anything but a warehouse. And yet, all of this is merely an illusion: the Caramel Corn Warehouse is, in fact, just a store and not the starting point of a caramel corn distribution network. Its duplicity notwithstanding, the caramel corn is fantastic and the faux Teamsters hauling pallets of toffeecorn bricks are remarkably authentic.

The Corpulent Cowboy: Wanna dress like a cowpoke but can't find size forty-six chaps? The Corpulent Cowboy is the place for you. Stop cramming your fat head into ten-gallon cowboy hats—here, you can purchase fourteen-to-eighteen-gallon hick-headwear that doesn't make your flabby skull sweat. Plus, the Corpulent Cowboy offers products to help the dangerously obese survive their condition in style: combination bolo/heart monitors and boots equipped with blood-pressure gauges are bestsellers to the grossly overweight-but-responsible.

It Blows (The Air Conditioner Store): Offering air conditioners at fair prices was all well and good for It Blows during the spring and summer, but business tended to slow from the -ber months through the -uaries. Thus, the store now offers memorabilia from such films as *The*

WHAT'S RIGHT WITH SPRINGFIELD?

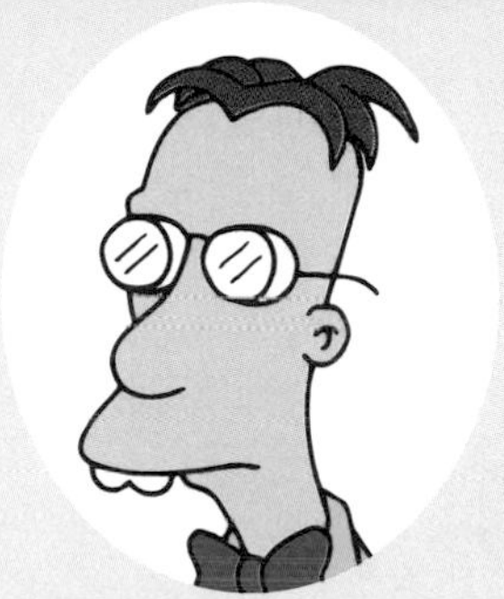

"Truth be told, the basement of the Springfield Natural History Museum is, ng-hey, in actuality, a top-secret compound used by a government financed biochem concern, woo-hoy, to create living, breathing, self-cleaning furniture and rugs. Ng-yag. It's a remarkable place and they're doing remarkable things."

—Prof. John Frink, scientist

Lost World, Godzilla, and *Lethal Weapon 3* during the fall and winter.

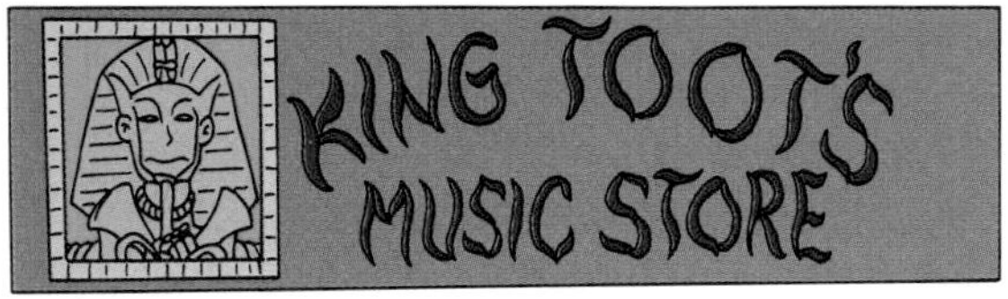
KING TOOT'S
MUSIC STORE

King Toot's Music Store: Stocking everything from electric guitars to violins to big annoying gongs, King Toot's Music Store is Springfield's number one musical-instrument store and America's fifth-highest-volume triangle reseller. King Toot's has also supplied musical equipment to such artists as The Be Sharps, Bleeding Gums Murphy, and noted nose flutist Ralph Wiggum.

Nick's Bowling Shop: Selling balls, shirts, and ball and shirt insurance policies, Nick's also services balls and shirts. They smoothify, re-inscribe, and widen finger holes for widening bowlers. Contrary to popular belief, Nick's does not flush balls.

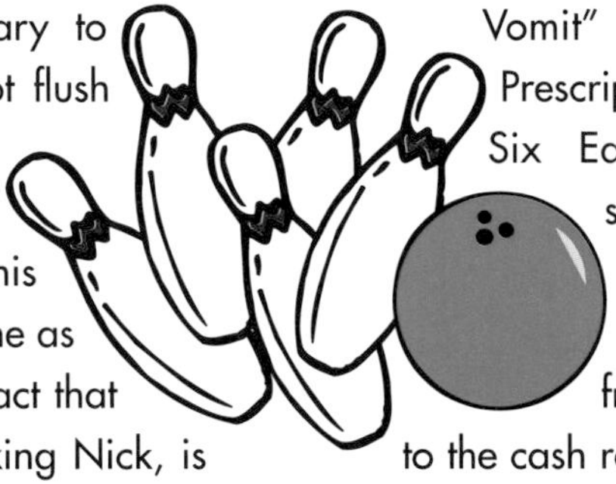

Nick's Bowling Shop: This Nick's is almost exactly the same as the other Nick's, save for the fact that this Nick's has a different-looking Nick, is located on the other side of town, and instead of a doorchime, greets customers with a digitized ball-and-pin crash. This Nick's also does not flush balls.

Yukingham Palace: At this guffawery, the joke's on you at incredibly reasonable prices. Yukingham Palace offers bulk specials on whoopee cushions, joybuzzers, and cigar explosives, as well as such kits for the do-it-yourself jokester as "Make Your Own Gag Vomit" and "How to Make Prescription Schnozz Glasses in Six Easy Steps." Those with sensitive dental work are advised not to buy any of the gumballs available from the new machine next to the cash register, as they explode on the first chew.

Shoelaces Plus: Shoelaces have been the rock of this Springfield institution for more than seven years; it's the "plus" that has changed over time. At first, "plus" meant

(At right) The geeky majesty of The Android's Dungeon.

ARTIFACTS

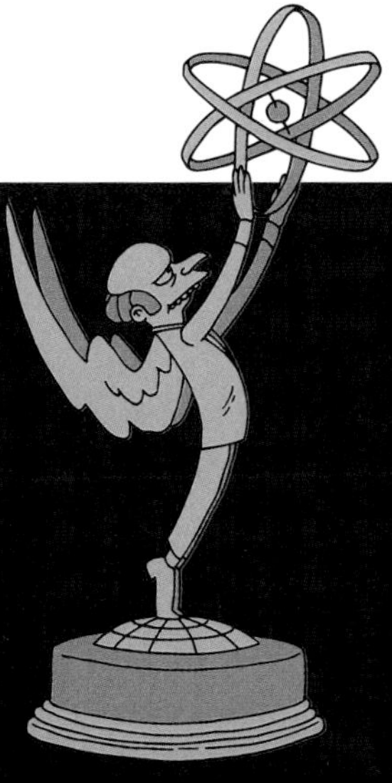

THE BURNSIE:

What It Is:
This statuette was given to Springfield Nuclear Power Plant employee Homer Simpson for winning the first annual Montgomery Burns Award for Outstanding Achievement in the Field of Excellence.

Where It Resides:
Simpson's safe deposit closet, somewhere near the bottom.

Its Rumored Condition:
Slightly melted after Simpson tried to make it into a lamp.

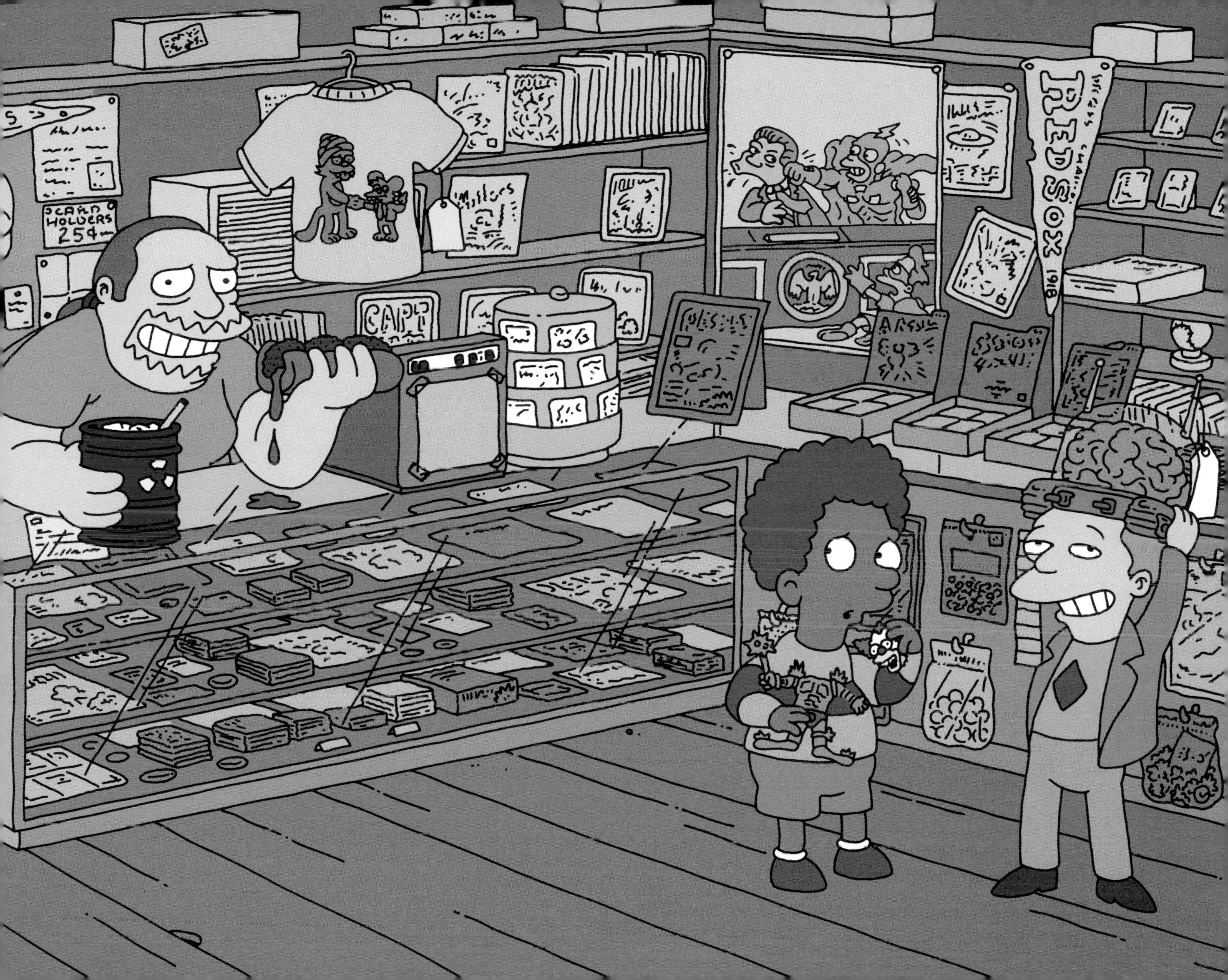
CARD HOLDERS 25¢
CAPT
RED SOX
1918

WHAT'S RIGHT WITH SPRINGFIELD?

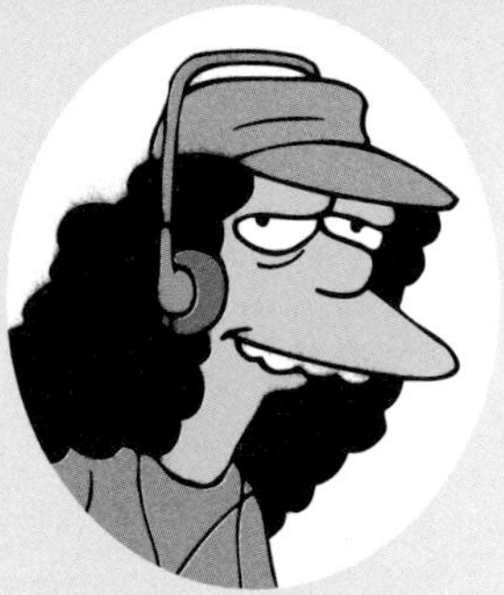

"I like the Abnormal D' Flume at Mt. Splashmore. The only lame thing about it is that they don't let you slide it naked anymore."

—Otto, bus driver

shoelace accessories: shoelace repair kits, automatic shoelace detanglers, and gold-plated shoelace-end laminations. Although the shoelaces sold steadily, the accessories didn't catch on and were discontinued. To justify the "plus" in its name, the store turned to the world of shammies. However, like the shoelace accessories, the shammies failed to perform. Since then, the store has stocked "plus" items like mustache trimmers, wood sealants, velvet paintings of political leaders, butter, and mini-rotisserie ovens for office cubicles.

Miscellaneous, Etc.: Specializing in expensive items with ultra-specific purposes, Miscellaneous, Etc. wants you to walk into the store, slap yourself on your surprised head, and cry out, "This is what I've been saving up for, something exactly like this!" Items for sale include insoles that make you shorter, the World's Best Refrigerator Magnet, and a device you hang around your neck to make other people's breath smell better.

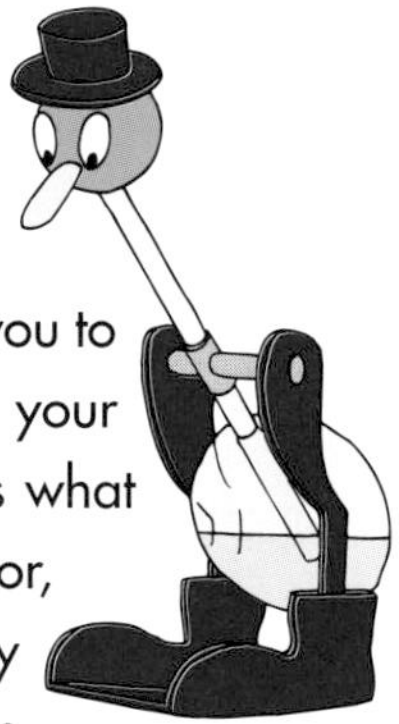

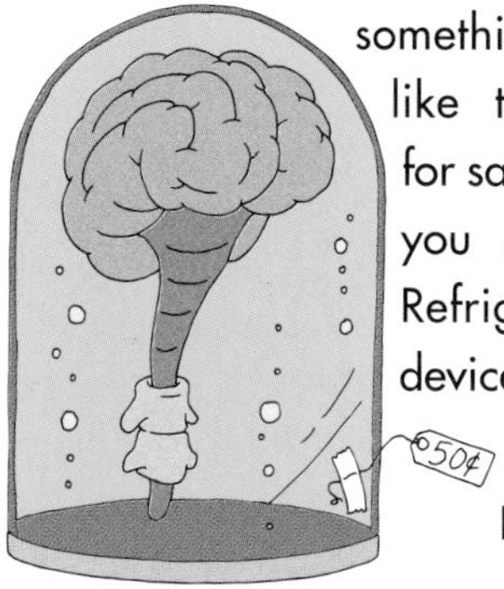
50¢

Herman's Military Antiques: Need something interesting for the jingoistic gun-and-sword nut in your family? Among its many offerings, Herman's stocks a full line of flags from every militaristic regime in the world, old undergarments previously owned by famous generals, and rusty weapons from past wars and police actions. Plus, it's an excellent place to do some freak watching and go trolling for featured fugitives from *America's Most Wanted*.

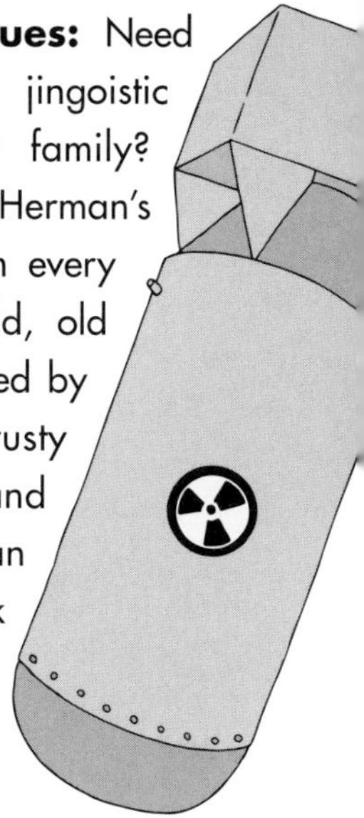

The Tam O' Shanter Connection: A haven for plaid-hat enthusiasts, this store features a myriad of Scottish berets with poofy balls on top. It also features incredibly long pipes (both tobacco and bubble), humorous plaques ("Erin Go Bra-less!"), and vacuum-packed salmon. The store also has a poofy-ball repair/replacement counter that has been voted "Best Tam O' Shanter Maintenance in Springfield" for ten years running.

Kwik-E-Mart: With the Kwik-E-Mart, shopping convenience is available twenty-four hours a day, under the constant hum of fluorescent lights. But

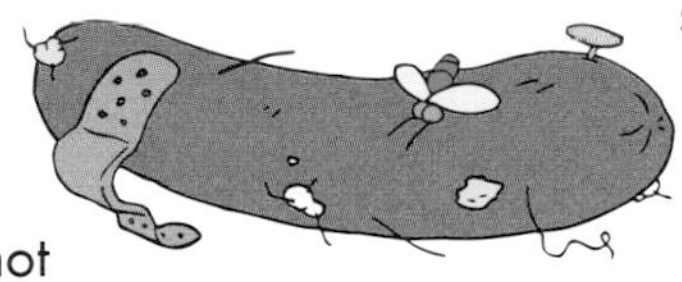

besides providing its customers with top-flight Squishees, dangerously old hot dogs, and indestructible snack cakes, there is often something unusual happening at this beloved stuff-and-snackery. Movie actor James Woods worked here researching a movie role; a frozen senior citizen was once put on display; the store was briefly converted into a strip club/convenience mart; and, on the day it installed gas pumps, an errant round of artillery struck and instantly destroyed the innovative store. Anytime, day or night, the Kwik-E-Mart's manager and operator, Apu Nahasapeemapetilon, can be found standing behind the counter, happily greeting customers, occasionally wounded by an armed robber. If he loses consciousness, customers who call 911 for him receive a coupon for a free fried pickle.

Top It Off: This discount warehouse sells only top hats and the film *Top Hat* on video. Its motto: "If you've got a head, then we have a top hat and classic movie for you." Indeed, the store does have a top hat for everyone: mini-top hats for kids, industrial hard plastic top hats for construction workers, and top hats fitted with small explosive devices for supervillians are just a few of the selections available.

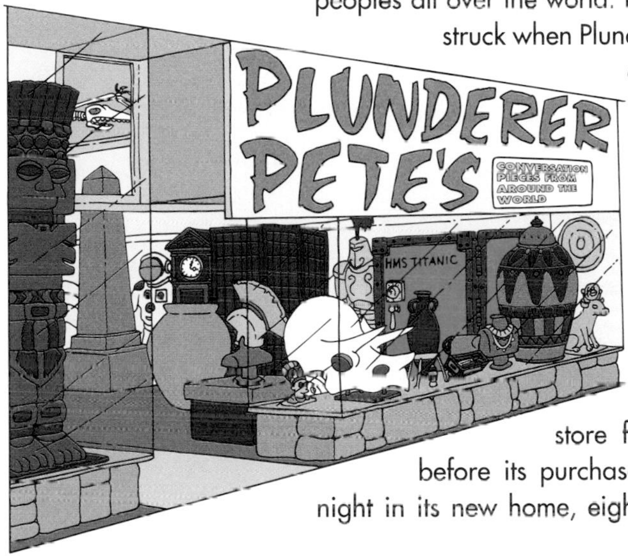
PLUNDERER PETE'S
CONVERSATION PIECES FROM AROUND THE WORLD
HMS TITANIC

Plunderer Pete's: For years, this store sold quality artifacts plundered from the ruins (and sometimes, active communities) of indigenous peoples all over the world. Recently, tragedy struck when Plunderer Pete's made a sale of a large stone god worshipped by natives of a South Pacific island. It seems that, although the stone god had sat peacefully in the store for many months before its purchase, during its first night in its new home, eight native warriors

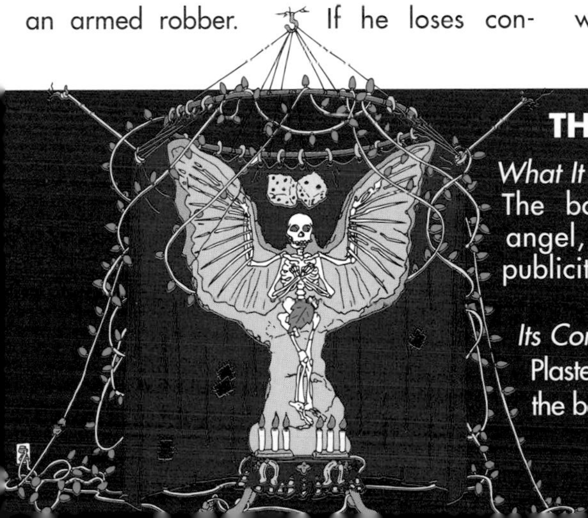

THE SPRINGFIELD ANGEL:

What It Is:
The bogus, fossilized skeleton of an angel, put together as a successful publicity stunt for the Heavenly Hills mall.

Its Composition:
Plaster of Paris, cement pterodactyl wings, the bones of a former mall employee.

Its Former Home:
Next to the rakes in Homer Simpson's garage.

Its Current Home:
Above the doors to mall entrance C. (It's the one closest to the Pottery Barn.)

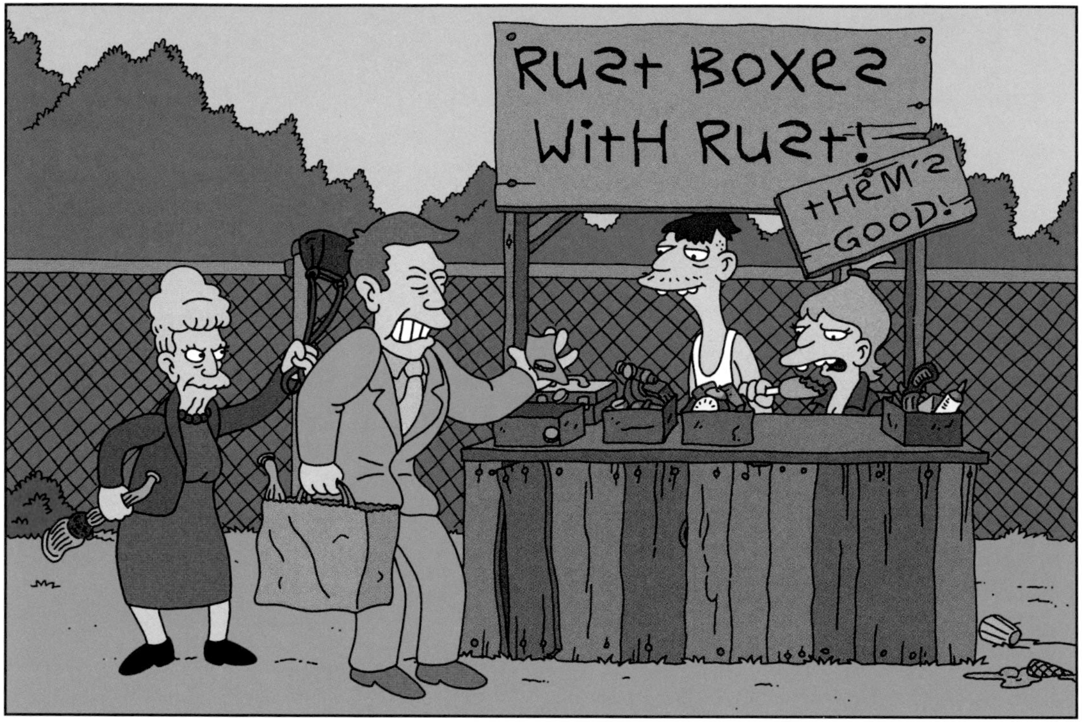
RUST BOXES WITH RUST!
THEM'S GOOD!
A family dispute plays out at the Springfield Swap Meet.

emerged from hiding inside the statue and proceeded to take over the house, claiming it as their own. The unfortunate owners suffered superficial blow-dart wounds to their rumps and mother-grabbing headaches when they woke up on their front lawn. Plunderer Pete's is now mired in litigation, and Pete himself has been heard to say, "I think I'm a-gettin' too old for all this a-plunderin'."

It's a Wonderful Knife: This is the store that made cutlery shopping fun again. First, customers must step lively when entering, lest they be slightly chopped by an oversized novelty knife that perpetually swings toward the door. Next, they're greeted by salespeople dressed like the store's best-selling knives. And if that weren't enough, lucky customers are chosen at random to be strapped to a spinning wheel and have knives thrown at them. Knives that do not pierce them are theirs to keep.

J.R.R. Toykin's: A two-story wonderland that accepts most major credit cards. It's not just that the store is incredibly well-stocked: J.R.R. Toykin's features giant playthings hanging from the ceiling, a mini-railroad to transport customers throughout the massive store, and whimsical rides to get families in the toy-purchasing mood. The rides include the Big Ben Slide, the Plunging Space Needle, the Really Large Erector Ferris Wheel, and Up Escalator.

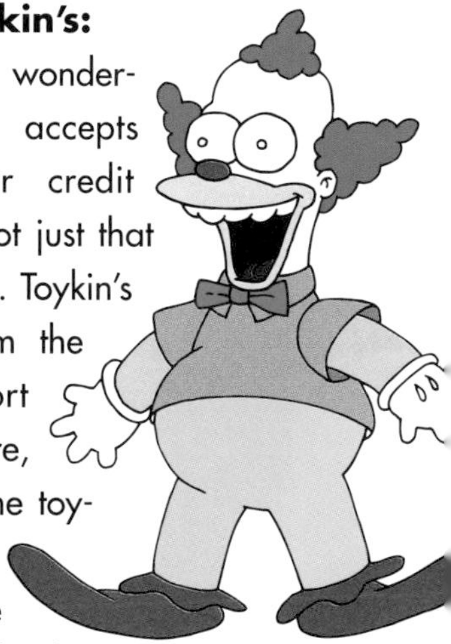

The Android's Dungeon: The regulars of this establishment are composed of a group of ill-mannered ten-year-olds who stand around and argue about who would win a fight between Radioactive Man and Fallout Boy. Despite the preposterous nature of the question itself (Fallout Boy is Radioactive Man's partner and charge, and the only way they would fight is if they were under the control of Hypnohead, a villain they have defeated thirty times), the portly owner of this establishment will invariably chime in with the authority of a Supreme Court justice, handing down decisions that all must obey lest they be exiled from Eden. When purchasing goods from this man, don't say anything or make direct eye contact: you'll just give him room for a put-down regarding your pathetic lack of knowledge on Romulan diplomatic protocol.

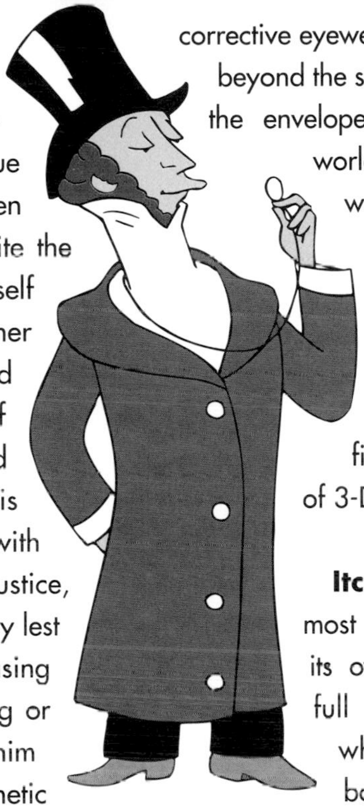

Kliff's Kar Chalet: Price gouging, morality-impaired salesmen, and bad coffee make this dealership much like every other one in the world. The only difference? They spell car incorrectly.

Heinrich's Monocle Shop: If Springfield had a true king of mono-ocular corrective eyewear, it'd be Heinrich. Why? He's gone beyond the simple lens and chain and has pushed the envelope to develop the Monogcle™—the world's first safety monocle, designed for woodworking and yard work. He also created the Mr. Monocle Wet/Dry 3000, a simple kit that helps convert a regular monocle into an all-weather wonder. Currently, Heinrich is feverishly at work on the world's first monocle that can be used in place of 3-D glasses.

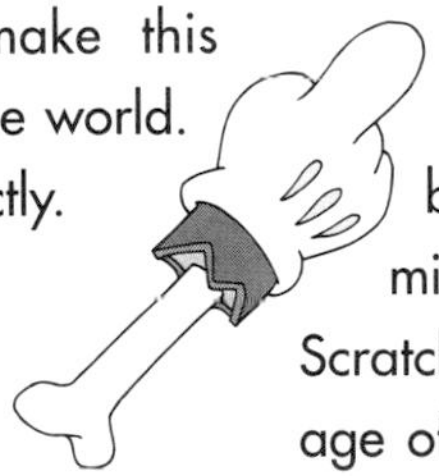

Itchy & Scratchy Store: The world's most violent cat-and-mouse team now has its own charming boutique, full of elegant and/or whimsical items for both the neophyte and hardcore devotee. Not surprisingly, most of the Itchy items come with fake (yet extremely realistic) weapons, while the Scratchy items are identified by custom-shot bulletholes, burned areas, or missing limb coverings (such as the sleeveless Scratchy AmpuTee-shirt). Yes, if you are above the age of nine (or are extremely mature for that age),

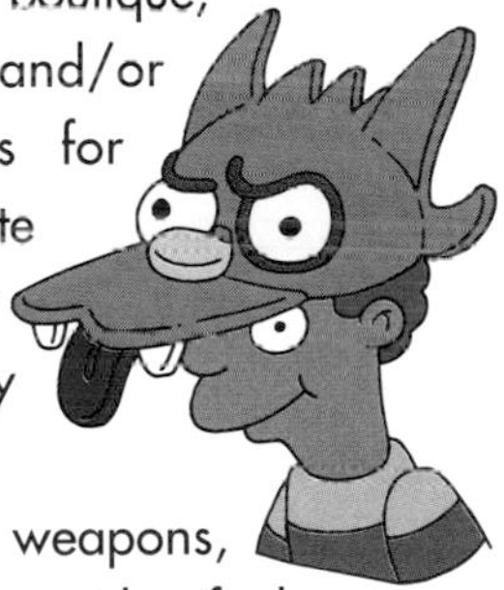

WHAT'S RIGHT WITH SPRINGFIELD?

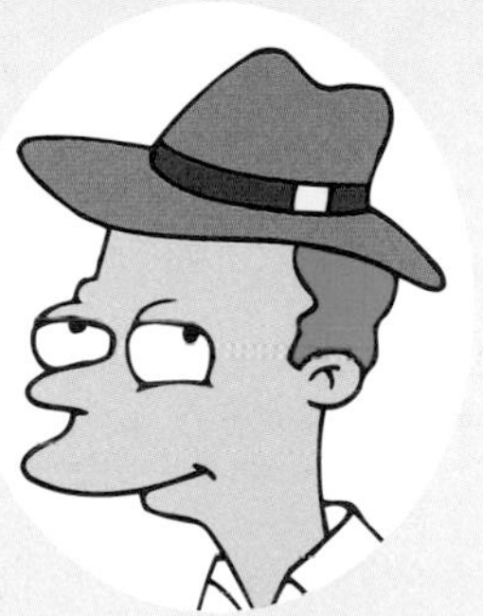

"I'm a newspaperman by trade. Over the years, nothing in town has made my job easier than the Springfield Nuclear Power Plant. Whether it's a near meltdown, a strange new species of fish evolving out of the core-coolant water, or their illegally dumped radioactive waste reanimating Dr. Marvin Monroe, the SNPP has always given me a great scoop by deadline. Heck, the phone's ringing now. Maybe ol' Monty Burns is firing upon protesters again."

—Dave Shutton,
columnist,
the *Springfield Shopper*

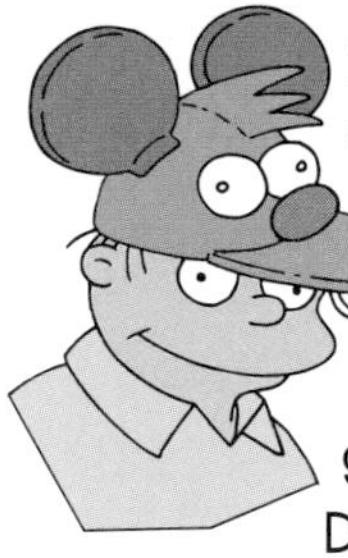

you will be offended—but, at least you'll be offended by high-quality apparel and well-crafted home-decorative items. (For you gardeners, the Scratchy Dancing Guts lawn sprinkler is a terrific, beautifying addition to any front yard.)

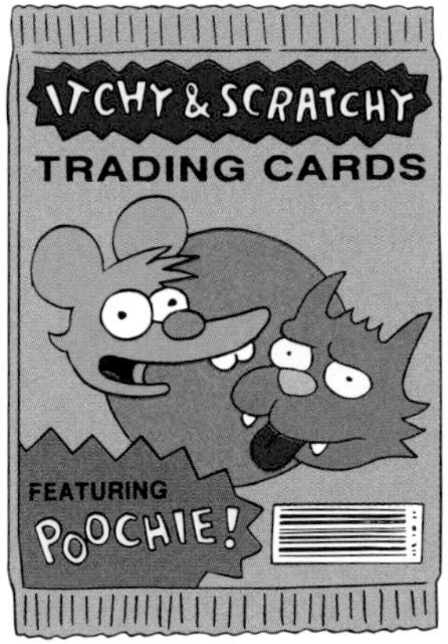
ITCHY & SCRATCHY
TRADING CARDS
FEATURING
POOCHIE!

House of Tires: Due to a lack of foresight, House of Tires is located atop a six-story building. This presents a bit of a problem, as customers cannot get their cars within a couple of stories of the store, and even if they do, the cars are only there for a millisecond, suspended in midair during some sort of illegal jump. To remedy this shortcoming, House of Tires has a strict, cash-and-carry-and-eventually-drag-down-the-stairs policy which dictates that customers must install their own tires. The prices are low, but odds are good that customers will hurt themselves trying to negotiate the narrow stairway with a steel-belted radial on each arm. The store does loan out jacks and lugnut removers for fifteen minutes at a time, so if you're strong, quick, and can find a good parking space in front of the building (fat chance), you may want to try your luck. If not, just go to Sears.

Turban Outfitters: Local Sikhs agree: there's no finer head-fabric windery in all of Springfield. But Turban Outfitters doesn't merely offer turbans in the style of the Punjab region of India. In fact, it offers turbans from every country in the world—including those nations that have made sporting the headwear punishable by death. The management of the store maintains that a turban craze is going to hit the United States very, very soon; customers are encouraged to make the plunge now, before it becomes too hip.

The Lumber King: What better souvenir to bring back from a long trip than lumber? Many things, actually. But it still may be worth your while to visit this store just to see the owner walk around in his crown, "knighting" customers who make purchases over one hundred dollars.

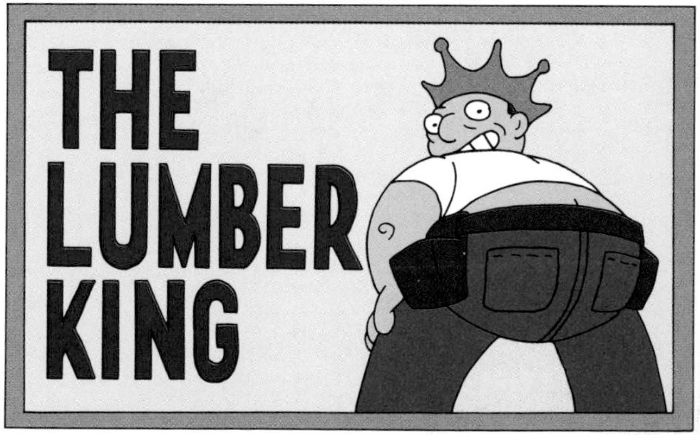
THE
LUMBER
KING

Springfield TV Store: If you happen to find yourself in Springfield during some sort of tumultuous event, why not go to the Springfield TV Store to watch the coverage on the several televisions in the front window, where you can be part of the time-honored cliché of people learning about big news from TV-store displays. To heighten the effect, say something aloud like, "Gee!" or "I can't believe it, I just can't believe it!" or "Boy, looks like we're all in the soup now!"

Try-N-Save: This huge store has everything one would possibly need for the home: aisles upon aisles of housewares, lawn-care items,

THE APPLIANCE EVERYONE'S TALKING ABOUT!

leisure wear, cooking supplies, toys, medical equipment, low-grade munitions, groceries, and pets. Competition is keen for weekly specials; some shoppers have been known to attach twirling spikes to the wheels of their carts to dispatch any comers *Ben Hur*-style. Needless to say, in the vast commerce ecosystem that is Try-N-Save, shopping Darwinism rules the day. Be prepared to evolve into one bad-ass shopping machine if you expect to survive.

Springfield Harmonica Shop: Go into this store and you will no doubt catch "harmonica fever" (especially if you try out a nonsterilized harmonica). The enthusiasm of the employees for these little metal musical wonderments is infectious; it's practically impossible not to leave the store thrilled about the big harmonica you've just purchased. You'll have visions of yourself playing your harmonica to a rapt, smiling crowd around campfires, on transatlantic flights, in movie theaters, waiting in the emergency room.... And yet, during the first week, after you fail to learn a jaunty version of "Pop Goes the Weasel," the harp will invariably wind up in the bottom drawer of a desk, where it will lay dormant, except for its occasional use as an emergency paperweight or cheese grater. It's all right—go in and buy that harmonica, but just don't spend too much money, okay?

Hailstone's: For department store shopping at department store prices, Hailstone's is the obvious choice. While shopping here, do watch out for the women with perfume and cologne—they strike quickly, silently, and with laserlike precision. One moment, you're standing around looking at tube socks, smelling normal. The next, you're awash with the pungent scent of Krusty Sport No. 5.

Swap Meet: Who knows what treasures you'll find among the tripe at this magical stuff-people-have-already-used-for-years bazaar? Among the favorite booths at the meet are "Paintings, Wishbone Necklaces, and Tuning Fork Windchimes by Marge," "Chief Clancy Wiggum's Unsold Evidence Explosion," and "Barney Gumble's Just-Emptied Collectible Beer Cans." Somehow, between the old, rusting lunchboxes and the yellowing board games, shoppers have found astounding bargains on such items as the lost Ark of the Covenant and the New Orleans Saints.

SPRINGFIELD SWAP MEET

Goody New Shoes: A children's shoe store for those who don't care to consider fashion or comfort. The scene inside forms a depressing tableau of sad children, practical mothers, a jaundiced shoe salesman, and a shiny statue of a depression-era boy wearing a tam and proudly holding up new shoes. Parents will appreciate the low prices, while kids will enjoy punching the statue.

Everybody into the Cool:
A Kid's Guide to Springfield

by Bart Simpson, Esquire, Age 10

If you're over thirteen, turn the page, man. But if you're under thirteen and your parents are actually thinking of coming to Springfield, YOU GOTTA READ THIS. Unless you're extremely lucky, you're probably gonna wind up at some kind of monument, museum, or (and I don't even wanna think about this) an educational walking tour while on your trip. If your mom's anything like mine, it's inevitable. But, if you get on top of it now, you can buy yourself at least ONE DAY free of tour guide-led boredom and possibly get through your whole vacation without learning anything.

PHONY ILLNESS = GENUINE FUN

The first thing to do is figure out how you're gonna weasel out of the conventional sightseeing. My advice? Remember two magical words: INTESTINAL PARASITE. You'll only have to say 'em once, but make sure you throw in some pathetic groaning for believability. Just in case, give yourself a sickly sheen by thinking of the possibility that you might actually have to go to a crafts fair and clutch your stomach while bending your knees a little to clinch the deal. The folks will probably buy it, tuck you into your hotel bed, and take off for the bore-itoreum. That's when you spring into action. That's when you spring into Springfield.

HIT THE SIDEWALK, MAN

To take the edge off, start your adventure with a Squishee. I recommend the "Twenty-One Syrup Salute," available only at Springfield's legendary Kwik-E-Mart. The heady rush of ice, sugar, and stabilizers will help you hit the bricks running. Also, drop a few quarters into "Escape From Death Row" before you split— it's an incredibly realistic game that actually lets you use rusty spoons as lethal weapons (the publishers won't let me give you the gory details. Let's just say that you WILL get virtually wet!). Before you leave, the back wall behind the Kwik-E-Mart (right next to the dumpster) is a perfect place to let everyone know that you've been here. Just don't spray over any of El Barto's tags—I hear that guy is one bad mammer-jammer. Other good places to spray paint for posterity are the Springfield Library, the Springfield Anti-Vandalism Council Building, and anything belonging to or on the person of School Principal Seymour Skinner.

A splendid way to kill a couple hours is to do some quality spitting off of the bridge at Elm Street. It's got some good height, heavy traffic flow below (cars and people), and there's just something about the architecture that creates a great splat-echo. A cool game I play with my pal Milhouse is "Roy G. Biv's A Drooler." That's where we try to spit on cars colored in the order of the rainbow (or, as my geeky sister says, the "natural spectrum.") You start with a red car, then to an orange, then to a yellow... If you hit the wrong colored car or you miss entirely, you gotta start over at red. Although it's tempting, don't waste your whole day here. There's a helluva lot more Springfield to see.

If you bring your board, you're in for a treat. Springfield has surprisingly smooth sidewalks that are always being replaced (so heads up). If you're lucky, you may come across a still-wet slab where you can sign your name for

(At right) At the Noise Land Video Arcade, a young delinquent loses games of "Escape From Grandma's House II" and "Quarter on a String", respectively.

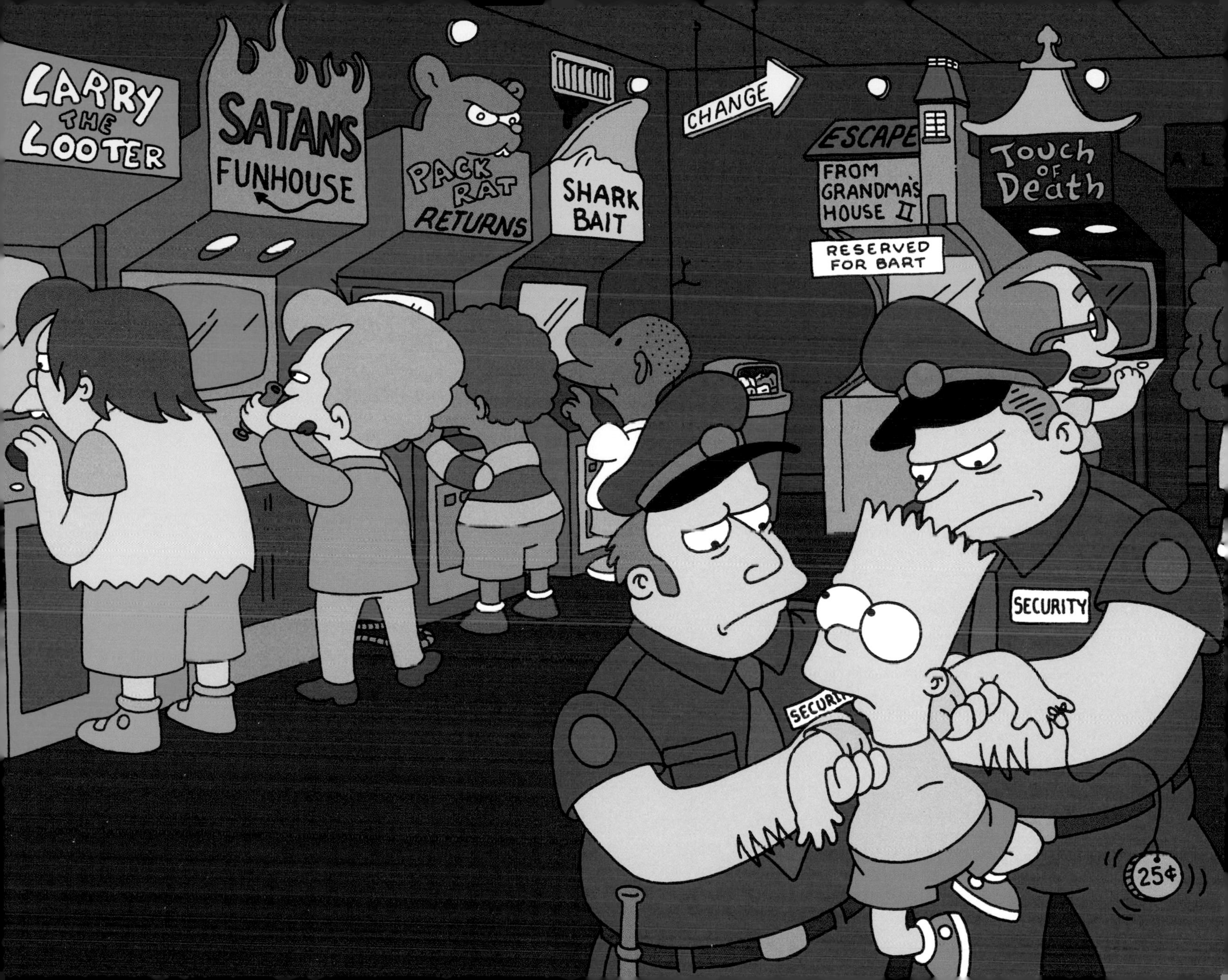
LARRY THE LOOTER
SATANS FUNHOUSE
PACK RAT RETURNS
SHARK BAIT
CHANGE
ESCAPE FROM GRANDMA'S HOUSE II
RESERVED FOR BART
Touch of Death
SECURITY
SECURITY
25¢

future generations to worship. If you find yourself near Moe's Tavern, watch out for my Dad's friend who usually sleeps it off on the sidewalk outside. There's one killer hill in town that's so dangerous I nearly died a horrible death trying to skate down it, so have a blast! Don't fear the reaper, man!

If you're up for a memorable Springfield experience, take a trip to the condemned Morningwood Penitentiary. Ever since they lost the lock to the front gates, any kid with the brains God gave a pork rind can sneak in and out without having to carry heavy lock-picking kits (for the record though, I use Lil' Bastard brand). At the Pentitentiary you can see the cracked walls and rusty bars that once contained the tortured screams of society's most-blackhearted criminals (but be careful... this comes awfully close to being a learning experience). Plus, there are rats aplenty, so bring your slingshot.

A great Springfield pay phone activity is prank calling Moe's Tavern. Some guy (probably that unbelievably cool El Barto dude) has been harrassing Moe for years, but why should he have all the fun? Drop a dime and give Moe one of these zingers: ask to speak to Moe Deodorant, Mike Raphouse, or I. M. Dorkified and then laugh as Moe threatens to use your rib cage for a cactus planter.

Got an irresistible itchin' to throw rancid food products at houses, cars, and other unsuspecting tourists? Well, Springfield is the place for you! The best spoiled meat, sour sauces, and rotten produce in the universe can be found in the dumpster behind any Krustyburger location. Remember, always wear gloves—that way they can't catch you horrifyingly stink-handed.

THE BART SIMPSON SPRINGFIELD SPOTS

Of course, maybe you just wanna do the staples; fast food, video games, shopping... Well, here's what I recommend:

If you want burgers, you hit the previously mentioned Krustyburger (forget Berger's Burgers. It's old school, old style, old fashioned, and they don't give out any toys with their meals). For all your various practical joking needs, try Yukingham Palace where you can select from 73 varieties of fake vomit and the biggest collection of rubber doggie-do in the state. You wanna go coin-op? Visit Noise Land Video Arcade and try to beat Jimbo Jones's record on "Dirt Nap II." Downtown, there's a 24-hour rub-on tattoo parlor, an all-night models and model decals store, a triple-G-rated movie theater, and a place to pick up bicycle seat covers that's open 'til 3 AM. My bedtime is currently ten o'clock, so I'm just going on unsubstantiated

rumor and the blurry memories of a recent Squishee binge. For toys, J.R.R. Toykin's is a must-go-to-and-spend-at; it's got the best selection, relatively cheap prices, and a crooked stock boy who'll sell you an impossible to find Scarlet Floozy action figure at an unusually low 25% markup. The Android's Dungeon is my comic book store of choice; it always fulfills my *Radioactive Man* needs and if I have to make a quick escape, the owner is too fat chase me.

GET BACK, MAN

You should plan to head back at least an hour before dinnertime, just to be on the safe side. When you hear your family walking in, try to look as sick as possible to generate the maximum output of parental guilt. (I mean, they've been out havin' the time of their lives while you were stuck with stomach cramps and illness-related hallucinations.) When your mom asks how you feel, start crying, telling her you were so hoping that the family could take a day trip to Duff Gardens. Then, when their hearts are nearly breaking, bring it on home with a remarkable twenty-minute recovery. If your family has any heart at all, you'll be riding the Barrel Roll within twenty-four hours.

Good luck, man.

ANNUAL EVENTS

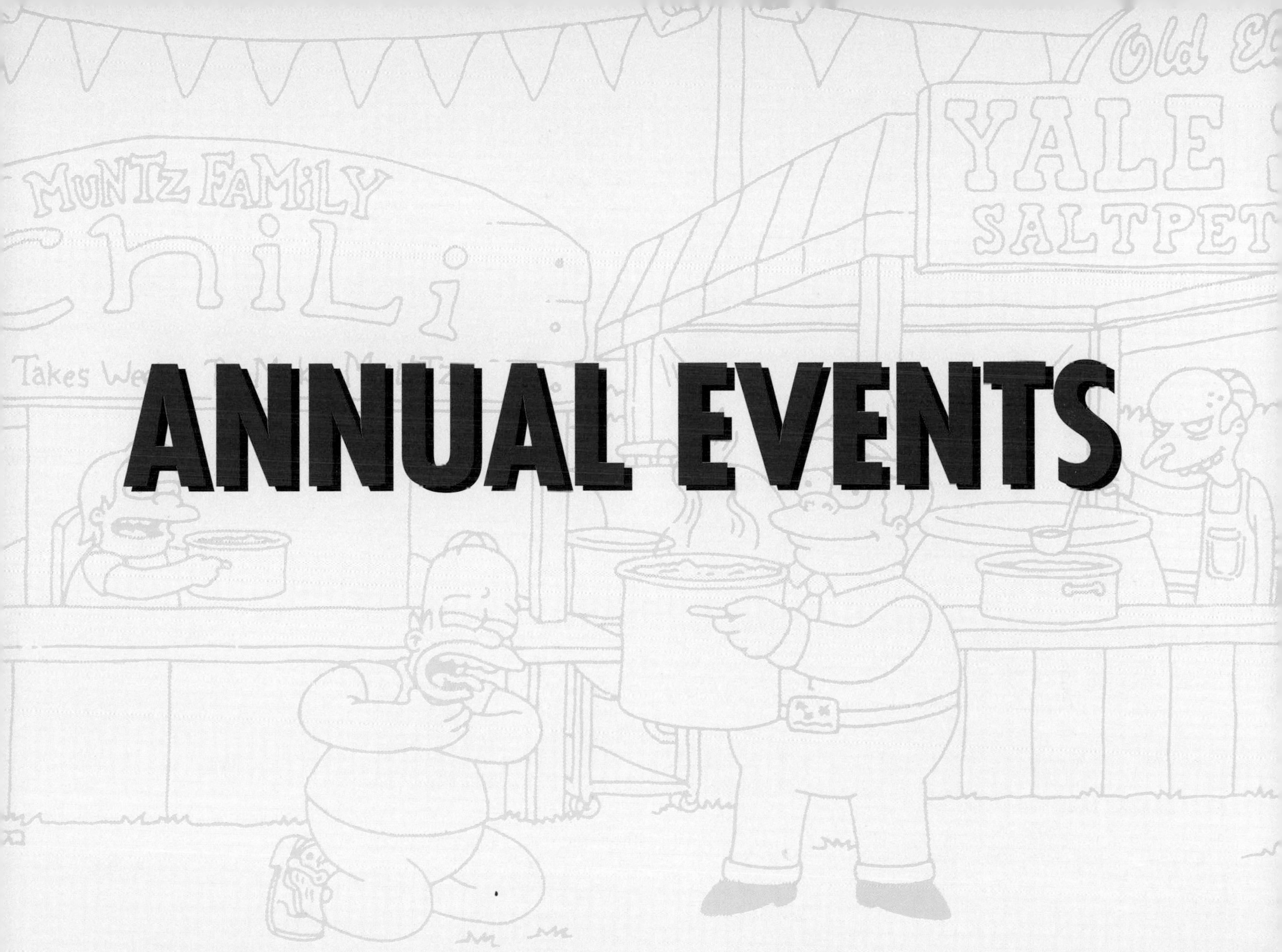
MuNTz FAMiLY

Thinking of planning your Springfield trip around one of the town's special annual events? Well, that could be a problem. If only the Springfield Elementary School hadn't sold a record amount of calendars at its annual fundraiser several years (or more) ago. The defective, thirteen-month timetable seems to have set daykeeping off permanently in Springfield (the calendar included the month "Smarch"); thus, correct dates are unavailable for the following events. Check the Springfield Chamber of Commerce, as exact dates for annual events are subject to change annually.

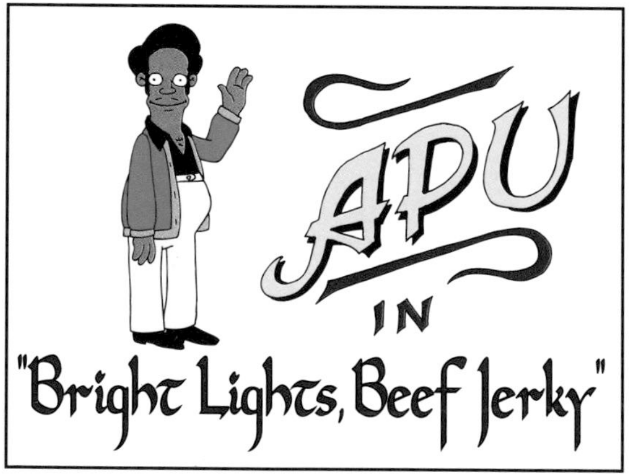
APU
IN
"Bright Lights, Beef Jerky"

Perhaps the most glamorous yearly event held in the city is the **Springfield Film Festival**. Featuring films made by local residents and judged by other local residents and flash-in-the-pan celebrity movie critics, the festival culminates in a tense, gala evening, during which finalists' films are screened before the entire town. Recent audience favorites include Selma Bouvier's *Jub-Jub Goes to Venus* and Milhouse Van Houten's *Egg Salad Sick Day*.

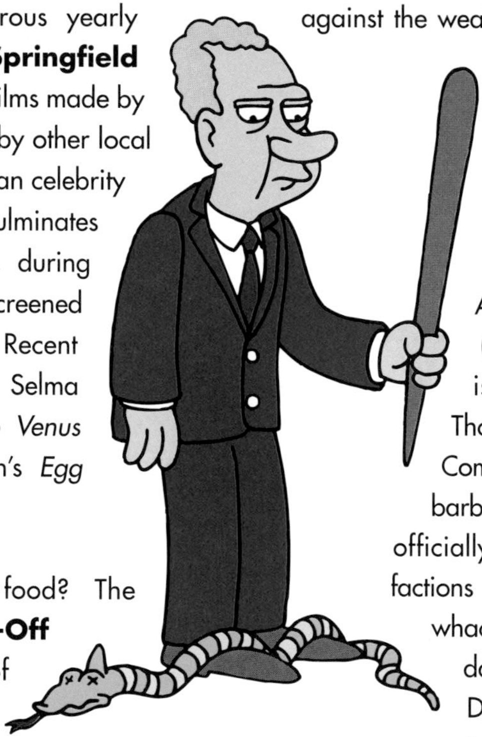

Did someone mention food? The **Springfield Chili Cook-Off** is an amazing day of ground meat, spices, hot peppers, and inhuman consumption of beer. In the past, some men have been driven to hallucination by select samples of chili, while others have broken into never-ending sweats. Needless to say, this is no place for the chili neophyte. The festival is full of men and women who consider chili more as a weapon against the weak than as a fun, family foodstuff. Bring your own metal spoon (many of the chilis tend to eat through wood rather quickly).

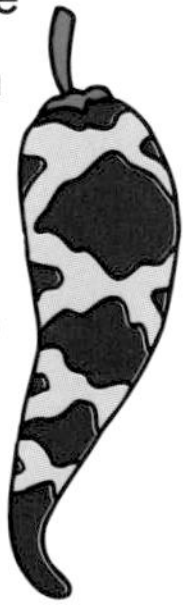

A less dangerous holiday (for humans, anyway) is **Whacking Day**. Though the Chamber of Commerce contends that the barbaric holiday is no longer officially celebrated, rebel factions of still-dedicated snake whackers promise that the day will go on. Whacking Day supposedly dates back to Springfield pioneer days, when town founder Jebediah Springfield drove local snakes to the center of town and proceeded to beat them all to death. On Whacking Day, Springfielders follow in Jebediah's footsteps, killing hundreds of innocent snakes in the name of tradition, senseless cruelty, and cheap entertainment.

(At right) The thrill of chili and the agony of peppers hot enough to strip paint off of wood at the annual Springfield Chili Cook-Off.

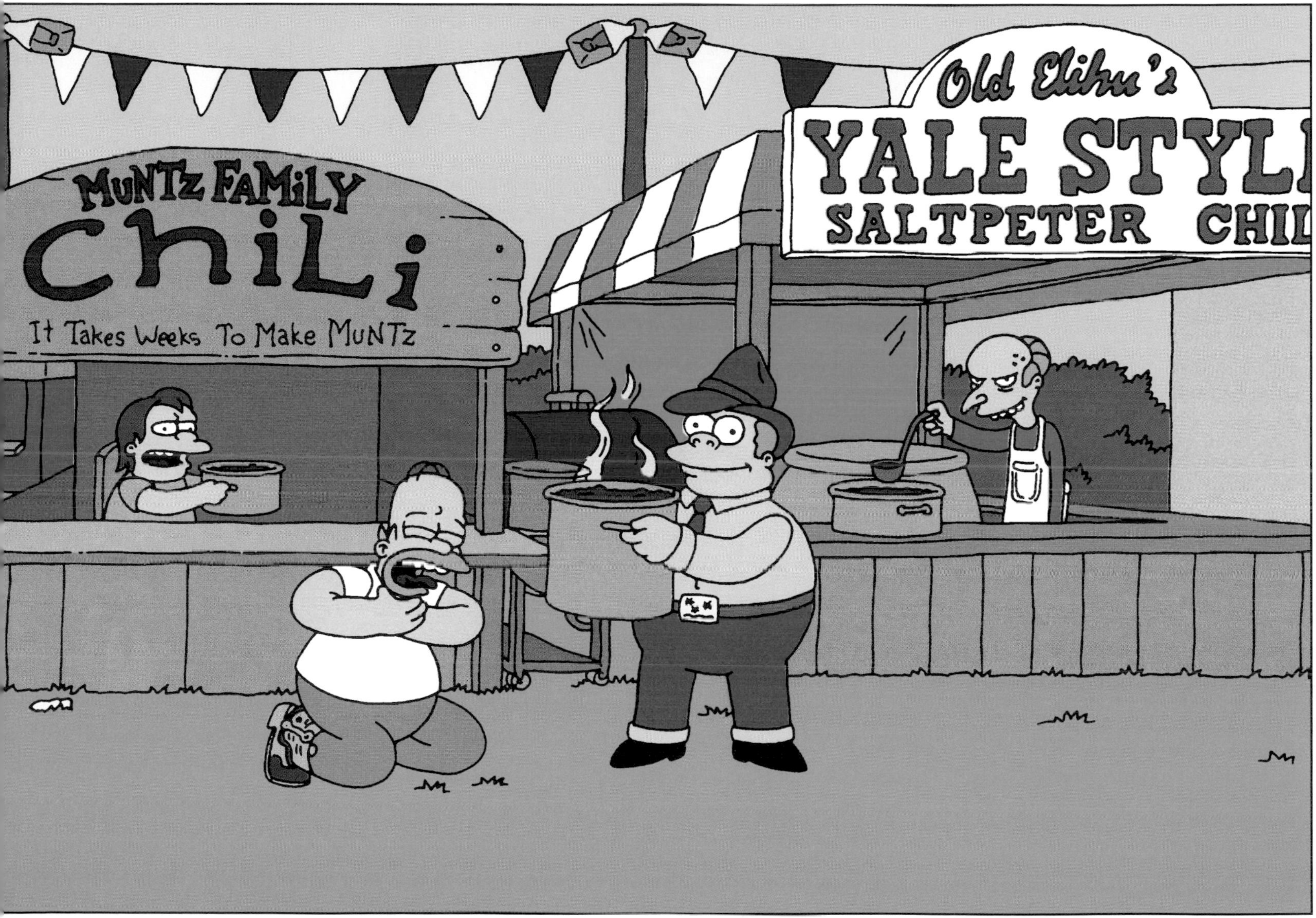
MUNTZ FAMILY
ChiLi
It Takes Weeks To Make MUNTz
Old Elihu's
YALE STYL
SALTPETER CHI

WHAT'S RIGHT WITH SPRINGFIELD?

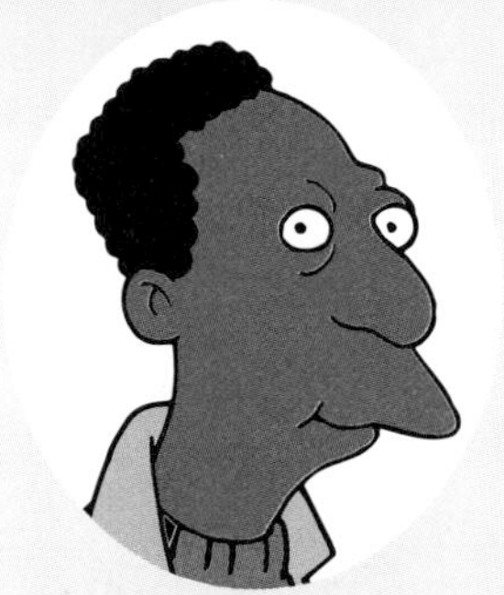

"Me, I like Springfield Stadium. They serve peanuts in the oil they used to fry the corn dogs in."

—Carl,
nuclear technician

The **Do-What-You-Feel Festival** is another Springfield event that may or may not be celebrated

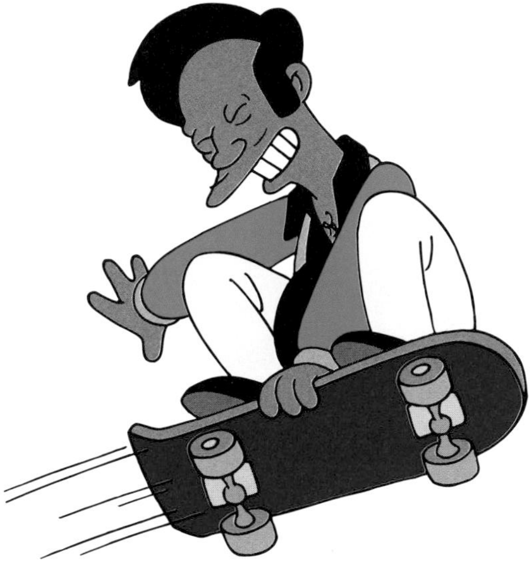

again. Originally conceived as a celebration of people surrendering to the voice of their inner child, the first (and only, thus far) DWYF Festival broke down into one of Springfield's famous city-wide riots, in which people were celebrating the "owning of your okayness" one minute and throwing neighbors through store windows the next.

A decidedly more low-key event is Springfield's yearly **Regional Ace Awards.** Dick Cavett has hosted the proceedings for the past several years, telling meandering stories about Elliott Gould before announcing the winners of such awards as Best Public Access Talk Show (featuring naked people and/or local politicians). It doesn't make for an exciting evening, but the chances of a riot breaking out are fairly slim—unless, of course, the Ace goes to the less-deserving nominee for Best City-Wide Riot Coverage.

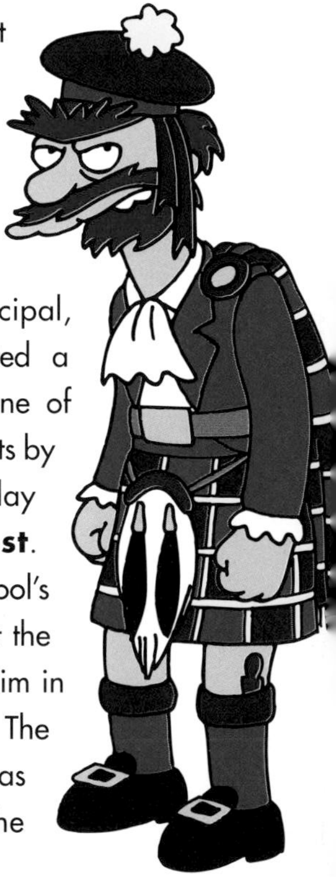

Although this annual event has never actually been celebrated, there are a determined few who wish to see it become a reality. Recently, Springfield Elementary School's principal, Seymour Skinner, conducted a sting operation to catch one of the school's worst delinquents by creating a phony holiday called **Scotchtoberfest**. Skinner convinced the school's Scottish groundskeeper that the holiday was real and put him in charge of the festivities. The sting operation proceeded as planned, and when the smoke cleared, the hapless groundskeeper realized he'd been played for a patsy. Since that day, he has vowed to make Scotchtoberfest a Springfield-wide reality. So far, his grand vision of the town wearing kilts, eating haggis, and listening to traditional Scottish bagpipe music hasn't caught on.

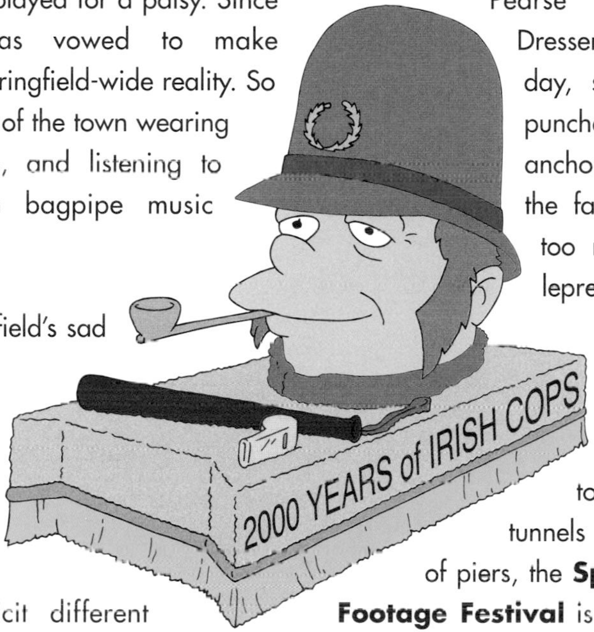
2000 YEARS of IRISH COPS

Called both "Springfield's sad day of shame" and "the most righteous Springfield shinny-bang-bang of the year," Springfield's **St. Patrick's Day** festivities elicit different emotions from its residents, depending on how much they drink at the event. For an entire day, the main street of town is choked with drunks trying to convince one another that they're having a good time while attempting to keep down their lunch of corned beef, cabbage, and fried marshmallow clover. Meanwhile, those sober enough to pay attention watch a parade featuring such floats as "When Irish Eyes Are Smiling They Have Opticians to Thank!" and "Patrick Pearse Was a Snappy Dresser." By the end of the day, someone will have punched Channel 6 news anchor Kent Brockman in the face for making one too many references to leprechauns.

Featuring everything from rockets launching into space to trains heading into tunnels to mules diving off of piers, the **Springfield Stock-Footage Festival** is one of the greatest nonnarrative, nondocumentary film festivals in the world. Over thirty-six hours of indirectly suggestive and directly non-suggestive films are shown over four days to Springfielders, who are always left clamoring for more. The big hit of the last festival was *Boring Shots of Toledo,* which swept all the major categories, including Best Rear-Projection Film Used to Make People Appear to Be Driving.

If you like dressing up as your favorite comic book superhero and then going out in public with no regard for your dignity as a human being, then **Close Encounter of the**

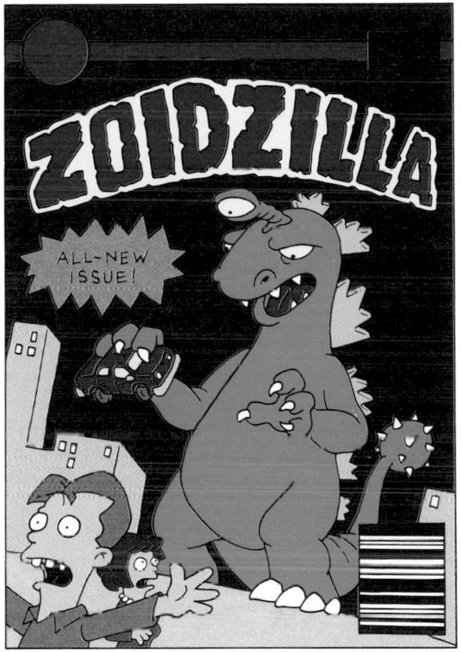
ZOIDZILLA
ALL-NEW ISSUE!

Comic Book Kind, Springfield's annual comic book convention, is for you. Featuring dozens of horribly under- or overweight comic book dealers, a handful of bitter editors and artists, and at least three actors who appeared onscreen once or twice in some sort of science-fiction program, this nerdfest is an excellent place for the nonfan to come out and observe really weird people having a great time. Add to this the opportunity to purchase overpriced merchandise and ogle convention models in revealing costumes and you have one heck of a Sunday.

Another just-as-strange but nongeeky convention held in town is the annual **StaceyCon**—Springfield's celebration of America's favorite plastic girl, Malibu Stacey. The town scored a cutie-coup when it somehow wrested the right to hold the Con from the San Diego Airport Hilton. Thus, every year Springfield is flooded with young girls, nostalgic professional women, and well-dressed men with one single objective in mind: purchase as many collectible Malibu Stacey items as possible. The big seller last year was the Four-Armed Super-Shopping Stacey. But cash purchases aren't the only thing going on at the Con: there's a contest to come up with Talking Malibu Stacey's new phrase (a recent winner: "Let's not eat, so we can look good at the beach!"), a cotillion, and a high-pitched screaming-only auction.

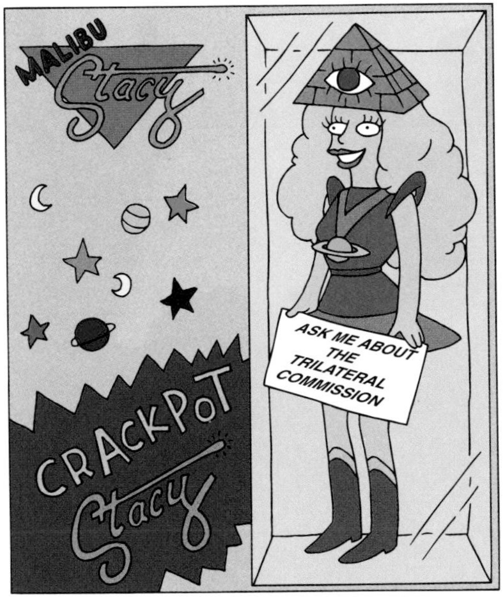
MALIBU
Stacy
CRACKPOT
Stacy
ASK ME ABOUT THE TRILATERAL COMMISSION

For those who truly want to immerse themselves in Springfield tradition, the annual **Evergreen Terrace Rummage Sale** literally reeks of the town's past. During the event, residents of the street sell items purchased from other sales over the years, keeping alive a rummage continuum that's been in existence since the time of the Springfield pioneers. In fact, it's rumored that Jebediah Springfield may have purchased his legendary coonskin cap at the town's first rummage sale. It's also rumored that it was alive at the time.

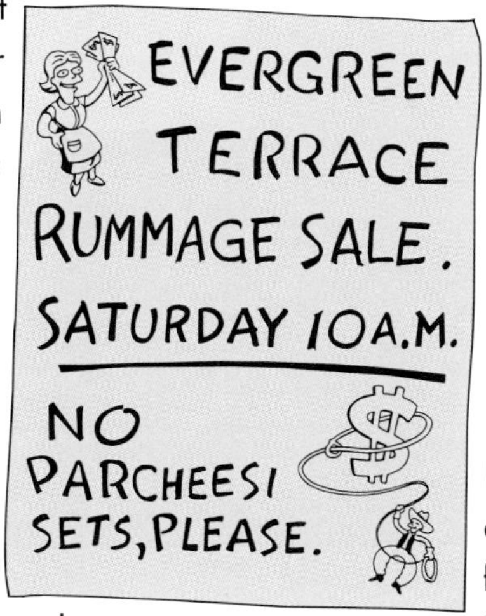
EVERGREEN
TERRACE
RUMMAGE SALE.
SATURDAY 10A.M.
NO
PARCHEESI
SETS, PLEASE.

Finally, an interesting, smaller event to attend is Springfield Elementary School's **Diorama-Rama**, for many (including the aforementioned Principal Seymour Skinner) the most exciting day of the school year. Dioramas have always been taken seriously at the elementary school, and thus the competition at DRR is keen. Do bring your video camera—titles of past amazing dioramas have included "The Story of the Bible as Told in a Nike Box" and "Run, Forrest, Run! A Novelization I Soon Won't Forget."

SURVIVAL GUIDE

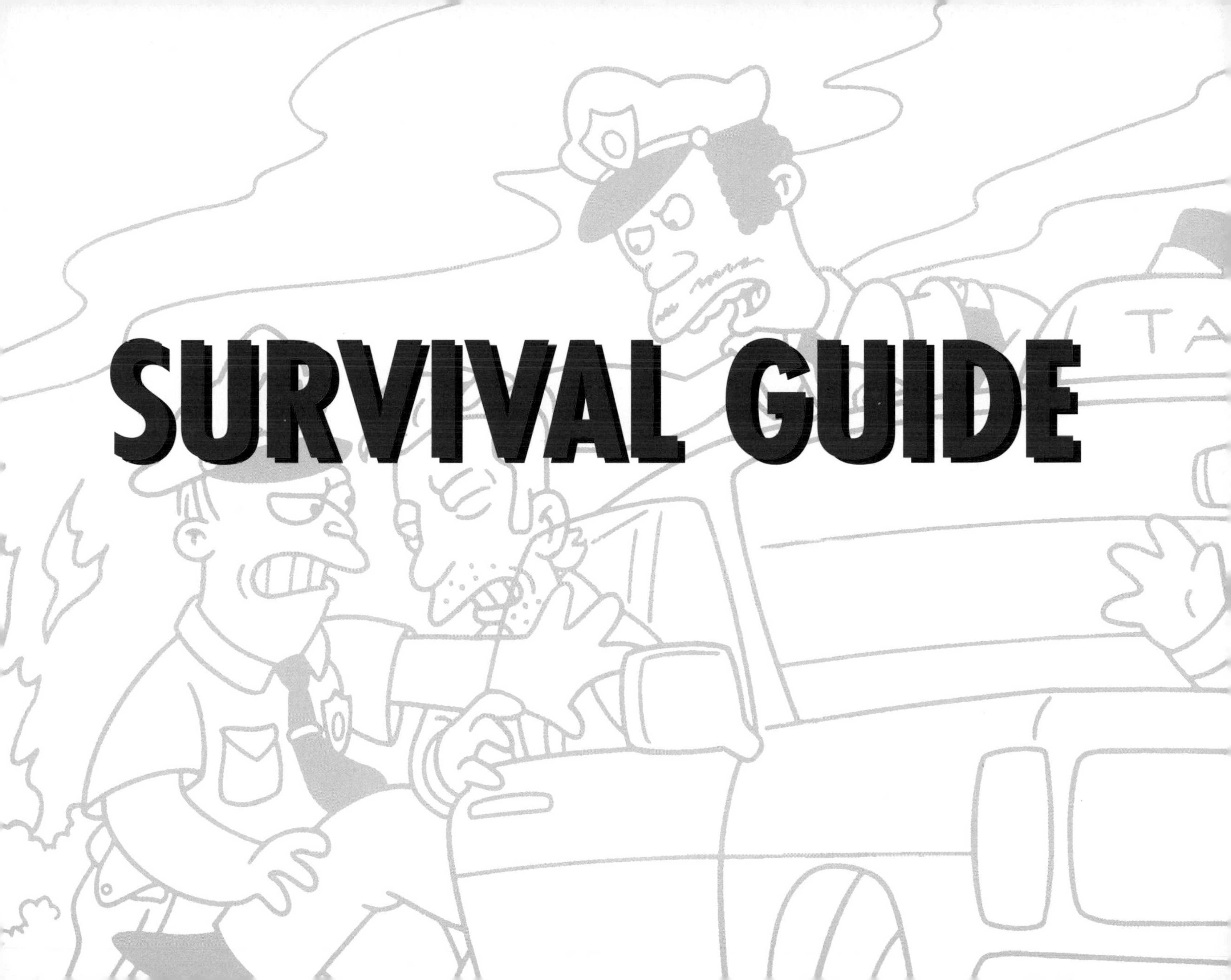

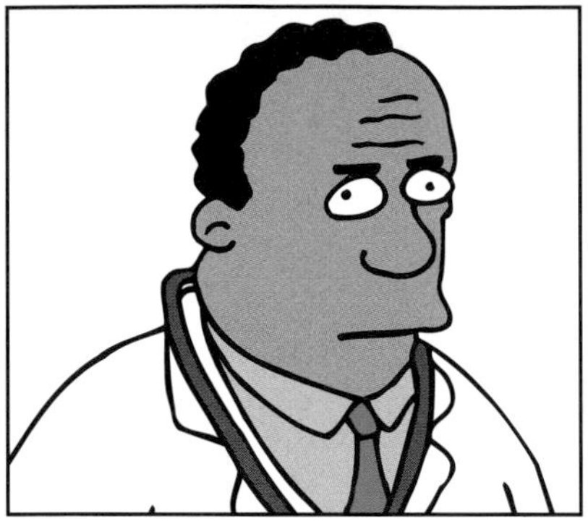

Surviving Springfield: How to Do It

by Dr. Julius Hibbert, M.D.

There is no good reason on God's green Earth why someone should not survive a trip to Springfield: all it takes is thinking ahead and taking some basic precautions. As a physician, a father, a churchgoer, and a mildly compassionate human being, I implore you to read this survival guide and take all the necessary precautions before embarking on your fun-filled trip to this dangerous city fraught with peril. Below, I've outlined the various hazards you'll need to plan for if you want to leave our glorious city of joy unscathed.

You've heard about it in the movies, but in Springfield, it's all too real: **radiation**. Usually not much of a problem in most American cities, radiation is the persistent scourge of Springfield, finding its way into the most innocent places, such as confessionals, hall closets, and antique cannons. Why so much radiation? Well, for one thing, the Springfield Nuclear Power Plant was built during a particularly laissez-faire period of the Nuclear Regulatory Commission. Usual precautions to contain radiation were set aside in favor of using folk remedies. For example, instead of installing proper radioactive shielding for the power core, the management decided to use drywall with a big horseshoe nailed to it. The other cause of excess radiation in Springfield is the plant's "Be a Plant Pal" program, in which employees who store a drum of nuclear waste in their basements get to attend Nuclear Plant Employee, Spouses, and No-More-Than-Three-Children Night at Springfield War Memorial Stadium. But please, don't let the rampant presence of radiation throughout the city stop you from visiting: again, all you need is a little common sense to keep you from being slowly poisoned. First, bring a lightweight Geiger counter, perhaps a model that could be hung around your neck, much like one of Mr. T's medallions. Second, bring a high quality, fashionable *radiation suit*. Why fashionable? Because that's all you'll be wearing for the duration of your stay in Springfield. UNDER NO CIRCUMSTANCES SHOULD YOU REMOVE YOUR RADIATION SUIT WHILE IN THIS CITY.

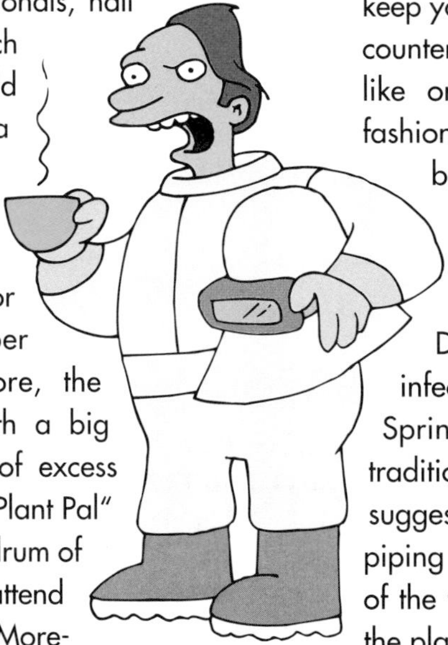

Despite worldwide strides across the world in preventing infection, **infectious disease** is alive and well and living in Springfield. These are the facts: health codes in Springfield traditionally have not been considered to be laws, but rather friendly suggestions. The sewer system and the sewage system share some piping interchanges. Plus, there's been a great deal of talk about one of the town's more prominent scientists accidentally contaminating all the playing cards in Springfield with

(At right) Dr. Julius Hibbert stitches up an under-anesthetized patient at Marvin Monroe Memorial Hospital.

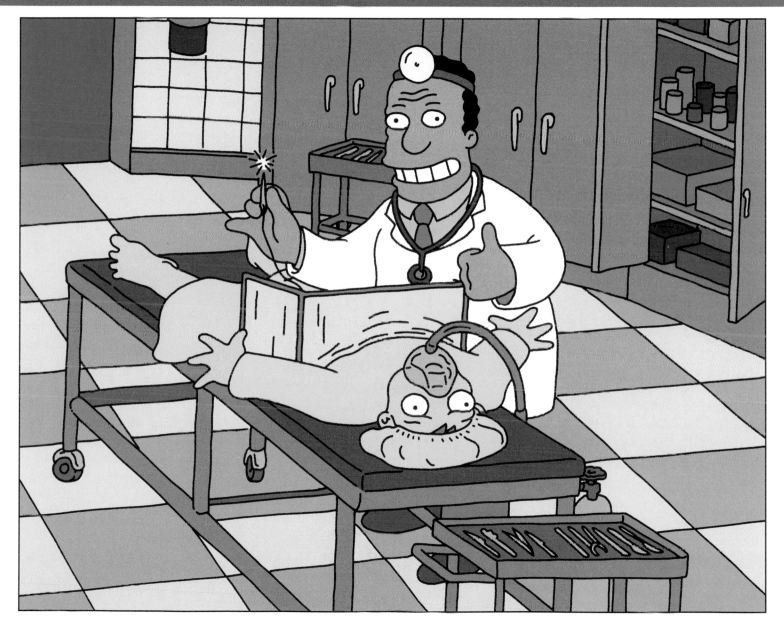

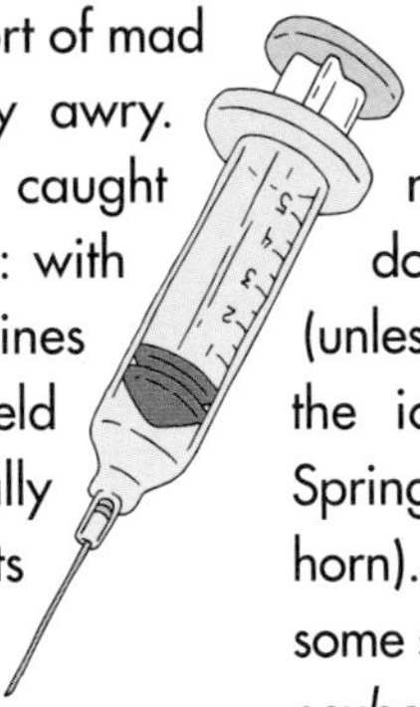

traces of the Black Plague—some sort of mad experiment gone horribly, horribly awry. Luckily, modern science may have caught up with this enemy of good health: with the *Memminger Regimen* of vaccines and antibiotics, visitors to Springfield can dine and drink tap water virtually without worry. The regimen consists of twenty-four shots administered four times each week over a six-week period. Though expensive and painful, this procedure teaches the body to fight off the myriad of bacteria, spirochetes, and mutant viruses that are present throughout the Springfield municipal area. Of course, no vaccine or antibiotic is fail-safe, so, just to be on the safe side, try to limit your water drinking in Springfield to one shotglass a day. (And regarding that shotglass of water—the townspeople have a saying, "If it's black, send it back; if it's brown, drink it down.) As far as food goes, avoid meats, fish, grains, and vegetables—highly processed candy, for the most part, is okay. Also, do not buy playing cards under any circumstances.

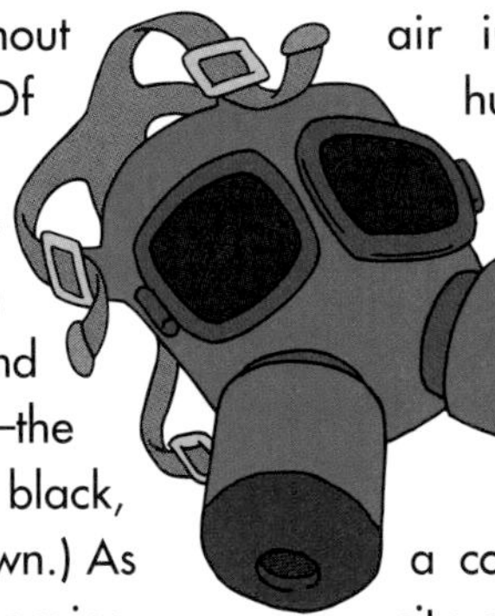

Air pollution isn't much of a concern for native Springfieldites—their organs have been utilizing this city's hazardous air for years and have adapted. But to visitors, the oxygen-to-carbon monoxide ratio may prove challenging, and even if that doesn't get you, the ozone surely will (unless you're high above the city, breathing the icy, pure-yet-under-oxygenated air of Springfield's highest mountain, the Murderhorn). The only sensible precaution is to wear some sort of *highly effective filtration device* (*or scuba gear*) throughout your stay in Springfield. Your radiation suit most likely will have to be altered to accommodate this equipment, but it will be well worth it, as the air in Springfield ages normal human lungs about two years for every day spent breathing here. Luckily, there have been benefits from this awful pollution: the thick layer of smog once burned up a comet that was threatening the city, and because of the adulterated CO_2 content in the air, dandelions and crabgrass will not grow in certain upscale neighborhoods (like the one I live in), keeping front lawns weed free and beautiful.

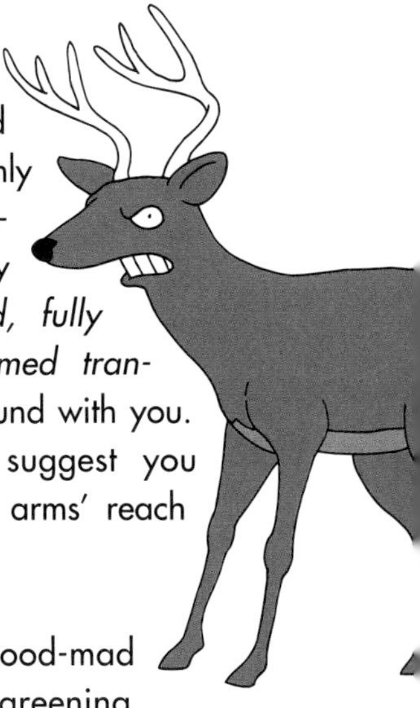

Animal rampages are simply something Springfielders have come to live with. Whether it's a curious bear that's come out of the forest to forage among the garbage cans and maim locals or a spooked domesticated elephant that has decided to take it on the lam, at least one large mammal runs crazed through downtown Springfield every other month. Local politicos have downplayed the problem, even trying to exploit it for publicity, by taking out ads in travel magazines that proclaim Springfield, "America's monthly Pamplona, except with rabid monkeys and annoyed reindeer instead of bulls." The only reasonable safeguard is to carry a *high-powered, fully loaded and armed tranquilizer gun* around with you. Additionally, I suggest you keep one within arms' reach while you sleep.

When a blood-mad animal isn't careening through the streets of Springfield, odds are good that some sort of **runaway vehicle** is. Whether it's the Springfield Elementary School bus, a giant snowplow, or a Pinto

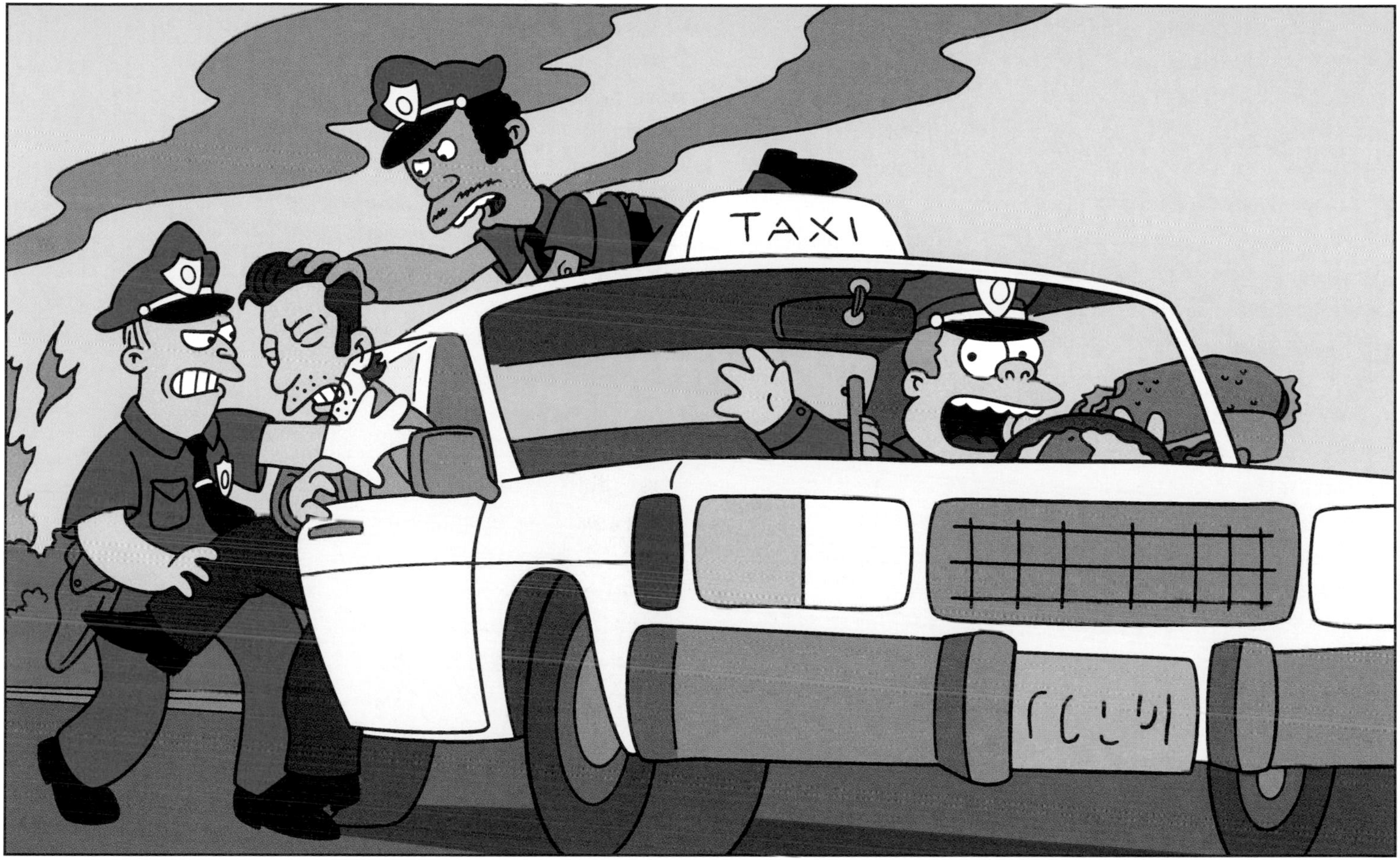
TAXI

After commandeering a cab and grabbing some lunch, Springfield's Finest nab a potential looter during the most recent riots.

driven by Springfield's worst driver, Hans Moleman, somewhere in Springfield, four wheels are racing toward disaster. Thus, I must recommend that you *stay off the streets and spend as little time as possible on the sidewalks,* which are viewed by many local motorists as cute, little, traffic-free mini-streets.

Of course, there are times when everyone decides to "take it to the streets." About every three years, **city-wide riots** tend to break out in Springfield for one reason or another, whether it be over a statue of Jimmy Carter or an especially boring soccer match. During these three-or-four-day periods of civil lawlessness, it's best to *remain inside, preferably with the lights off, and staying away from windows.* To ensure safety, you might want to put all of your valuables and a tasty snack *in a paper bag labeled "Looters"* and place it in front of your door. Marauders will appreciate your thoughtfulness and may decide to leave you unharmed.

The forces of nature probably won't have the same sense of generosity. Springfield's unique geography is subject to **near spontaneous hurricanes** that wreak havoc upon the landscape, reducing giant fast-food mascots and orphanages to rubble within moments. There is very, very little forewarning for hurricanes in Springfield, so the best safety measure to take when traveling there is to always know where the closest storm shelter is. Because visitors aren't very familiar with the lay of the land, I suggest you carry around a *global positioning device and a map, marked with all municipal storm shelters*—these items could make the difference between several days in a dank, crowded, miserable concrete bunker and serious injury.

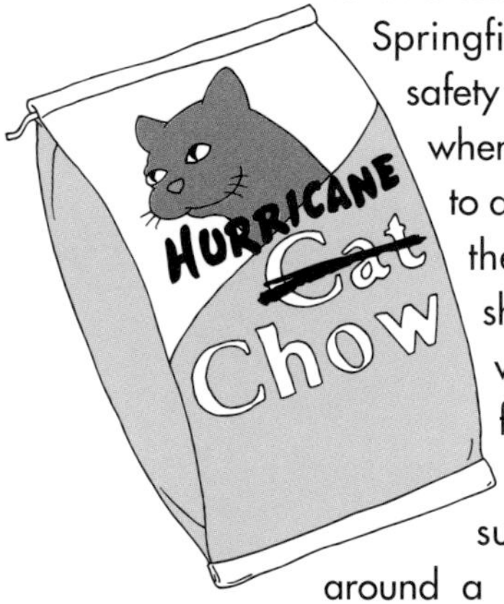
HURRICANE
Cat
Chow

Finally, Springfield has a threat to safety completely unique to any other city in the world: the **Sideshow Bob Factor**. On more than one occasion, Sideshow Bob, former kiddie-TV sidekick, attempted murderer and bon vivant, has threatened to destroy Springfield—it's quite possible that he'll try it again. Some say he's reformed and is interested in getting a fact-checking position on *The New Yorker*. Others report that he's joined with his brother, Cecil, in becoming a fearful fraternal force of fury, hell-bent on destroying the lives of every man, woman, child, and vacationer in the city. If the latter is the case (and I truly hope it isn't, as I do believe *The New Yorker* could benefit from Bob's keen literary eye), there is absolutely nothing one can do as a preventive measure against this man's murderous madness. The only thing I can suggest is making your peace with whatever estranged relatives you have before you depart for Springfield and—if Sideshow Bob strikes—depart this Earth.

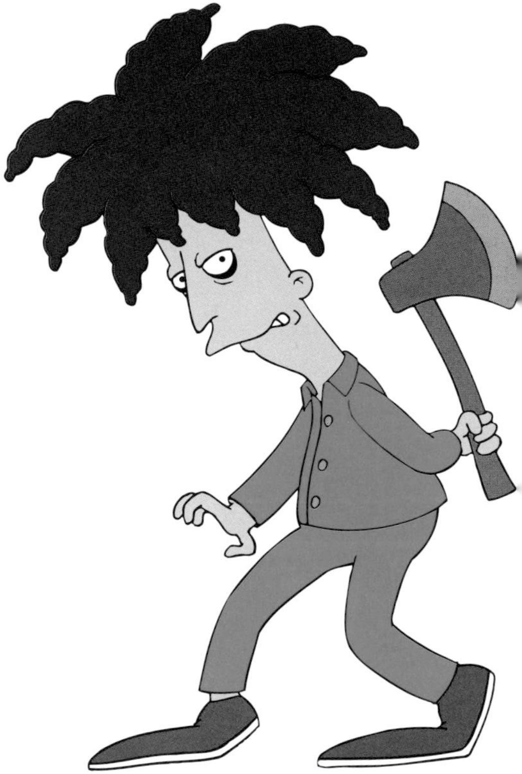

With these simple precautions, you can enjoy your trip to Springfield with very little fear about suffering a horrible fate. That said, I offer you this prescription: 100ccs of fun, 100ccs of leisure, with a booster shot of common sense. The only side effects you'll suffer are a little itching, some mild chafing, and one terrific Springfield vacation.

INDEX

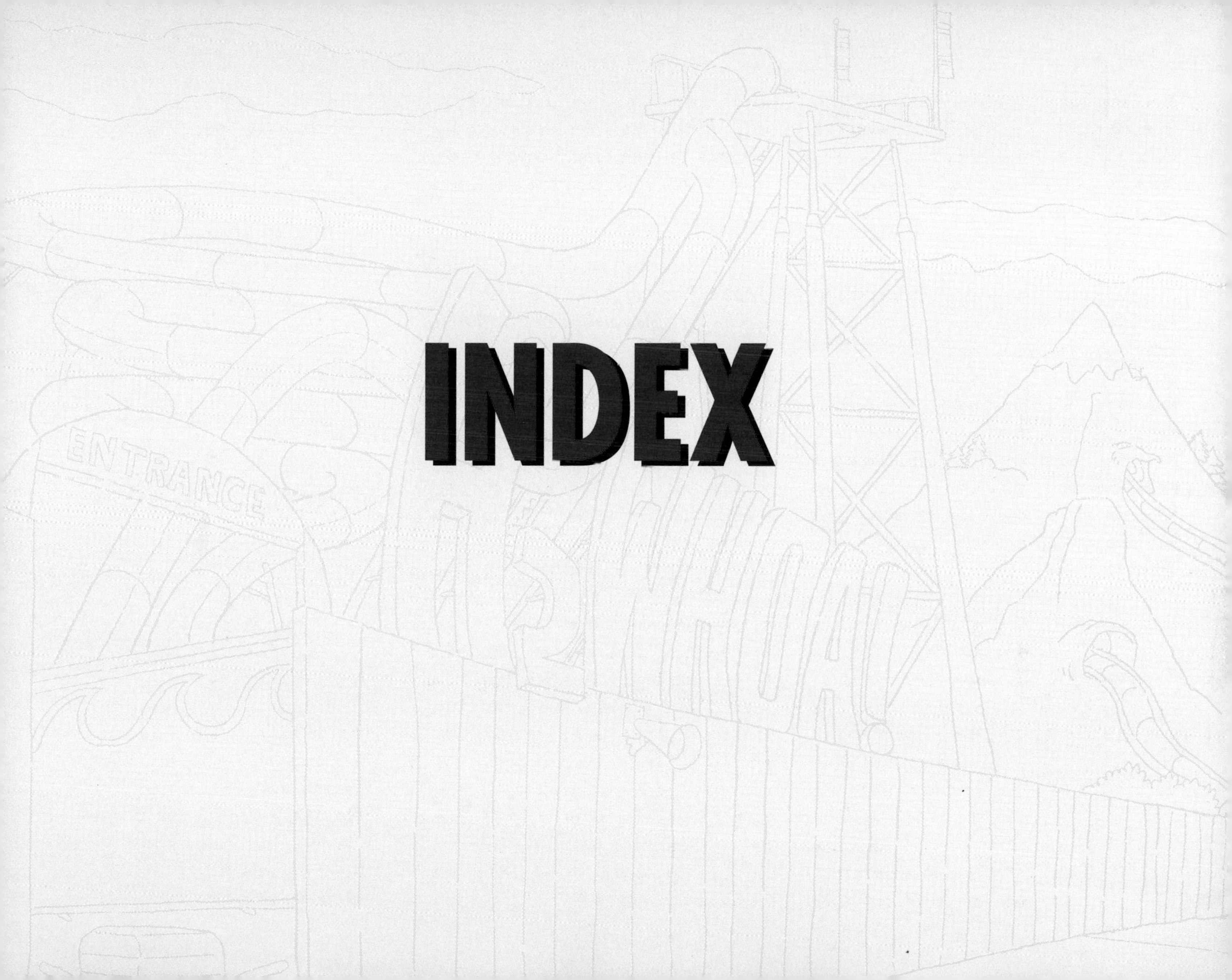
ENTRANCE
WHOA!

INDEX

Look for these other fine publications in the *Are We There Yet?* series:

Are We There Yet? Shelbyville

Are We There Yet? North Haverbrook

Are We There Yet? Ogdenville

Are We There Yet? Brockway

Are We There Yet? Crackton

Are We There Yet? Little Pwagmattasquarmsettport

Are We There Yet? Little Newark

Are We There Yet? New Bedrock

Are We There Yet? Cape Feare

Are We There Yet? Terror Lake

Are We There Yet? New Horrorfield

Are We There Yet? Screamville

Are We There Yet? Frigid Falls

Are We There Yet? Mount Seldom

Are We There Yet? Lake Flaccid

Are We There Yet? Capital City

Are We There Yet? New York City

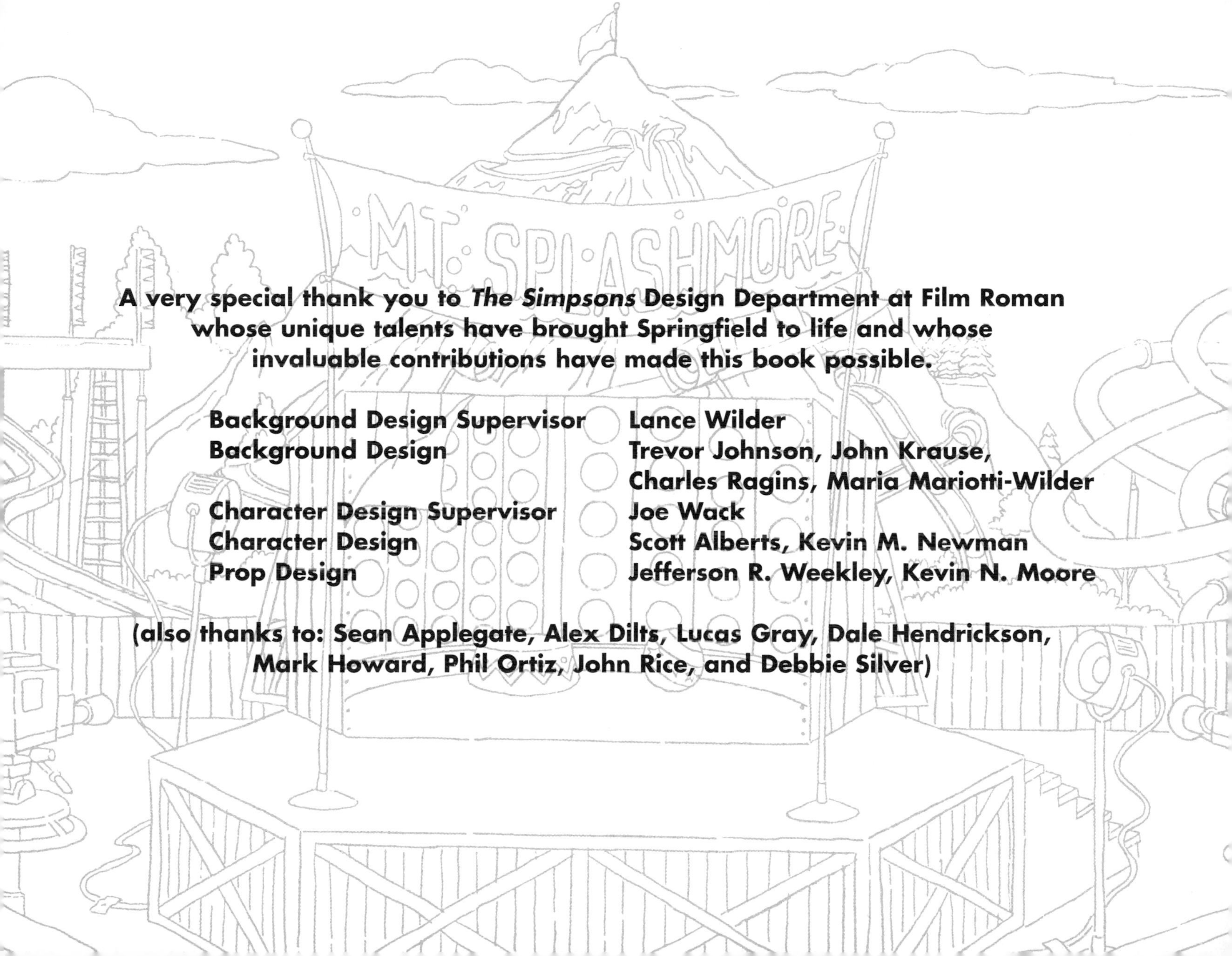
MT. SPLASHMORE

A very special thank you to *The Simpsons* Design Department at Film Roman whose unique talents have brought Springfield to life and whose invaluable contributions have made this book possible.

Background Design Supervisor	**Lance Wilder**
Background Design	**Trevor Johnson, John Krause, Charles Ragins, Maria Mariotti-Wilder**
Character Design Supervisor	**Joe Wack**
Character Design	**Scott Alberts, Kevin M. Newman**
Prop Design	**Jefferson R. Weekley, Kevin N. Moore**

(also thanks to: Sean Applegate, Alex Dilts, Lucas Gray, Dale Hendrickson, Mark Howard, Phil Ortiz, John Rice, and Debbie Silver)

TRAVEL NOTES

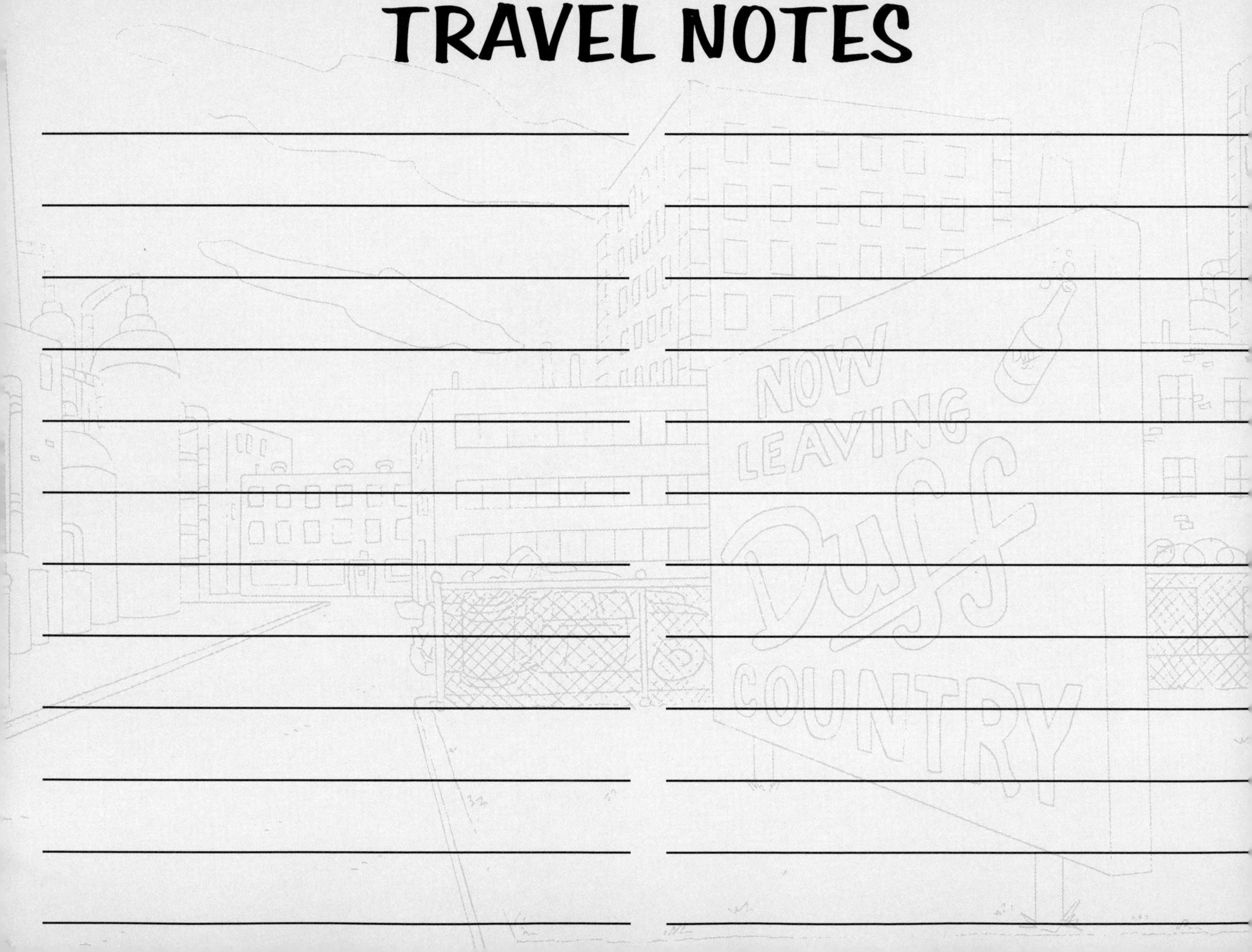
NOW LEAVING
Duff
COUNTRY

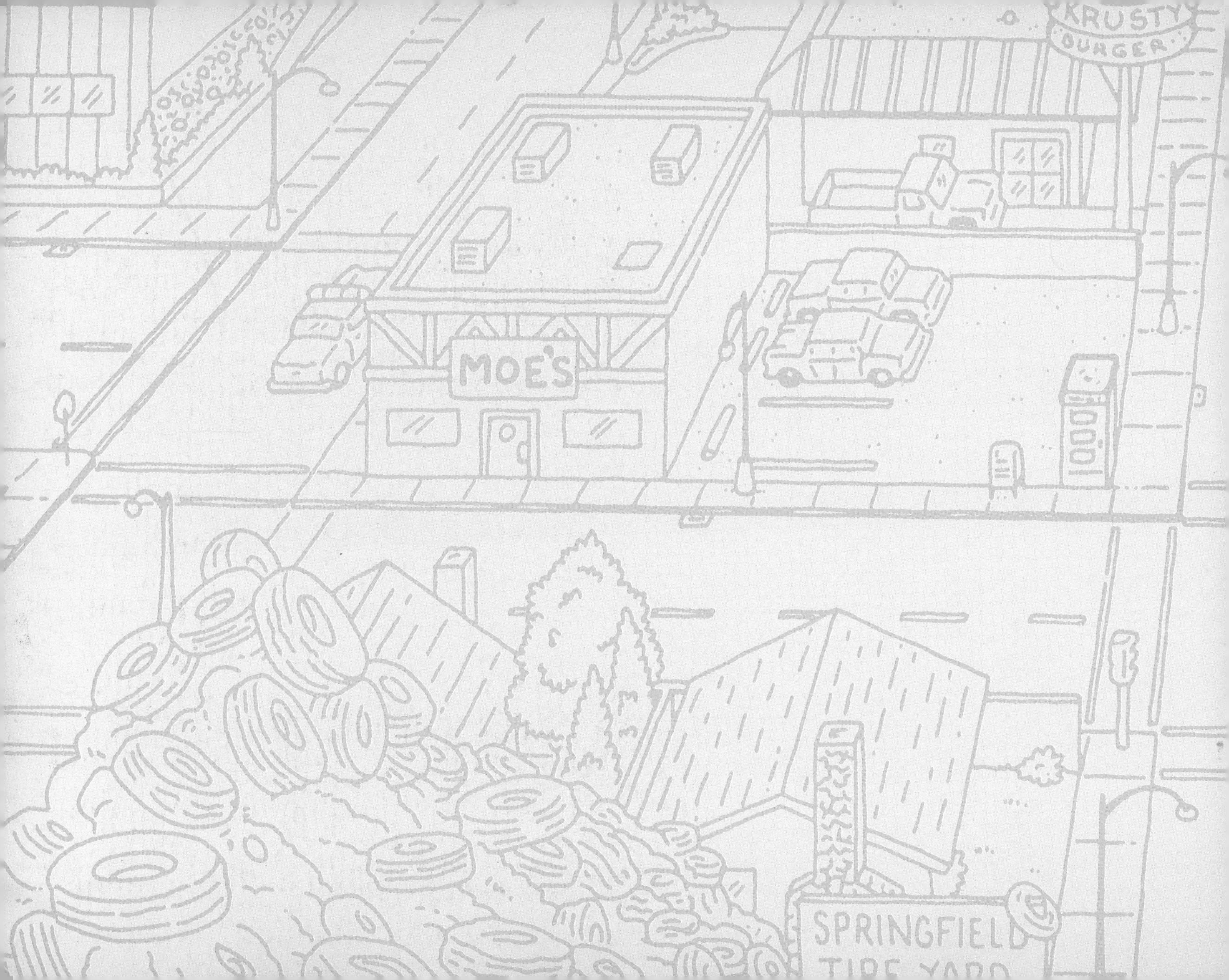
KRUSTY
BURGER
MOE'S
SPRINGFIELD